"Who Set You Flowin'?"

RACE AND AMERICAN CULTURE

General Editors:
Arnold Rampersad and Shelley Fisher Fishkin

Love and Theft
Blackface Minstrelsy and the American Working Class
Eric Lott

The Dialect of Modernism:
Race, Language, and Twentieth-Century Literature
Michael North

Bordering on the Body
The Racial Matrix of Modern Fiction and Culture
Laura Doyle

"Who Set You Flowin'?"
The African-American Migration Narrative
Farah Jasmine Griffin

Doers of the Word
African-American Women Reformers in the North (1830–1880)
Carla L. Peterson

"WHO SET YOU FLOWIN'?"

The African-American Migration Narrative

FARAH JASMINE GRIFFIN

O)
Ne

11 18826 3

Oxford University Press

Oxford   New York
Athens   Auckland   Bangkok   Bogota   Bombay
Buenos Aires   Calcutta   Cape Town   Dar es Salaam
Delhi   Florence   Hong Kong   Istanbul   Karachi
Kuala Lumpur   Madras   Madrid   Melbourne
Mexico City   Nairobi   Paris   Singapore
Taipei   Tokyo   Toronto

and associated companies in
Berlin   Ibadan

Library of Congress Cataloging-in-Publication Data
Griffin, Farah Jasmine.
"Who set you flowin'?":
the African-American migration narrative /
Farah Jasmine Griffin.
p. cm.—(Race and American culture)
Originally presented as the author's thesis (doctoral—Yale University).
Includes bibliographical references and index.
ISBN 0-19-508896-4—ISBN 0-19-508897-2 (pbk.)
1. American fiction—Afro-American authors—History and criticism.
2. Rural-urban migration in literature.
3. Migration, Internal, in literature.
4. City and town life in literature.
5. Afro-Americans in literature.
6. Narration (Rhetoric)
I. Title. II. Series.
PS374.N4G75   1995   813.009′895073—dc20   94-22860

For
My Grandmother,
Willie Lee Carson
(1904–1981),
who migrated from Eastman, Georgia,
to Philadelphia in February 1923;

and

Her three Philadelphia-born Daughters,

Eunice Cogdell
(1924–1991)
Eartha Mordecai
Wilhelmena Griffin

Acknowledgments

During the course of writing this book I have had the privilege of gathering advice from some of the wisest and most generous people I know. By introducing me to new paradigms Evelyn Higginbotham upset my intellectual equilibrium on more than one occasion. In so doing she greatly helped my personal growth as well as the growth of this project. I am grateful for the attention she has given to my work. James A. Miller was always there to answer a question, lend a book, debate a point, read a draft, and make me laugh. Likewise, Jerry Watts challenged my thoughts and read an early draft of this project. Cornel West's careful reading of the manuscript provided me with wisdom, insight, and critical affirmation.

This book had its beginning as my dissertation for the American Studies Program at Yale University. Many of my teachers supported the project in its initial stages. I am especially grateful to my dissertation committee. Professor Robert Stepto was an ideal mentor and advisor. He always provided me with insight and enthusiasm, and his occasional "you can do more with this" impelled me to try. Michael Denning's thoughtful comments and his ability to anticipate the shape of the project were invaluable even before I put pen to paper. Working with him throughout graduate school was clearly an intellectual high point. Hazel Carby's close attention to my work, her vast store of knowledge, and her published writings made her an important member of the dissertation committee. Professors Nancy Cott and Jean-Christophe Agnew helped to clarify my thinking about issues of history and power. Their classes and written comments were especially helpful. I appreciate Alan Trachtenberg's careful reading and valuable suggestions for revision.

Werner Sollors, Carol Bernstein, Kimberly Benston, Susan Pennybacker, Ron Thomas, Errol Louis, Paul Rogers, The Wesleyan-Trinity-Yale Feminist Writer's Group (Ann du Cille, Indira Karamachetti, Barbara Sicherman, Joan Hedrick, Laura Wexler, and Gertrude Hughes), and my intellectual sisters, Lisa Sullivan and Saidiya Hartman, all contributed enormously to my writing and thinking about cities, literature and African-American life and culture. Herman Beavers, Ines Salazar, and Houston Baker, my colleagues at the University of Pennsylvania, were very supportive.

With grace and patience Crystal Lucky and Cheryl Dorsey did the very tedious but invaluable job of proofreading and checking my notes and bibliography. I love both of them dearly. Ian Strachan helped me to proofread the entire manuscript. Tim Lucky offered much-needed computer assistance. Tricia Rose generously helped me with acquiring permission for rap lyrics.

Students in my African-American Literature and the City courses at Trinity College and Bryn Mawr College helped me to sharpen my thoughts and flesh out my ideas; I am especially grateful to Felicia Bradley, Denise Burgher, Charles Wallace, Joy Wright, Aimee Anctil, and Valerie Brown.

Without the financial and technical support of the following institutions and fellowships I never would have completed the project: Ann Plato Fellowship, American Studies Fellowship (Trinity College); Yale University; Bryn Mawr College Dissertation Fellowship; American Association of University Women Dissertation Fellowship; and the University of Pennsylvania Faculty Research Grant.

Librarians at Sterling Memorial Library (Yale University), Trinity College, Bryn Mawr College, Widener Library (Harvard University), Van Pelt Library (University of Pennsylvania), and the Library of Congress were especially helpful. A few deserve special mention: Sam Brylawski of the Recorded Sound Reference Center, Library of Congress, Sylvia Harris of the indexing department at ASCAP, and Clarence Washington of the Crisis Publishing Company.

Liz Maguire, Elda Rotor, and Paul Schlotthauer of Oxford University Press have provided enthusiasm and answers to many tiresome questions. I am also grateful to Arnold Rampersad and Shelley Fisher Fishkin for their support of this project.

For providing me with food, shelter, love, and peace of mind, I want to thank my family, especially my beautiful mother, Wilhelmena Griffin; my five "sisters," Shaun Biggers, Cheryl Dorsey, Lynelle Granady, Nina Henderson, and Karen O'Neal; and my friends F. Joseph Rogers and Edjohnetta Miller. Finally, Sylvia Ardyn Boone provided me with a model of serenity, kindness, and excellence. She passed away before this project was completed, but my memory of her sustained me nonetheless.

Contents

Introduction, 3

1. "Boll Weevil in the Cotton/Devil in the White Man":
   Reasons for Leaving the South, 13

2. The South in the City:
   The Initial Confrontation with the Urban Landscape, 48

3. Safe Spaces and Other Places:
   Navigating the Urban Landscape, 100

4. To Where from Here?
   The Final Vision of the Migration Narrative, 142

5. New Directions for the Migration Narrative:
   Thoughts on *Jazz*, 184

Notes, 199

Bibliography, 219

Index, 227

"Who Set You Flowin'?"

This new phase of Negro American life . . . will doubtless prove to be the most significant event in our local history since the Civil War.

Carter G. Woodson (1918)

Move. Walk. Run.

Toni Morrison (1987)

Take me to another place, take me to another time.

Arrested Development (1992)

The fundamental theme of New World African modernity is neither integration nor separation but rather migration and emigration.

Cornel West (1993)

Introduction

From the publication of Paul Laurence Dunbar's *Sport of the Gods* in 1902 to Toni Morrison's *Jazz* in 1992, the migration narrative emerges as one of the twentieth century's dominant forms of African-American cultural production.[1] Through migration narratives—musical, visual, and literary—African-American artists and intellectuals attempt to come to terms with the massive dislocation of black peoples following migration. Given the impact of migration and urbanization on African-Americans in particular and American society in general, it is not surprising that this century has witnessed the emergence of this new form.

Most often, migration narratives portray the movement of a major character or the text itself from a provincial (not necessarily rural) Southern or Midwestern site (home of the ancestor) to a more cosmopolitan, metropolitan area. Within the migration narrative the protagonist or a central figure who most influences the protagonist is a migrant. The representation of the migration experience depends on the genre and form of the narrative as well as the historical and political moment of production. Also, each artist's conception of power is directly related to the construction of his or her text.

The narrative is marked by four pivotal moments: (1) an event that propels the action northward, (2) a detailed representation of the initial confrontation with the urban landscape, (3) an illustration of the migrant's attempt to negotiate that landscape and his or her resistance to the negative effects of urbanization, and (4) a vision of the possibilities or limitations of the Northern, Western, or Midwestern city and the South. These moments may occur in any given order within the context of the narrative; in other words, it is not necessary that there be a straightforward linear progression from the South to a vision of the consequences of migration, although this is most often the case.

The migration narrative shares with the slave narrative notions of ascent from the South into a "freer" North. Like the slave narrative and the fiction it inspired, the migration narrative has its own set of narrative conventions. If the slave narrative revolves around the auction block, the whipping, the separation of families, and miscegenation, the migration narrative provides us with lynching scenes, meetings with ancestors, and urban spaces like kitchenettes, dance halls, and street corners. The migration narrative is marked by an exploration of urbanism, an explication of sophisticated modern power, and, in some instances, a return South. Finally, the migration narrative takes shape in a variety of art forms: autobiography, fiction, music, poetry, photography, and painting.

Although literary critics have noted migration as an important theme in African-American fiction, until recently they have been less attentive to the relationship between migration and African-American literary production. The study of twentieth-century black migration has been the province of social scientists, historians, and scholars of African-American music and folklore. Prompted by Robert Stepto's *From Behind the Veil: A Study of Afro-American Narrative* (1979), in the past decade, literary and cultural critics Susan Willis, Hazel Carby, Lawrence Rodgers, and Charles Scruggs have started the important project of situating twentieth-century migration as a major factor in African-American cultural production.[2]

Hazel Carby's work is particularly noteworthy. Carby documents the emergence and development of a black women's blues culture that created "a music that spoke the desires which were released in the dramatic shift in social relations that occurred in a historical moment of crisis and dislocation."[3] For Carby, the 1920s marked a time when established black Northern intellectuals were confronted with large numbers of migrants who challenged earlier notions of sexuality, leadership, and any sense of a monolithic black culture.

Charles Scruggs stresses migration as an important starting point in the study of black literature of the city. Lawrence Rodgers is the first to identify migration with the emergence of a new genre of African-American literature: the Great Migration novel.

This book departs from the foregoing studies in its interdisciplinary focus and in its discussion of a variety of literary, musical, and visual works that were created during the height of the Great Migration and the years that followed it. I have chosen to call these texts migration narratives. The paradigm "migration narrative" provides a conceptual umbrella under which to gather these African-American creative artifacts. In addition to identifying the migration narrative as a dominant form of African-American cultural production in the twentieth century, I have tried to create a way of talking about African-American art that provides comprehensive space for the diversity of gender, class, and sexuality. Through critical readings of migration narratives, I reveal paradigms like "ancestors" and "strangers" that cross class, gender, and genre. This interpretation finds no one static migration narrative; instead these narratives are as diverse as the people and the times that create them.

Most migration narratives offer a catalyst for leaving the South. Although there are different reasons for migrating, in all cases the South is portrayed as an immediate, identifiable, and oppressive power. Southern power is exercised by people known to its victims—bosses, landlords, sheriffs, and, in the case of black women, even family members. To the extent that power is exercised psychically, it relies on the potential victim's fear of the violence that awaits him or her. In fictional texts especially, Southern power is inflicted on black bodies in the form of lynching, beating, and rape. It is dramatized in the spectacle and torture of elaborate lynching and burning rituals.[4] The degree to which Southern power is stressed differs from genre to genre, but there is a consensus that this power is unsophisticated in nature.[5]

Although the narratives tend to represent the South as a site of terror and exploitation, some of them also identify it as a site of the ancestor. The role of the ancestor in the Southern sections of the migration narrative is of great significance to the development of the text. If the ancestor's role is mitigated, then it is likely that throughout the course of the narrative, the South will be portrayed as a site of racial horror and shame. In this instance, the ancestor will be of little use on the Northern landscape. If, on the other hand, the early Southern sections stress the significance of an ancestor, or the blood of any recently deceased black person, then the South becomes a place where black blood earns a black birthright to the land, a locus of history, culture, and possible redemption. If the South is thus established as a place of birthright, then the ancestor will be a significant influence in the migrant's life in the North.

After leaving the South, the next pivotal moment in the migration narrative is the initial confrontation with the urban landscape. This confrontation often shapes the fate of the South (embodied in the migrants themselves, the ancestor, and any retention of the South) in the city. The confrontation with the urban landscape— usually experienced as a change in time, space, and technology as well as a different concept of race relations—results in a profound change in the way that the mechanisms of power work in the city. Here, it seems, power is more subtle and sophisticated. The more sophisticated use of power is not beyond resorting to acts of physical violence on black bodies. The prevalence of police brutality in urban areas is one example of this. In this instance it is often necessary for migrants to evoke the presence of an ancestor or certain aspects of their Southern folk culture in order to combat the harsh confrontation with the urban landscape.

I have borrowed the concept "ancestor" from Toni Morrison, who argues: "[Ancestors] are sort of timeless people whose relationships to the characters are benevolent, instructive, and protective, and they provide a certain kind of wisdom."[6] I want to extend Morrison's definition of the ancestor to include an understanding of the full ramifications of the term. The ancestor is present in ritual, religion, music, food, and performance. His or her legacy is evident in discursive formations like the oral tradition. The ancestor might be a literal ancestor; he or she also has earthly representatives, whom we might call elders. The ancestor's presence in Southern cultural forms such as song, food, and language sometimes provides the new migrant a cushion with which to soften the impact of urbanization. In *Moorings and Metaphors: Figures of Culture and Gender in Black Women's Literature,* Karla Holloway argues that the ancestor figure "serves as a recursive touchstone" and that "the ancestral presence constitutes a posture of remembrance." (p. 115).

Toni Morrison's Pilate Dead and Julie Dash's Nana Peazant are the quintessential representatives of the ancestor. Pilate is the central female figure of Morrison's *Song of Solomon.* As the daughter of Macon Dead I she is a direct descendant of the flying African. She embodies the history of the Dead clan in her earring and her song. Self-born, possessing no sign of her connection, she is nonetheless the most connected character in the text. She sits on the boundaries, dwells in the borderlands. In her mind she houses not only the songs and stories of the past, but also the remedies, the recipes for nurturance and survival. Pilate is both root and leaf, the transitional space between the ground where the ancestors reside and the sky to which they direct all who revere them. She is both tall and short; both eloquent and illiterate. She speaks freely to the dead, the living, and the unborn.

Similarly, the character Nana Peazant in Julie Dash's film *Daughters of the Dust* possesses the qualities of the ancestor. As family griot, Nana holds her family's history in a box filled with "scraps of memory," her Yoruba-based religious rituals, and her stories. This elder advises her migrating grandchildren: "I'm the one that can give you strength. . . . Take me wherever you go. I'm your strength."

Ancestors are a specific presence in the text. They are found in both its content and its form. Toni Morrison best articulates the role of the migration narrative as repository of the ancestor when she says that her storytelling, like that of the characters in *Song of Solomon*, is an attempt to preserve and pass on the stories and the songs of the African-American past.[7] As far as she is concerned, urbanization and "the press toward upward social mobility would mean to get as far away from that kind of knowledge as possible." According to Morrison, such a fiction "recognizes what the conflicts are, what the problems are. But it need not solve those problems because it is not a case study."[8] In an interview, Morrison even suggested that fiction as ancestor serves as a space for enlightenment, sustenance, and renewal: "There is a confrontation between old values of the tribes and newer urban values. It's confusing. There has to be a mode to do what the music did for blacks, what we used to be able to do with each other in private and in that civilization that existed underneath the white civilization."[9]

While Morrison's fiction seeks to be the repository of the ancestor and eschews becoming a "case study," other migration narratives strive toward a more objective stance. These are dominated by the "stranger." On the pages of the written migration narrative and in the lyrics of many of the musical ones, the migrant often meets a literal stranger who offers (mis)guidance, advice, and a new worldview. The stranger exists in a dialectical relationship with the ancestor. While the ancestor originates in the South and lives in the North, for the most part the stranger is a Northern phenomenon.

My concept of the stranger is greatly influenced, but not circumscribed by, the stranger "who stays" in the work of the German-Jewish sociologist Georg Simmel. Simmel's stranger is a figure whose membership within a group involves being at once outside and within its boundaries.

Simmel characterizes the stranger who stays as "a potential wanderer . . . [who,] although he has gone no further, has not quite got over the freedom of coming and going. He is fixed within a certain spatial circle—or within a group whose boundaries are analogous to spatial boundaries."[10] Simmel's stranger does not initially belong to the group; instead, he brings qualities into it that are not, and cannot be, indigenous. The stranger is a cosmopolitan figure.

Simmel created his concept of the stranger as a means of understanding the process of migration and urbanization in a European context. In American sociology, "the stranger" evolves into "the marginal man" and is best described in the work of Robert Park.[11] For Park, human migrations produced new personalities, one of which he characterized as the newly emancipated individual, or the marginal man. For this character type, "energies that were formerly controlled by custom and tradition are released. . . . [Such persons] become . . . not merely emancipated, but enlightened."[12] Park continues, "The emancipated individual invariably becomes in a certain sense and to a certain degree a cosmopolitan. He learns to look upon the world in which he was born and bred with something of the detachment of a stranger. He acquires, in short, an intellectual bias." This figure has severed all ties with the ancestor, yet, under Parks's definition, this will not inhibit but will further his access to freedom.

In relation to the dominant white society, all migrants are strangers—foreigners driven by persecution to wander in search of a new home. However, within the context of the African-American community, the stranger is that figure who possesses no connections to the community. Migrants who seek to be strangers can never occupy that space fully, but those who come closest "change their discomforts into a base of resistance."[13]

Like Simmel's "stranger," the omniscient narrators of these texts play the role of journalists, streetwise reporters who detach themselves and present the readers with a case for consideration and action. Gwendolyn Brooks has in fact likened herself to a reporter in her attempts to record the daily lives of ordinary black urbanites. Ann Petry used her skills as a newspaper reporter documenting black Harlem of the forties to write her classic novel *The Street*, and with *Native Son* Richard Wright provides us with the novel-as-stranger par excellence. In "Blueprint for Negro Writing," Wright argues that writers are "agents of social change who possess unified personalities, organized emotions [and an] obdurate will to change the world."[14] Wright credited the social sciences for providing him with objective, critical frameworks in which to place his stories.[15]

Richard Wright is an exemplar of the migrant as stranger. In his essay "How Bigger Thomas Was Born," Wright explains how he himself avoided becoming Bigger. Wright's description resembles that of Julia Kristeva's stranger, who, according to Kristeva, "had he stayed home, might have become an outlaw." Wright the protagonist shares with Bigger a sense of disconnection from the stifling folk tradition of the race. The protagonists Bigger and Wright mark the negative and positive consequences of stranger status, respectively. Bigger is devoid of any human connection and does not fill that void with a critical consciousness until he has already become an outlaw. Wright becomes the stranger who possesses the critical consciousness and who occupies the position of cosmopolite.

In terms of form, the texts seem to oscillate between the two encounters with the stranger and the ancestor. In fact, the most sophisticated texts, like Morrison's *Song of Solomon* and Jean Toomer's *Cane*, strive to be sites of the ancestor. Wright's *Native Son* and Petry's *The Street* strive to occupy the space of the stranger, the observer, the social scientist shedding light on a familiar but strange situation. Stevie Wonder's "Living for the City" embodies the conflict between the stranger and the ancestor in both its content and its musical form. The figurations of ancestors and strangers provide useful conceptual tools for understanding the migration narratives; they are both masculine and feminine, male and female, concrete and abstract. In their extremes, ancestors and strangers are polar opposites; in more sophisticated texts they overlap. Sometimes the stranger and the ancestor seem to exist in the same figure. In fact, the most effective ancestors possess qualities of the stranger and the most effective strangers can pass as ancestors. For instance, Pilate glides through the pages of *Song of Solomon* walking a line between the familiar, ancestral mode and that of the "stranger."

The third moment of the migration narrative is the portrayal of the way migrants negotiate the urban landscape. Once situated on the urban landscape, domestic, street, and psychic space are all sites of contestation for migrants and the powers that seek to control them. Again, the ancestor is of great significance in this struggle. These spaces are often sites where the ancestor is invoked; at other times they are sites from which he or she is banished. Often, rejection of the ancestor leads to further alienation, exile, the status of stranger, or sometimes death. The ancestor in turn is a site of negotiation for the construction of a new self. The creation of a new self may be one of the most crucial aspects of resistance to the complexities of the North. However, for many, the sites of the ancestor are stifling and provincial and as such they inhibit the progress and the development of the protagonist.

These spaces are either the locus for producing and maintaining the negative effects of urbanization—fragmentation, dislocation, and material and spiritual impoverishment—or "safe havens" from these negative effects. In the latter instance, they help the migrant to construct an alternate urban subjectivity. (Subject is here used to connote an object of social and historical forces as well as a historical agent.)

I borrow the term "safe spaces" from Patricia Hill Collins, who defines them

8

as places where black women "speak freely" and where domination does not exist as a "hegemonic ideology." She identifies as safe spaces extended families, churches, and African-American community organizations, as well as cultural traditions like the black women's blues and literary traditions. According to Collins these spaces form a site of "resisting objectification as Other." Collins claims such sites "house a culture of resistance."[16]

My use of "safe space" seeks to complicate Collins's definition. First, hegemonic ideology can exist even in spaces of resistance. Second, these sites are more often the locus of sustenance and preservation than of resistance. While sustenance and preservation are necessary components of resistance, I do not believe they are in and of themselves resistant acts. Moreover, safe spaces can be very conservative spaces as well. For my purposes safe spaces provide a way of understanding the possibilities of such sites in the migration narrative. However, the narratives often point out the irony of the term "safe." For instance, in some cases the black church is not necessarily a safe space for black women in light of its gender hierarchy, its stand against birth control and abortion, and its homophobia. In other cases the church is the only site that recognizes and affirms black humanity.

In the migration narrative, safe spaces are available to both male and female characters.[17] At their most progressive, they are spaces of retreat, healing, and resistance; at their most reactionary, they are potentially provincial spaces which do not encourage resistance but instead help to create complacent subjects whose only aim is to exist within the confines of power that oppress them. In many instances these spaces contain both possibilities. In some cases safe spaces are sites where the South is invoked—not just in its horror, terror, and exploitation, but as a place that housed the values and memories that sustained black people. The South emerges as the home of the ancestor, the place where community and history are valued over Northern individualism.

Safe spaces are both material and discursive. Narrative safe spaces are often resistant to traditional narrative form. They appear in song, food, elements of oral culture, the silences around ritual, and in dream sequences. Literal safe spaces in the city are places where rituals can be enacted to invoke the presence of the ancestor in the North: Pilate's kitchen in *Song of Solomon*, Mary's boarding house in *Invisible Man*, the Savoy Ballroom in Harlem, the Jungle Room on Sixty-eighth Street in Manhattan, where new migrants shouted "Let's go home" to band leader James P. Johnson in a call for Southern music.[18] These are all safe spaces where the ancestor is invoked. In this sense, the South is no longer simply a "historical locus" but also a figurative one.

On the other hand, for writers like Richard Wright and James Baldwin, sites like the library provide "safe" space as well as exposure to a world from which their protagonists are excluded.[19] This newfound knowledge can both empower and anger them. In any case, they are aware of the racism of the dominant society as well as the provincial nature of their own communities.

Because safe spaces are created by as well as resistant to sophisticated urban power, they have a tenuous and contradictory existence. A woman's safe space—the home, for instance—might be inhibiting for a man. Similarly, a woman might find the culture of the street, which nurtures an urban black manhood, somewhat dangerous and detrimental to her well-being. Both men and women might find that these spaces are under the control of people and forces that oppress them.

The fourth moment of the migration narrative provides a consideration of the sophistication of modern urban power, an evaluation of the consequences of migration and urbanization, and a vision of future possibilities. For many artists, the North ensures the death and demise of the migrant; for others migration is one step on the road to a cosmopolitan status. Still others, like the rap band Arrested Development, require a return to the South as a means of acquiring racial, historical, and cultural redemption.

The chapters of this book are organized around these four moments in an effort to provide a kind of critical migration narrative. This mode of organization best reveals the contours of the narratives as well as the manner in which the portrayal of migration changes over time and is contested at any given historical and political moment. In an attempt to address the obvious limitation of this organization, the closing chapter initiates a more sustained reading of Toni Morrison's *Jazz* using the framework described within.

The moments described here are constantly revised and challenged. At any given time different interpretations exist side by side. Nevertheless, one interpretation usually emerges as dominant.[20] The major shift in the representation of the migration is prompted by a shift in the understanding of power and the different forms it takes in the North and the South.

During the years following the Harlem Renaissance throughout the Depression to World War II, Richard Wright's version of the migration narrative was the dominant portrayal. For Wright, the South is never a site of possibility for the migrant. Unless he acquires a critical consciousness of the stranger, unless he distances himself from folk culture, he is assured a certain literal or metaphorical "death on the city pavements." Although Zora Neale Hurston provides an alternative to Wright in that her fiction is situated in a racially monolithic South, Wright's is nonetheless the dominant vision. I measure Wright's hegemony not only by the critical attention received by his work, or by the accolades of Book-of-the-Month Club selection and best-seller lists, but also by the degree to which he influenced other African-American writers: Although authors like Chester Himes, William Demby, and Ann Petry differ from Wright in significant ways, they nonetheless have been influenced by him.

The period following the war serves as a kind of transition from Wright's dominance to the emergence of Ralph Ellison. This era is marked by the publication of Ralph Ellison's *Invisible Man* and James Baldwin's *Go Tell It on the Mountain*. Despite both writers' very public disavowals of Wright's influence on their work—

indeed neither presents a picture as bleak as that of Wright—they nonetheless share his vision in many ways. Baldwin shares Wright's sense of the stifling nature of black life, yet both he and Ellison appreciate the complexities of African-American life much more than Wright. In so doing, they also suggest the possibilities of the South by privileging the importance of certain elements of black Southern culture to the survival of urban blacks.

Following the Civil Rights and Black Power movements, Toni Morrison's version of the migration narrative emerges as the dominant one. In her work the South becomes not only a site of racial redemption and identity but also the place where Africa is most present. It is not surprising that this emerges as the dominant portrayal of African-American migration following the Civil Rights Movement. If, in fact, the South is a premodern power, it is more susceptible to the forms of social protest that take place there during the Civil Rights Movement. Therefore, it is more likely to be affected by social change. Because of this it can be reconsidered as a burial ground, as a place of cultural origins, home of the ancestors, as a place to be redeemed. The North, however, as a more complex and omniscient power, is not susceptible to the same strategies of the Civil Rights Movement; thus the failure of Martin Luther King in Chicago. Artists who recognize this begin to represent the South in ways only alluded to by their predecessors and to reimagine the possibilities the South holds for African-American people.

Morrison is not the first to have the South reemerge as a site of African-American history and culture; Ralph Ellison, Albert Murray, and Alice Walker precede her. However, Morrison is the first whose texts not only tell the story of the ancestor in the South, but also embody the ancestor.[21] In this way, her significance is not only in the story she tells, but also in the way in which she tells it. I measure Morrison's dominance by the number of scholarly books and articles devoted to her work, the almost automatic appearance of her work on bestseller lists, and her winning of the Pulitzer Prize and the Nobel Prize for Literature.

Although one interpretation of migration may reign at any given moment, it is always challenged by other visions. At times those challenges come from other forms; for instance, film or music may challenge the dominance of a literary artist's interpretation. Oftentimes the challenge comes from within genres; thus one novelist challenges another. Challenges may even come within the work of one artist. As we shall see, Toni Morrison revises and rewrites many of the tropes that she helps to establish.

The pages that follow document the existence of the migration narrative and illustrate the various changes that occur throughout its history. This study builds upon the foundations of the last twenty years of African-American cultural criticism. It is not a social history, but an attempt to provide historically and theoretically informed close readings of selected migration narratives. In a project of this scope, there are of course many important narratives that have been left out.

However, I think that the framework discussed within provides room for the inclusion of a variety of works not discussed in depth: texts of migration from the Caribbean to North American cities like Paule Marshall's *Brown Girl Brownstones*,[22] texts of migration to the West such as Chester Himes's novel *If He Hollers Let Him Go*, Charles Burnett's films *To Sleep with Anger* and *Killer of Sheep*, and Carrie Mae Weems's photograph series *Family Pictures and Stories* or the plays of August Wilson.[23] The migration narrative is also embedded in the arenas of sport: the integration of baseball, the entrance of blacks into the urban, ethnic game of basketball, and the subsequent stylistic innovations of each game are also possible areas for exploration. It is my hope that this book will encourage further studies of these various forms of the migration narrative.

"Boll Weevil in the Cotton / Devil in the White Man": Reasons for Leaving the South

The lynched body is missing from panel 15 (Figure 1.1) in Jacob Lawrence's *The Migration of the Negro Series*. The caption beneath it reads: "Another cause was lynching. It was found that where there had been a lynching, the people who were reluctant to leave at first left immediately after this." The painting is chilling yet simple; there are no complex figures. The most striking object, the hanging body, is striking by its absence. However, all the organic forms of the painting are linked to a lynching.

The small 12" × 18" tempera on masonite is divided by a diagonal into two large horizontal planes. Light dominates the top of the painting; the bottom is dark brown. The harsh brown of the branch and the noose interrupt the otherwise peaceful pastel plane. The noose falls in a perpendicular from the branch, echoing in shape and line the vertical figure at bottom left. Both the noose and the branch from which it hangs are brown, like the earth and the figure who occupies it. The round and twisted noose mirrors the hunched human figure at the bottom.

A black-skinned, bent body—unseen, unnamed, anonymous—is connected to the noose through its circular shape and color. The figure's blood-red clothing stand out because red is the only primary color of the painting. Like the rock on which it sits, the figure is round. The landscape is cold, bleak; there is no sun. We do not know if it is dawn or dusk. The immediate horror is gone, but an aura of mourning and sadness remain.

This depiction of a lynching is unique among other Lawrence works with the same subject matter: In other paintings and drawings, Lawrence focuses on the hanging bodies. In his John Brown series, the lynched body dominates. Lawrence's *New Republic* drawings portray heads of lynched men that have become the branches of the trees. Yet in this painting he chooses to rid the scene of the body, of the evidence. It is as though the landscape and the mourning figure embody the horror of lynching. In this sense it is not the horror of one single individual, but the horror, the shame, and the burden of the land. The viewer is

Figure 1.1 Jacob Lawrence, *The Migration of the Negro*, 1940–41. Panel 15. "Another cause was lynching. It was found that where there had been a lynching, the people who were reluctant to leave at first left immediately after this." Tempera on masonite, 12″ × 18″. (The Phillips Collection, Washington, D.C.)

familiar enough with the visual tropes of trees, noose, and black figure to read the meaning of the painting. She does not speculate, "Of what crime is he accused?" Instead, her attention turns to the bleakness of the landscape, the branchlike noose, the earth, and the mourning figure. The figure is linked to the noose in color and in shape; the noose in turn, is linked by the same elements to the ground. The horror of lynching in this painting is the horror of a land and entire people. The body of the mourner is weighed down by it, the beauty of the tree is marred by it. For Lawrence, this is cause for leaving the South. Power, as exercised here, enters the landscape and the individuals who inhabit it.[1]

The Migration series was exhibited at the Harlem Community Arts Center in June 1941; it was moved to New York's Downtown Gallery the following December. At the Downtown Gallery, the series appeared as part of the historic American Negro Art Exhibition. The American Negro Art Exhibition included works by other young African-American artists as well. Both Romare Bearden and Elizabeth Catlett were among the artists whose work appeared in the exhibition. However, Lawrence's series made him one of the first African-American artists to receive widespread critical attention. Twenty-six of the paintings appeared in the February 1941 issue of *Fortune* magazine. In February 1942, the Museum of Modern Art in New York purchased the odd-numbered panels of the series and the Phillips Collection in Washington purchased the even-numbered paintings. The *Fortune* feature, as well as the subsequent showings launched by a traveling exhibition, brought Lawrence's work to a larger audience.[2] Much of that audience was already familiar with the relationship of Southern violence and black migration.

What Lawrence suggests with the subtlety of his painting, Billie Holiday aggressively asserts in her haunting interpretation of "Strange Fruit." Holiday introduced the song in 1939, early in her tenure at Cafe Society in New York. According to her biographer Robert O'Meally, the song "propelled her into the ranks of the 'crossover' stars." At Cafe Society, Holiday sang to an integrated audience made up of "leftists, jazz lovers, and New Yorkers in the know."[3] The song became so popular among the Cafe Society crowd that Holiday recorded it in 1939 at their urging. O'Meally notes that her recording company, Columbia, refused to record the song out of fear of the Southern white market. Determined to have the song recorded, Holiday sought out independent record producer Milt Gabler, who agreed to do it. Holiday's singing and recording of the song was meant to be interpreted as a political act as well as an artistic one. For a certain left-leaning audience, it came to symbolize the injustice of the American South, thus becoming joined with other works of art of the same period that sought to carry a similar message: Richard Wright's *Uncle Tom's Children* (1938) and *Native Son* (1940) and the Lawrence paintings (1941). This period obviously marked a growing sense of assertiveness on the part of African-American artists. Through both the media and the cultural production of these African-American visual, literary, and musical artists, lynching became a dominant symbol of the South.

Wright's *Native Son* and Billie Holiday's version of "Strange Fruit" continue to resonate the temperament of that period for contemporary audiences. Although the song is based on a poem by Lewis Allen, it truly belongs to Holiday.[4] The words are as follows:

> Southern trees bear a strange fruit:
> Blood on the leaves and blood at the root;
> Black bodies swinging in the southern breeze;
> Strange fruit hanging from the poplar trees.
>
> Pastoral scene of the gallant South:
> The bulging eyes and the twisted mouth;
> Scent of magnolia sweet and fresh;
> Then the sudden smell of burning flesh.
>
> Here is a fruit for the crows to pluck;
> For the rain to gather, for the wind to suck.
> For the sun to rot, for the tree to drop;
> Here is a strange and bitter crop.

No newspaper account, no graphic photograph, no literary description matches the haunting pathos with which Holiday emphasizes words like "root," "pluck," and "suck." Her portrayal of the naturally beautiful "pastoral South," marred by the realities of burning black bodies, gives meaning and emotion to the descriptions written by the novelists. Unlike Lawrence, Holiday places the black body at the very center of the pastoral. Its blood nourishes the fertile earth which in life it tilled. She is the only woman artist we consider who focuses so intently on the body of the lynched. Interestingly, the body at the center of Holiday's song is not a gendered body. One does not know if she is speaking of a male or female. Robert O'Meally argues the imagery of trees "that 'bear' and 'fruit' that is 'plucked' or 'dropped,' also gave expression to her role as a woman who discerned a sexual motive in the act of lynching."[5] However, I would argue by not naming the gender of the lynched body, Holiday is asserting the "sexual motive in the act of lynching," as well as the possibility that the lynched body may be that of a black woman.

Holiday's Southern earth is fertilized with the blood of black people. "Southern trees bear a strange fruit: / blood on the leaves, and blood at the root." Her emphasis and phrasing, stressing fruit and root, link black blood to the tree organically. There is even an organic connection between the wind and the trees: "Black bodies swinging in the Southern breeze; / Strange fruit hanging from the poplar trees." The wind carries the scent of the burning body: "Scent of magnolia, sweet and fresh; / then the sudden smell of burning flesh." The juxtaposition of the sweet and bitter affirms the basic contradiction of the South. On the surface it is a land of great physical beauty and charm, but beneath it lay black blood and decayed black bodies. Beneath the charm lay the horror. Like the cotton they pick, the lynched black bodies are also a Southern crop. Violence, death, and terror in the midst of natural serenity are made even more chilling by Holiday's whisper-soft, rapier-sharp phrasing. The horror is organically linked to the place, a place where even the crows and the wind act violently upon the black body.

These two different portrayals of a lynching, one emphasizing the effect on the community and the land, the other focusing on the lynched body, illustrate the range of representation in the migration narrative. Hanging bodies, burned and mutilated, women, raped and tormented—such figures populate the migration narrative. The texts are filled to the brim with the portrayal of an institutionalized terrorism that daily inflicts itself on the lives of black characters. Lynching becomes a metaphor for all such acts of violence on Southern blacks. The black body—be it lynched, raped, working in the fields, working in kitchens, or acting in resistance—is a site of struggle. The power of the South is one of spectacle and torture. It infiltrates black bodies, leaving them dismembered, bent, old beyond their years. It also reaches into the very depths of the land which they occupy, as is suggested by Lawrence's painting.

According to Michel Foucault, "Nothing is more material, physical, corporal, than the exercise of power."[6] Although Foucault attributes this exercise of power to an earlier era, one which begins to decline in the nineteenth century, the authors of migration narratives assert that it typifies the exercise of power in the American South well into the twentieth century. For the African-American migrant protagonist, a shift in the way power is exercised is spatial, not temporal. In

Figure 1.2 *The Reason.* (*The Crisis* [March 1920].)

1920, the Chicago Urban League noted: "After a lynching, colored people from that community will arrive in Chicago inside of two weeks"; historical and sociological literature, however, often list lynching as a secondary factor in the decision to migrate. It falls into a category with disenfranchisement and lack of educational opportunity. For the most part the primary causes cited are economic, the

17

failure of the South's single-crop economy, the desire of blacks for better, more stable wages.

It seems that the reasons cited for leaving the South differ with the nature of the sources consulted. Sociologists, historians, novelists, poets, painters, journalists, politicians, and the migrants themselves all have added their voices to the chorus of reasons for leaving the South. The voices of the migrants and those who research their creative work stress their agency. Until recently social historians and sociologists have tended to stress economic and political forces outside of the migrants' control as the primary cause for migration.[7] The vast majority of literary texts focus on violence as the principal catalyst for migration.

I

> I pick up my life
> And take it on the train
> To Los Angeles, Bakersfield,
> Seattle, Oakland, Salt Lake,
> Any place that is
> North and West—
> And not South.
>
> Langston Hughes, "One Way Ticket"

Carol Marks's *Farewell, We're Good and Gone* (1989) claims that the migration was primarily "orchestrated by northern industry." According to Marks, the destruction of the South's single-crop dependence, disenfranchisement and segregation, and the war in Europe, which sharply reduced European migration, all helped to make Southern migrants an attractive alternative source of labor. Northern industrialists precipitated the mass movement North through the use of labor agents.[8] Marks's assertion denies agency of the migrants.

Lawrence Levine warns against relying entirely upon this interpretation of the migration:

> As indisputably important as the economic motive was, it is possible to overstress it so that the black migration is converted into an inexorable force and Negroes are seen once again not as actors capable of affecting at least some part of their destinies, but primarily as beings who are acted upon—southern leaves blown North by the winds of destitution. . . .
> Black songs too make it clear that migration was more than the product of pure economic forces.[9]

Levine agrees with Amiri Baraka, who states emphatically: "It was a decision Negroes made to leave the South, not an historical imperative."[10]

Both Baraka and Levine are concerned with the culture of the mass of migrants. Perhaps this is why they so strongly stress issues of migrant agency. It is in the cultural histories, rather than in the sociological texts, that Southern blacks emerge as agents involved in their own destiny. It is the cultural creations of the migrants—particularly letters and blues lyrics—that present the most well-rounded and complex picture of the factors that motivated them to leave.

According to William Barlow, rural blues "articulated the call for urban migration." For Barlow, "Many rural blues artists were in the forefront of the exodus; they were the oracles of their generation, contrasting the promise of freedom with the reality of their harsh living conditions." However, for the most part, blues lyrics, the migration narrative of the mass of migrants, tend to focus on floods, the boll weevil, sharecropping, and failed love. Blues of the northbound genre stress the persona's decision to leave as an attempt to escape various factors that equal "blues." These include Jim Crow and bad working conditions, but most often the persona seeks to leave in order to follow a lover.[11] The vast majority of blues lyrics tell of migrant men leaving their women, or women who are trying to escape the "blues." The overall pathos of the blues haunts the atmosphere, and this is the reason for leaving. "The blues" encompasses the psychological state of someone who is exploited, abused, dominated, and dispossessed. Other lyrics draw specifically on the natural disasters which haunt the South, causing economic destruction and displacement. The final, and most rare group of lyrics focus on social injustice or violence as the cause for migration.[12]

Examples of the first type abound in migration blues. The railroad, long a symbol of freedom in the African-American oral tradition, reappears in the northbound blues. By invoking it, the blues lyricist calls upon an image packed with cultural significance for his audience. However, as Hazel Carby has illustrated, the meaning of the train image differs significantly according to the sex of the persona. According to Carby, "The train, which had symbolized freedom and mobility for men in male blues songs . . . [for women signified] a mournful signal of imminent desertion and future loneliness."[13]

Both men and women sing the second type of blues, those that focus on natural disasters. One such example of this type of blues song and performance is Bessie Smith's "Homeless Blues." Framed by an opening and closing instrumental refrain of "Home Sweet Home," Smith's voice narrates the tale of a dispossessed, dislocated persona who has become homeless as a result of the flood:

> Mississippi River, What a fix you left me in.
> Oh Mississippi River, What a fix you left me in.
> Pot holes of water clear up to my chin.
>
> House without a [inaudible], didn't even have a door.
> House without a [inaudible], didn't even have a door.
> Plain old two room shanty but it was my home sweet home.
>
> Ma and Pa got drowned, Mississippi you's to blame.
> My Ma and Pa got drowned, Mississippi you's to blame.
> Mississippi River, I can't stand to hear your name.

Homeless, yes I'm Homeless. Might as well be dead.
Oh you know I'm Homeless, yes I'm Homeless. Might as well be dead.
Hungry and disgusted. No place to lay my head.
Wish I was an eagle, but I'm a plain old black crow.
Wish I was an eagle, but I'm just a plain old black crow.
I'm gonna flap my wings and leave here and never come back no more.[14]

While the song specifically focuses on the Mississippi River flood, it reveals much more about the conditions under which poor blacks lived in the South and it articulates their relationship to American society in general. Though Smith chides the Mississippi River, the listener senses that the objects of her critique are those who have created the conditions of poverty under which she lives. Her house is a two-room shanty. The flood causes the loss of both her parents, leaving her orphaned. There are no relief measures in place to assist her in light of this loss. The Mississippi River, symbol of mobility and freedom, gateway to the West and notions of manifest destiny for the likes of Huck Finn, is here responsible for taking away loved ones. This is an image with which many African-Americans identify. For African-American slaves "downriver" connoted a geographical place where slavery was most harsh and inhumane. The slave narratives and spirituals reflect the pain of being sold downriver and literally separated from family and community. For twentieth-century African-Americans, the Mississippi River still signals the terror of the South. When authorities dragged the Mississippi River for the bodies of civil rights workers James Chaney, Andrew Goodman, and Michael Schwerner, they pulled from the river numerous black bodies, whose disappearances had never been investigated. With "Homeless Blues," Smith foreshadows her artistic daughter Nina Simone, who forty years later sang "Mississippi Goddamn!!"

Finally, the persona situates herself in opposition to another symbol of American freedom, the eagle, by calling herself a "plain black crow." As a dispossessed denizen, she maintains no identification with the patriotic symbol. In the guise of the crow, she asserts her intention to flee the South, the land of injustice. The image of the crow is packed with cultural significance for Smith's audience. The term "Jim Crow" can be traced back to the early nineteenth century and was initially used to describe black people who were "lost in obscurity."[15] Following Reconstruction, the term came to define the segregation statutes of the American South. The changing definition of Jim Crow is exemplary of the black condition in the United States, a condition characterized by a constant wandering in "search" of a "freer" space. Yet the spaces to which generations of African-Americans have roamed are marked by attempts to further constrain and control them. The notion of Jim Crow as a lost black soul is especially fitting in the context of the "Homeless Blues." The persona as "an old black crow" is at once conflated with the image of lost Africans on the American landscape as well as the image of the South's system of racial apartheid.

Smith utilizes familiar images and rearticulates them into new forms of black cultural resistance. The images of the eagle and the Mississippi River have one meaning for the dominant, oppressor society and an altogether different meaning for the oppressed, whom she represents. By voicing the alternative meaning, by recording it for posterity, she ensures its continued presence in the discourse around notions of American democracy and freedom.

Smith's performance dramatically asserts the persona's anger and disgust. This is not the song of a passive victim; Smith defiantly articulates her frustration and anger with the Mississippi River, confronting it harshly, with the accusation, "Mississippi, you's to blame." Her opposition to cherished American symbols is evident in the music itself. The use of the sweet and familiar instrumental "Home Sweet Home" refrain which opens this song is in stark contrast to the clear, assertive voice of the singer, who speaks of a doorless two-room shanty. Like her slave foremothers who sang "Sometimes I feel like a feather in the air and I spread my wings and fly,"[16] Smith also employs the image of flight as escape from the oppressive conditions she records. Smith paints a picture with which her audience is familiar; then she tells them that their only option is to flee it through the act of migration.

"Homeless Blues" was recorded on September 28, 1927, and was one of the many blues and vaudeville songs Smith performed in the North and the South. According to Chris Albertson, Smith did not change her songs to suit the racial makeup of her various audiences. Though she performed to both black and white audiences (in segregated theaters), surely her black audience experienced "Mississippi River Blues" as documentation of their own experience. By 1927, Smith was widely recognized as one of the best classic blues singers of the day. She performed in theaters as well as tent shows. Much of her inspiration came from the black audiences who attended her shows and she used her songwriting ability to voice their concerns. In fact, prior to recording "Homeless Blues," Smith wrote and recorded "Back Water Blues." The song and its title were inspired by her visit to a small Southern town. Maud Smith, one of the performers employed by Bessie Smith, recalled:

> After we left Cincinnati, we came to this little town, which was flooded, so everybody had to step off the train into little rowboats that took us to where we were staying. It was an undertaker parlor next door to the theater, and we were supposed to stay in some rooms they had upstairs there. So after we had put our bags down, Bessie looked around and said, "No, no, I can't stay here tonight." But there was a lot of other people there, and they were trying to get her to stay, so they started hollerin', "Miss Bessie, please sing the 'Back Water Blues,' please sing the 'Back Water Blues.' " Well, Bessie didn't know anything about any "Back Water Blues," but after we came back home to [Philadelphia] where we were living, Bessie came in the kitchen one day, and she had a pencil and paper, and she started singing and writing. That's when she wrote the "Back Water Blues"—she got the title from those people down South.[17]

While Smith sang of the homelessness that resulted from the Mississippi flood others sang more directly of social injustices as cause to migrate. An anonymous blues lyric from Mississippi asserts:

> Times is gettin' might hard
> Money gettin' might scarce
> Soon's I sell my cott'n 'n corn
> I'se gon' leave dis place.

Both Fae Barns and Maggie Jones sang of their disgust with Jim Crow.[18]

These more overt lyrics imply that violence is the cause of migration. I stress the word imply because most often, blues lyrics do not mention lynching or the threat of violence as the cause of migration. In blues lyrics lynching is usually the punishment bestowed on a man or woman for killing his or her beloved. The absence of lynching as a reason for migration in the blues is best explained by Lawrence Levine:

> Overt protest was less common in blues than in other folk forms for a number of reasons. As blues developed, the black situation in the US was changing—indeed, the blues themselves were one of the manifestations of that change—and other outlets for protest were opening up . . . probably most crucially, blues were usually intended for an exclusively black audience and were a perfect instrument for voicing internal group problems, the individual personal difficulties and experiences, while work songs, though they too expressed personal dilemmas, were more openly sung, often with white auditors close by and frequently aimed at letting those outsiders know what the black singers felt about their situation.[19]

The closest one gets to the threat of violence as a catalyst to migration is

> Boll Weevil in the Cotton
> Cut worm in the corn.
> Devil in the White man.
> I'm good and gone.

Here the devil in the white man associates a full range of characteristics to the white boss, which might include the threat of violence. The meanings of these lyrics are often hidden beneath a complex web of metaphor and metonymy. Just as violence is implied in blues lyrics, so too is the desire for better economic or educational opportunity. Usually, the lone blues persona asserts his or her individual initiative as the reason for leaving.

The second set of migrant-created documents, letters to the *Chicago Defender*, are slightly more explicit and concrete about the reasons for migration and they are less individualistic than the blues lyrics. Letters are more communal in nature and are often couched in terms of wanting to contribute to "the betterment of the race." A review of migrant letters at first suggests that the primary reasons for leaving are economic. The vast majority are from men and women in search of work and access to education for their children. They stress the able-bodiedness of the writer, his willingness to work long and hard, and a strong commitment to participate in any effort to uplift black people.

Yet, upon closer reading, the threat of violence emerges from the silences of these notes.[20] The first suggestion in migrant letters that economic reasons are not the only motive for the desire to migrate is in the urgent request for anonymity: "Things is awful here in the South. . . . Whatever you do, don't publish my name in you paper," wrote one person from Georgia in 1917. Another, writing from New Orleans, pleaded, "Please help me get away from the South. Please keep this letter and not put it in public print." Such requests are sprinkled throughout the letters. Fear of violent reprisal for trying to leave was a realistic fear. Southern whites did resort to violence when persuasion and warnings about the harshness of the North did not work.[21]

Other letters are more explicit in their descriptions of Southern terrorism. From Troy, Alabama: "Dear Sirs: I am enclosing a clipping of a lynching again, which speaks for itself. . . . So many of our people here are almost starving." From Macon, Georgia: "We have to be shot down here like rabbits for every little offense and I seen an occurrence happen down here this afternoon when three depties from the sheriff's office and one Negro spotter come out and found some our race in a crap game and it made me want to leave." From Palestine, Texas: "I am sure ancious to make it in the North because these Southern white people are so mean and they seems to be getting worse and I wants to get away."

Finally a letter from Dapne, Alabama, expresses the full range of the desire to leave: "We work but can't get scarcely any thing for it and they don't want us to go away and there is not much of anything here to do . . . begging to get away before we are killed. . . . We see starvation ahead of us here."[22] In the letters unemployment and the imminent threat of violence are primary catalysts for migrating. There is a significant difference between the letters and artistic creations of the black masses and the portrayals of migration by some scholars which suggest ways that issues of genre and class affect meaning and interpretation.

Letters differ from blues lyrics in that they are more explicit about the daily terror under which the writers live. This difference is very important, because it illustrates that the primary purpose of the blues lyrics is not protest or resistance but the creation of cultural pleasure. This is not to deny the relationship between cultural pleasure and protest or resistance; it is simply urging us not to blindly conflate the two. In spite of their differences, the blues and the letters, along with scholarly studies of black creativity, stress the decision to migrate as an active choice, a decision accenting both the subjectivity and agency of the migrant. Sociological texts stress the power of industrial capitalism over the undeveloped South and the black Southerners who inhabit it. The creations of the migrants themselves straddle the gap between sociologists like Marks and artists like Lawrence and Holiday. If social scientists stress economic factors, then artists emphasize violence as a cause of migration.[23]

Lynching survives as the dominant literary image that provokes the protagonist's migration.[24] Interestingly, this focus on violence and the body continues the tradition established by the slave narratives, which portray a violent physical encounter as the primary catalyst to the protagonist's escape. Similarly, for writers of the migration narrative, a lynching or the imminent threat of lynching often serves as the single most important event to push the movement of the text and the protagonist North. The portrayal of violence seems to be chosen as a literary device which most effectively demonstrates the relative powerlessness of black people in the pre–Civil Rights Movement South. For early writers, who focus on the body of the black victim, the violence enacted on black people in the forms of lynchings, burnings, shootings, and rapes helps to paint a picture of the South as a place of no redemption, as a site of racial horror and shame to which we can return only with fear and trepidation.[25] As Amiri Baraka notes, "The South would remain . . . the scene of the crime."[26] For the later writers, violence against blacks is significant in that it stakes a claim on the land itself, making the South a battleground where black people shed their blood. It is a place needing and in some instances providing racial redemption. This shift in representation is the focus of the remainder of the chapter.

II

Hair—braided chestnut,
   coiled like a lyncher's rope,
Eyes—fagots,
Lips—old scars, or the first red blisters,
Breath—the last sweet scent of cane,
And her slim body, white as the ash
   of black flesh after flame.

Jean Toomer, "Portrait in Georgia"

Jean Toomer's *Cane* (1923) is a bittersweet elegy to the beauty and the horror of the South. "Portrait in Georgia" and "Blood-Burning Moon" foreshadow and document, respectively, the lynching which spurs the movement of the text North. "Portrait in Georgia" might also be a portrait *of* Georgia. In this poem, Toomer establishes some of the major tropes of the migration narrative—tropes that are later revised and revisited by those African-American artists who follow him. The object of this poem is a woman whose braided hair is likened to a lyncher's rope and whose slim white-skinned body is actually made of the ash of burned black flesh. As is always the case with Toomer, the land is compared to a woman. This time it is a white woman.

In the poem and the story, the races are bound together in a relationship of interdependence. The image of Southern white womanhood is fragile and dying because of this dependence. The poet identifies the matrix linking Southern white womanhood to the lynching of black men.[27] He is neither the first nor the last to do so: A black woman, Ida B. Wells and a white woman, Jessie Daniel Ames, precede and follow him, respectively. In publications like "Southern Horrors," (1892) "A Red Record: Tabulated Statistics and Alleged Causes of Lynching in the United States 1892–1894" (1895), and "Mob Rule in New Orleans" (1900), Wells explored the connections between the sexual exploitation of black women, the economic exploitation of black people, and the practice of lynching. According to Wells, the political and economic threat to the Southern status quo posed by black people invited the violence enacted upon them. As the founder of the Association of Southern Women for the Prevention of Lynching, Ames articulated an understanding of the connections between white women and lynching from the perspective of a Southern white woman. According to Ames's biographer, Jacquelyn Dowd Hall, for Ames, "Lynching, far from offering a shield against sexual assault, served as a weapon of both racial and sexual terror, planting fear in women's minds and dependency in their hearts."[28]

Toomer uses the political critique in establishing the defining tropes of the African-American migration narrative: Nature imagery, ideals of white womanhood, and lynching are all partners in the lynching scenes of this art form. In selecting lynching as the major reason for migration, Toomer departs from the first migration narrative, Paul Laurence Dunbar's *Sport of the Gods* (1902).

For Dunbar, the South is not a site of racial terror. His migrating black family, the Hamiltons, are sent North because of the duplicity of one white man, Francis (Frank) Oakley. Oakley is portrayed as an outsider to the South. He is the younger brother of the Hamilton's employer, the kind and fair Maurice Oakley. Frank steals money from his brother and then accuses Berry Hamilton of having taken it. Berry is convicted of the crime and sent to prison. His family is forced to leave the South and migrate to New York. Frank is different from the text's white Southerners in that he is an unambitious artist who lives in France and depends on his brother for money. His "difference" is stressed through implications of his questionable sexuality. Although Frank steals the money for a woman with whom he claims to be in love, early descriptions paint him as an effeminate dandy. In creating this character and making his duplicity the root cause of injustice experienced by the black Hamiltons, Dunbar seems to displace the unfairness of the South onto one individual character who does not belong there.[29]

In the tradition of migration narratives, James Weldon Johnson's *The Autobiography of an Ex-Colored Man* (1912) is the first to suggest a lynching as the cause for the protagonist's final migration. However, Toomer is the artist most responsible for establishing violence on the black body as a trope to signify the violence of the South and as the major catalyst for migration. Authors who follow him manipulate these tropes in different ways in order to express the role of violence as a catalyst to migration and to establish or deny the place of the South in the migrant's survival once he or she arrives in the North.

In "Blood-Burning Moon," Toomer portrays the lynching of a black man. The title "Blood-Burning Moon" is taken from the African-American religious tradition of sermons and spirituals where the image of the blood-colored moon serves as an omen for the crucifixion of Christ. In the context of *Cane*, this image is especially fitting because the moon, like all elements of nature, foreshadows and reflects the horror of lynching. Furthermore, it is a significant image because it initiates the notion that blood and the moon are symbols of both death and redemption. Whereas here, in the first Southern section of the text, the moon is linked with the crucifixion of a black man, in the final Southern section it will signal the possible redemption of black people. The title foreshadows the lynching in this particular story as well as the return to the South as a site of racial redemption at the close of the text.

In this story, Toomer chooses to ground a lynching in the sexual relationship between a white man and a black woman. In most works by black male writers, a lynching is the result of an accusation of impropriety by a black man toward a white woman.[30] In focusing on the more historically accurate relationship between white men and black women, Toomer reveals the larger issues involved in their liaison—issues of power and ownership. However, he does not focus on them as they are related to the black woman; instead this is a story about the struggle for power between two men.

Like "Portrait in Georgia," which at first resembles a love poem likening a woman to nature, this story at first seems to be a romance about the rivalry between two men for a desirable woman. Traditionally, this genre is more concerned with the men's desire for each other than their desire for the woman.[31] However, in "Blood-Burning Moon," everything is complicated because of race. So once again, Toomer toys with traditional literary forms by inserting the volatile ingredient of race. Louisa's body becomes the ground on which the two male characters, Bob Stone and Tom Burwell, fight.

Bob Stone, the white man, loves and has won Louisa through two factors: "By the way the world reckons things, he had won her. By the measure of that warm glow which came to her mind at thought of him, he had won her."[32] By both the status quo and her consent, Louisa belongs to Stone. Tom Burwell, on the other hand, has no material means to possess her. Tom loves Louisa reverently, and he begins to speak poetically when he speaks of her: "Seems like the love I feels fo yo done stole m tongue."[33] She is his muse. In contrast, Bob Stones's love is a possessive, lustful one: "She was lovely—in her way. Nigger way" (p. 31). Despite his position he resents the social changes that have occurred with the end of slavery. In his fantasies he regains the status of the master: "He went in as a master should and took her. Direct, honest, bold" (p. 31).

When Tom kills Bob Stone over Louisa, he sets into motion a string of events that are all too familiar. He does not choose to flee from them; instead, he seems to accept his fate. Tom leans against the woodwork of a well and, like a tree, "He seemed rooted there" (p. 34). This is a very significant image, for it links the black man, soon to be lynched, with the Southern land. He becomes one with the tree and is rooted to the ground. The white mob is an industrial machine out to destroy the black tree: "White men like ants upon a forage rushed about. Except for the taut hum of their moving, all was silent. Shotguns, revolvers, rope, kerosene, torches." With the tools of their trade these white men enact their ritual. "The taut hum rose to a low roar . . . The moving body of their silence preceded them over the crest of the hill into factory town. It flattened the Negroes beneath it."

Consistent with Toomer's imagery throughout the Southern section of *Cane*, the oppressed is described with natural metaphors, while the oppressor is described with industrial metaphors.[34] Instead of a tree and a pastoral scene, Tom, who is the tree, is burned at the stake in the remnant of failed industrialism, an abandoned factory; his death is a metonymy for the demise of the South. Like concentric circles telling the same tale on different levels, in *Cane* relationships between men and women are echoed by relationships between white and black Southerners, which in turn are echoed by the relationship of Northern industry to the undeveloped South. All on the bottom half of the equation are doomed. There are no characters left to migrate. Those who act like Tom or Barlo are dead or mad; the others in their complacency are metaphorically dead like the land and the culture. The only migrants in the world of *Cane* are the text and the reader, and after the lynching of Tom both head North.

In his study of African-American short fiction, *Down Home*, Robert Bone asserts that most early twentieth-century African-American writers worked in a pastoral mode. He claims Toomer as part of this tradition. Interestingly, however, in his exploration of *Cane*, he fails to talk about "Blood-Burning Moon." To do so would have forced him to question his identification of the work as a pastoral text. In "Blood-Burning Moon" the pastoral explodes into an antipastoral. Bone notes that pastoral traditions spill over into the antipastoral and that within African-American literary history, this change occurs with the emergence of Richard Wright. However, as is evidenced by "Blood-Burning Moon" this change is foreshadowed in *Cane*. Tom Burwell becomes one with the land, his ashes part of the portrait of Georgia. This connection between the murder of Tom and the Southern landscape makes it impossible for this to be a truly pastoral text. Though the beauty of the Southern landscape remains throughout the text, it is not serene.[35]

While no individual character in *Cane* migrates, it is significant that this lynching tale is the last Southern story in the first section of the text. This final image of the South is the most vivid, the one that haunts the creative imagination of the text's artist—Ralph Kabnis. When Kabnis returns to take the cultural sojourn South, he is paralyzed by the fear of lynching. For Kabnis, it is the *imaginary* threat of lynching that dominates. This is not the case for the migrants portrayed by Richard Wright.

The publication of Richard Wright's first collection of short stories, *Uncle Tom's Children*, in 1938 marked a significant shift in the portrayal of lynching and its effect on the African-American community. With the publication of *Uncle*

Tom's Children, Wright began his ascent to the position of major African-American literary personality. While *Native Son* secured his position, *Uncle Tom's Children* launched him onto the literary landscape. The collection was reviewed by figures as diverse and significant as black critics Zora Neale Hurston, Alain Locke, and Sterling Brown, and leftist critics like Granville Hicks, James Farrell, and Malcolm Cowley.[36] Reviews appeared in the *New Republic* and *New York Times Book Review.* Eleanor Roosevelt mentioned Wright's work in her syndicated newspaper column.[37] As was the case with Lawrence's Migration series, this collection of writing by the young Richard Wright brought him to the attention of a very broad reading public. He introduced a notion of the South that was very different from the nostalgia of Hollywood in films like *Gone with the Wind* (1939) and *Stormy Weather* (1943).

There is no Kabnis in Wright's stories or novels—no Northerners in search of a Southern past, for such a search is prohibited by the very *real* threat of lynching. Neither are there any Southern characters who return to the South in Wright's fiction.[38] In many ways Wright continues the project started by Toomer; however, he departs from it as well. As with Toomer, the South for Wright is a site of natural beauty and racial horror. In Wright's fiction black bodies, exploited, dominated, and mutilated, are an indelible part of the Southern landscape. However, unlike Toomer, for Wright there is nothing to be regained by returning to the South.

Because of this, Wright unabashedly creates a South where the possibility of lynching is imminent and the memory of this possibility so strong that return is impossible. This shift in the portrayal of the South and the representation of lynching can be attributed to several factors. The first is simply the element of time. By the 1930s the high sense of hope and possibility which characterized the Harlem Renaissance had given way to the harsh reality of the Depression. By the time Wright had published his stories as well as his aesthetic manifesto, "Blueprint for Negro Writing," the presence and constant threat of lynching in the South remained and was epitomized by the case of the Scottsboro Boys. Third, Wright's own political orientation—at this time, Marxism—left no room for romanticization of a racial past.

III

> Most of the flogging and lynchings occur at harvest time, when fruit hangs heavy and ripe. . . .
>
> Richard Wright, *12 Million Black Voices*

The threat and actual occurrence of lynching pervade much of Richard Wright's work. His Southern characters are either witnesses or victims; the specter of the mob has a prominent place in the imaginations of his Northern characters. The fear of violence infiltrates their very psyches: Bigger Thomas of *Native Son* acts out of fear of being caught in a compromising position with a white woman, the most certain way to find oneself in the hands of the lynch mob. Aspects of their folk consciousness are in large part a response to the fear of lynching. After admiring the legs of a white woman while riding a Chicago subway, Jake of *Lawd Today* and his friends joke about the possibility of their own lynching:

> "Oh, Lawd, can I ever, can I ever? . . ."
> "Naw, nigger, you can never, you can never . . ."
> "But wherever there's life there's hope . . ."
> "And wherever there's trees there's rope."[39]

Trudier Harris argues that "the lynching metaphor becomes for Wright's characters, the stimuli in reaction to which their life responses are made."[40]

In Wright's world violence, fear, and desire are bound in an intricate relationship and work together to evoke differing responses from different characters. At times the masses of black people are paralyzed by this fear; but that which distinguishes Wright's protagonists (with the exception of Jake) from their brethren is that they act. Their action takes the form of violence, flight, or in some cases both.

If his own autobiographies share with the slave narratives the assertion that the quest for literacy is the primary motivating factor for leaving the South,[41] then his protagonists are motivated by fear of violence, especially in the form of lynching. For the purposes of this study, *Uncle Tom's Children* and *12 Million Black Voices* serve to illustrate the power of violence in the decision to migrate. However, while for the fictional Big Boy violence is the sole cause of individual flight, for the historical community of *12 Million Black Voices* it is but one element in a matrix of oppression that causes them to leave.

The South of *Uncle Tom's Children* is a place where white-on-black violence is a way of life. In the preface to this collection, "The Ethics of Living Jim Crow," Wright establishes the fact of violence. It is the glue holding the Southern social order together; it is the means by which black parents instruct their children in the ways of white folks and on how to survive the Jim Crow South. Lynching, castration, and beating await any who appear to act in defiance. The Southern black of these stories lives in poverty and constant fear of violence by powerful white men. The ritual of lynching, its promise, and its enactment are pervasive, hovering over each and every story.

Although Wright establishes the social construction of complacent black subjects in the Jim Crow South, although he opens his collection with an explanation of the "ethics of living Jim Crow," he nonetheless writes out of a framework that does not preclude their agency. Even when death awaits his protagonists, it does not strike them prior to their acting in their own self-defense. The cost of this defiance is often a brutal, and at times an agonizing, death.

In "Big Boy Leaves Home" the title character and his friends play adolescent physical games amid the beauty and serenity of the Southern landscape. However, this serenity is soon interrupted by the appearance of the object of fear and desire, the catalyst to terror, the white man's most valued property—a white woman. "It's a woman. . . . A white woman."[42] Upon seeing her, their hands instinctively "cover their groins" in an attempt to hide desire and protect themselves from castration. A white woman immediately evokes both desire for the forbidden and fear of castration. Under a different set of circumstances, the presence of a woman on the shore of this already sensual and erotic scene would suggest a sense of continuity, continuity in the sensuality of nature and woman. Here, because the boys are black (and already nude), and because the woman is white, the sense of fear and terror invade the bucolic, Eden-like scene.

They have reason to be afraid. The white woman screams; her companion shoots two of the boys. Horror and death are juxtaposed against the serene pastoralism of the lake. "Buck toppled headlong, sending up a shower of bright spray to the sunlight. The creek bubbled." The black bodies of Buck and Lester become an indelible part of this scene. The beauty and serenity mock the horror, thereby making it all the more terrifying.

When Big Boy and Bobo act in self-defense the hurricane of events leading to death and flight is initiated. Big Boy murders his white assailant. Fear for their actions takes two forms: On the one hand Bobo is almost paralyzed, and on the other Big Boy is spurred toward movement and flight.

The final section of the story details Big Boy's escape. Here, by using the sound of a distant train to evoke the promise of escape to the North, Wright merges Big Boy with the collective history of black people. He stands as representative of the runaway slave as well as the bluesman. The image of the train is consistent with its use as a symbol of escape to freedom in African-American oral culture from the spirituals to the blues. In this section, Wright also makes the terror of the lynching part of the Southern landscape by juxtaposing descriptions of the white mob's lynching song with descriptions of the land: "Song waves rolled over the top of pine trees. The sky sagged low, heavy with clouds. Wind was rising. Sometimes cricket cries cut surprisingly across the mob song." As is the case in "Strange Fruit," here again the Southern landscape is linked with Southern terror.

As Big Boy escapes the mob, he witnesses the lynching of Bobo whose body is feathered, burned, and torn: "A black body flashed in the light. Bobo was struggling, twisting; they were binding his arms and legs. . . . He saw a tar-drenched body glistening and turning. . . . The wind carried, like a flurry of snow, a widening spiral of white feathers into the night. The flames leaped tall as trees" (p. 49). The black body is foregrounded and, as in Holiday's song, the wind carries the scent of the burning flesh and the feathers which have been tarred to the body. The feathers carrying the skin become one with the wind.

Wright makes no explicit connection between Bobo's body and the land. Instead, the sight of this imposition of power on one black man places the reins of power in the body of another. Big Boy is "numb, empty as though all blood had been drawn from him. Then his muscles flexed taut when he heard a faint patter" (p. 50). Big Boy experiences the lynching as though he himself were the victim. Again, it is similar to Lawrence's painting, the lynched individual is but a synecdoche for the black community. Although Big Boy physically escapes the mob, its presence and actions are brought to bear on his own body. Wright ends the story "The sun had risen" and Big Boy is headed northward, hidden in the back of a truck. With him he takes this consciousness of fear. The South will remain for him a place where the crickets sing along with the lynch mob, where brooks bubble with the last gasping breaths of a boyhood friend. The South will forever be associated with the taboo of white women and the horror of lynching. These images will influence his urban interactions and remain dominant in his memory of his "home."

Wright departs from the threat of lynching as the dominant cause for migration in his nonfiction work. In his own autobiographies, *Black Boy* and *American Hunger*, Wright is not unlike the bluesmen, who are agents and emphatically decide to leave the South. In *12 Million Black Voices*, a photographic essay for which Wright provided an eloquent manuscript documenting the black experience, the visual and literary images of lynching join other oppressive factors as catalyst to migration.

When it was published in 1941, *Voices* took its place among a line of documentary photo-text books that utilized photographs from the extensive Farm Securities Administration (FSA) files. John Tagg, author of *The Burden of Representation*, argues that most of the documentary books were simply tools of "the discourse of paternalistic, state-directed reform of the New Deal"; William Stott, author of *Documentary Depression and Thirties America*, contends that the thirties documentary shifted from criticizing America to celebrating it.[43] However, Wright's *12 Million Black Voices* not only reclaims the critical tradition, but it is also evidence of the contestation over the interpretation of migration. This contest is evident in the tensions between the written and photographic narratives and within the photographic narrative itself.

The photographs, selected primarily from the FSA files by Edwin Rosskam, a former FSA administrator, were not taken for the book.[44] The vast majority of the photographs seek to present a people in despair who nonetheless maintain a sense of dignity and whose countenances portray a sense of optimism. However, among the photographs, there are at least four which resist the visual narrative of dignity, beauty, and optimism in the face of profound poverty, instead asserting an alternative narrative—one of brutality, terror, and protest. Specifically, these include the photographs of the lynching in the Southern section and of the looting, police brutality, and protest march in the Northern section. Upon closer inspection, it is evident that these four photographs were not selected from the files of the FSA, but instead they come from the Associated Press. These resisting images are more in keeping with the narrative provided by Wright's text.

31

Many of the themes of *Uncle Tom's Children* reappear in this nonfiction work: the natural beauty of the South, the economic exploitation of black people, their ambivalent relation to the land, and the constant threat of violence. However, the black people of *12 Million Black Voices* are not always agents. More often than not they appear as the objects of history, as victims who are always acted upon. This is especially true of the Southern section where issues of economic exploitation are highlighted over the imminent threat of violence. The "we" of this section, black people, specifically black men, find themselves in a web of relationships that deny them humanity or historical agency. "When we are caught in the throes of inspiration, when we are moved to better our lot, we do not ask ourselves: 'Can we do it?' but: 'Will they let us do it?' Before we black folk can move, we must first look into the white man's mind to see what is there, to see what he is thinking."[45]

Wright recognizes three forms of agency in black Southerners. The first is agency in language:

> We stole words from the grudging lips of the Lords of the Land, who did not want us to know too many of them or their meaning. And we charged this meager horde of stolen sounds with all the emotions and longings we had; we proceeded to build our language in inflections of voice, through tonal variety, by hurried speech, in honeyed drawls, by rolling our eyes, by flourishing our hands, by assigning to common, simple words new meanings, meanings which enabled us to speak of revolt in the actual presence of the Lords of the Land without their being aware! Our secret language extended our understanding of what slavery meant and gave us the freedom to speak to our brothers in captivity; we polished our new words, caressed them, gave them new shape and color, a new order and tempo, until, though they were the words of the Lords of the Land, they became *our* words, *our* language. [p. 40]

This eloquent passage is extremely important to Wright's oeuvre. It marks one of the rare instances where Wright concedes that black Southerners were capable of *creating* a culture. It stands in opposition to his claim, just a few pages earlier, that "when we are caught in the throes of inspiration . . . we must first look into the white man's mind to see what is there, to see what he is thinking" (p. 3). It is hard to believe that the writer of this passage is the same person who wrote:

> I used to mull over the strange absence of real kindness in Negroes, . . . how bare our traditions . . . how shallow was even our despair. . . .
> When I brooded upon the cultural barrenness of black life, I wondered if clean, positive tenderness, love, honor, loyalty, and the capacity to remember were native with man.[46]

While Wright does concede black agency in black language, the only action he recognizes as significant to black opposition to the white status quo is the decision either to act in violence or to migrate. The only option for those who seek to maintain some remnant of dignity and humanity is flight: "If you act at all, it is either to flee or kill; you are either a victim or a rebel" (p. 57). These are the only viable avenues of agency allowed black men.

After his detailed description of the various economic injustices of the South, Wright cites other institutions of repression which act to ensure the status quo: the courts and the lynch mob. Again, lynching literally becomes part of the description of landscape. By lyrically describing the lay of the land, Wright establishes the rhythm of the narrative as the rhythm of nature:

> The land we till is beautiful, with red and black and brown clay, with fresh and hungry smells, with pine trees and palm trees, with rolling hills and swampy delta. . . . Our Southern springs are filled with quiet noises and scenes of growth. . . .
>
> In summer the magnolia trees fill the countryside with sweet scents for long miles. . . .
>
> In autumn the land is afire with color. . . .
>
> In winter the forests resound with the bite of steel axes eating into tall trees as men gather wood for the leaden days of cold. [p. 32]

This paragraph reveals a harmony between the land and black people. It exhibits an appreciation for the earth's gifts and beauty. Here, Wright establishes not only the connection between black people and the South, but also his own connection with the people by using the pronoun "we." At this point in the narrative, he becomes a blues singer, sharing in the experiences of the black Southerners about whom he writes. Here, the book is a kind of blues performance in itself, expressing the humanity of black people in the face of racial and economic adversity. The land is "ours," yet all the elements of "our" oppression are here also. "We" till this land; "we" do not own it. Those same trees will act as crucifixes for "our" lynched bodies. Here is the contradictory relationship between "us" and the South land. "We" admire its beauty, consider it "ours," and "our" blood fertilizes the rich, fertile ground.

The Southern section of the text opens with this poetic description of the land and closes with "our" leaving it. In between, Wright links the landscape opening and the migratory ending: the relationship between black people and the visually beautiful earth; the exploitation of the land and people by the white landowners and industrial bosses, whose rape of the land will leave it dead; the limited options of black people—to die with the land or flee. The specter of the lynching figures prominently throughout: "Most of the flogging and lynchings occur at harvest time, when fruit hangs heavy and ripe, when the leaves are red and gold, when nuts fall from the trees, when the earth offers its best. The thought of harvest steals upon us with a sense of an inescapable judgment. It is time now to settle accounts with the Lords of the Land, to divide the crops and pay old debts, and we are afraid" (pp. 41–42).

If earlier paragraphs established an affinity between black people and the land, this paragraph provides the vital link between the land and the lynching. As with Holiday's "Strange Fruit," here the heavy, hanging fruit is also a metaphor for black bodies; autumn signifies not only the harvest, but also a sense of imminent death. The trees are pregnant both with fruit and with justified fear.

The same imagery used to establish the beauty of the South is here used to introduce its horror. The paragraph is striking for the casual tone: Floggings and lynchings are a common occurrence, as certain as the coming of harvest. Black people, abused children, await anxiously what is sure to come. (Throughout this text black people are likened to children.) It is important to note the link here between economics and death. The beauty and bounty of the harvest lead to the "settling of accounts and old debts," which in turn leads to violence. In this nonfiction text lynching is linked not to a white woman, but to money and its distribution.

Significantly, the sharecropper comes face to face with those who flog and lynch him. He knows the forces that act against him, he can face them, can call their names, and is linked to them in intricate ties of blood, land, and money. They maintain control over him by the spectacle of torture:

> We know that if we protest we will be called "bad niggers." The Lords of the Land will preach the doctrine of "white supremacy" to the poor whites who are eager to form mobs. In the midst of general hysteria they will seize one of us—it does not matter who, the innocent or guilty—and, as a token, a naked and bleeding body will be dragged through the dusty streets. The mobs will make certain that our token-death is known throughout the quarters where we black folk live. Our bodies will be swung by ropes from the limbs of trees, will be shot at and mutilated. . . . (p. 43).

The photographic narrative of this section is made up primarily of portraits and outdoor work scenes, most of which illustrate the dignity and humanity of the individuals. The first serene photographs portray a beautiful landscape being worked by a people with soulful eyes—a people whose faces betray little, whose tattered clothing and living condition tell of their poverty, a people with the primitive tools of agriculture, hoes and mule-drawn tractors. These are people who seem satisfied, not terrified with their lot.

Arthur Rothstein's *Steelworker* (Figure 1.3) typifies the representation of the black worker in the visual narrative. In this frontal portrait he is clean, relaxed. His eyes gaze pleasantly away from the viewer. There is a gentle smile on his serene countenance. The figure itself seems bigger and broader than the boundaries it occupies, spreading above and over them. There is no explicit suggestion here of oppression or dissatisfaction; no evidence of the terror about which Wright writes. However, there is a certain sadness in the smile, the face itself is a mask put on for the photographer.

The photograph of the lynching of Lint Shaw (Figure 1.4) sits in the middle of this visual narrative. It is bound on either side by more serene photos, highlighting the land, the workers, the impoverished families. In their resemblance to the photos that precede the lynching, those that follow suggest that life goes on as usual except that we, the viewers, now know the secret that lies in those soulful eyes. This photograph stands out not only for its content but also for its form. Its boundaries, like those of the frontal portraits, are bled to three edges of the page.

Figure 1.3 Arthur Rothstein, *Steelworker.* Pennsylvania. Farm
Securities Administration. (Reproduced from the Collections of the
Library of Congress)

There is no text to accompany it. It is grainy and lacks the sharpness of the FSA
images. James A. Miller has noted that this along with the dress of the figures
lend a timeless quality to the photograph.[47] Because of these formal elements,
the picture disrupts the rest of the visual narrative and in so doing, subverts it.
The white men stare directly into the camera. Elsewhere their eyes focus on the
blacks to whom they speak or in the distance. Here, they confront the viewer—
boldly displaying their prize—the bloodied, lynched black body. In its disruption
of the visual narrative, this photograph identifies itself with the written text. It
exposes the horror beneath the serenity.

The photographic narrative attempts to present the dominant white narrative
of blacks' relation to the South. The lynching photo and Wright's written narra-

Figure 1.4 *Lynching.* Georgia. (AP/Wide World Photos)

tive subvert that effort by providing an alternative perspective, one that challenges the romanticized pastoral view and asserts the terror of Southern justice. After the exploitation, after the threats of corporal and mental violence, after having been denied access to adequate housing and education—"we" grow tired and heed the call of Northern industry: "Perhaps for the first time in our lives, we straighten our backs, drop the hoe and give a fleeting glance to the white man's face and walk off" (p. 87).

Although *12 Million Black Voices* did not receive the kind of media attention given to documentary texts that focused on white subjects, it was widely reviewed in both the black and mainstream press. According to Nicholas Natanson, it "received considerably more play than Claude McKay's *Harlem: Negro Metropolis*" (1940), the other major black documentary text of the time.[48] The attention it received, following the heels of the major success of *Native Son* (1940) asserts the dominance of Wright's view of the South and of black migration.

IV

A bastard people, far from God, singing and crying in the wilderness.

James Baldwin, *Go Tell It on the Mountain*

36

Wright's work of the thirties and forties stresses the horror of the South, and lynching is the most immediate image of this. There is no indication that the South holds any possibility or redemptive value. This view begins to shift with the publication of James Baldwin's *Go Tell It on the Mountain* in 1952. In this text, the reasons for leaving the South and the image of lynching grow more complex. In addition to lynching, the sexual exploitation of black women is portrayed as a direct cause for migration. Lynching in *Go Tell It* is directly linked with notions of racial redemption, and the South becomes a possible site of this rebirth.

It may be argued that Baldwin is not the initiator of this shift in perspective. Ralph Ellison begins to paint a picture of the South as a place to be valued in the African-American imagination; however, Baldwin, like Toomer before him, makes an explicit connection between black blood and black redemption. In many ways he seems to take up where Toomer left off, but he does not explore this possibility in full within the context of this first novel.

In light of the history of the migration narrative, Baldwin is significant because he initiates a change in the gender of the victim of Southern violence and contributes to the portrayal of the South as a place of possible redemption. In this sense Baldwin becomes a transitional figure in the tradition of the migration narratives under consideration. In his first novel, we see the beginning of a career and a perspective that would come to challenge Wright's hegemony.

In *Go Tell It on the Mountain*, Florence, the protagonist's strong-willed paternal aunt, is one of the first major characters of African-American literature to join the Great Migration on the heels of sexual harassment:[49] "This became Florence's deep ambition, to walk out one morning through the cabin door, never to return."[50] Her conviction makes her one of the most significant African-American women in literature.[51] Historian Darlene Clark Hine notes that scholars have failed to pay attention to the "noneconomic motives propelling black female migration." According to Hine,

> Many black women quit the South out of a desire to achieve personal autonomy and to escape from sexual abuse at the hands of southern white men as well as black men. The combined influence of domestic violence and economic oppression is key to understanding the hidden motivation informing major social protest and migratory movements in Afro-American history.[52]

In light of this, Baldwin is far ahead of his time in his portrayal of the reasons for Florence's migration north.

Baldwin not only explores the sexism that exists between white men and black women but also reveals the contours of repression within the black family. While Wright sees the black Southern family as a repressive institution of socialization, impeding the manhood of its male members, Baldwin reveals it to be one in which the ambitions of the females are sacrificed for those of males. He immediately sets Florence in competition with her brother, Gabriel. She is far more deserving and desiring of the opportunities afforded him. The opening prayer of

Florence's Southern flashback establishes the gender dynamics of the black family and the physical danger facing black women in the South. Following the rape of Florence's best friend, Deborah, Florence's mother kneels in prayer and Baldwin tells us: "This was the first prayer Florence heard, the only prayer she was to ever hear in which her mother demanded the protection of God more passionately for her daughter than she did for her son" (p. 68).

As we learn, the mother dotes on her male child and forces Florence to sacrifice so that he may live a life of relative comfort and have access to educational opportunities. "Gabriel was the apple of his mother's eye. If he had never been born, Florence might have looked forward to a day when she would be released from her unrewarding round of labor, when she might think of her own future and go out to make it. With the birth of Gabriel, which occurred when she was five, her future was swallowed up" (p. 72). Florence's penis envy is not of the organ itself, which she hates, but of the privileges the possession of it seems to guarantee. For Florence, the South is a place where black women are subjugated in the black family and where they are subject to sexual abuse by white men. Interestingly, the family, black and white, as well as the state or mobs, is a site of domination and oppression for black women.

Having experienced the sexism of her own family, Florence does not desire to become the wife of a black Southerner: "And Florence, who was beautiful, but did not look with favor on any of the black men who lusted after her, not wishing to exchange her mother's cabin for one of theirs and to raise their children and so go down, toil blasted, into as it were a common grave" (p. 74). While home and children usually mean life, for Florence (as for Nella Larsen's Helga Crane) they mean death.

White families are also problematic for the young Florence. In 1900, at age twenty-six, she is propositioned by a white employer, and this is the straw that breaks the camel's back: "She had been working as a cook and a serving girl for a large white family in town, and it was on the day that her master proposed that she become his concubine that she knew her life among these wretched had come to its destined end. She left her employment that day . . . and bought a railroad ticket for New York" (p. 75). Note the use of the term master where we might expect employer. Baldwin uses this term to denote that the South from which Florence flees is the same South as that which enslaved her mother. For the first time, the threat of sexual exploitation leads directly to a move North. There is no link here to the death of a black man.

This is a significant shift in the depiction of causes for leaving the South and it gives the woman a sense of agency over her own fate. Unlike so many blues women, or indeed her own sister-in-law Elizabeth, Florence does not follow a man North. It is especially significant that this shift occurs in the work of a male writer. Most black male writers focus on lynching. When Baldwin does portray a lynching it is to establish it as a crime against black humanity. In this text lynching even takes on biblical proportions.

The lynching in *Go Tell It on the Mountain* is not the lynching of one of the major characters and it is not directly related to the migration of any major character. Instead, the lynching of the black soldier in Gabriel's section is used to paint a climate of the South. (Interestingly, it is not portrayed in the sections that deal with the Southern pasts of the female migrants.) The specific lynching falls into the overall climate of terror and fear experienced by black people during the Nadir. Baldwin focuses on this climate:

> And blood, in all the cities through which he passed, ran down. There seemed no door, anywhere, behind which blood did not call out, unceasingly, for blood; no woman, whether singing before defiant trumpets or rejoicing before the Lord, who had not seen her father, her brother, her lover, or her son cut down without mercy; who had not seen her sister become part of the white man's great whorehouse, who had not, all too narrowly, escaped that house herself; no man, preaching, or cursing, strumming his guitar in the lone blue evening, or blowing in fury and ecstasy his golden horn at night, who had not been made to bend his head and drink white men's muddy water; no man whose manhood had not been at the root, sickened, whose loins had not been dishonored, whose seed had not been scattered into oblivion. . . . Yes their parts were cut off, they were dishonored . . . a bastard people, far from God, singing and crying in the wilderness! [p.137]

This apocalyptic vision of the South conflates historical reality with biblical chaos. Gabriel sees it as a curse upon his people. The horror of the South terrorizes, makes whores of both worldly and holy women; black men are forced to engage in sexual activity with white men and they are castrated and maimed. Again their blood flows through Southern streets. Baldwin's South, like Holiday's and Lawrence's, is the site of racial shame and horror. Through this passage, we know that the red clay of Georgia is colored by blood.

However, as was the case with "Blood-Burning Moon," the blood imagery begins to establish the South in a somewhat different light. Biblically, blood is often redemptive in nature ("washed in the blood of the lamb"). The language of this passage is derived from the Book of Numbers of the Old Testament where Moses leads the Hebrews out of Egypt into the Wilderness. Here they begin to question God and to rebel. The first generation dies without reaching the Promised Land, but God does fulfill this promise to the new generation. Baldwin's passage, like the book from which it is drawn, asserts the rebellion–redemption, death–promise dialectic. The fact that the death is linked to a lynching suggests that the bodies of the lynched are the sacrificed bodies that ensure the redemptive possibilities of the South. Though the earth is soaked with the blood of black people, it may hold redemptive possibilities for them as well. In fact, it may be a sacred ground, where their blood is sacrificed.[53]

Southern violence in *Go Tell It on the Mountain* takes on many forms, mentally, physically, and, most important, spiritually. It is a violence inflicted upon black men by white men in the form of lynching and castration; it is a violence inflicted upon black women by white men in the form of rape and concubinage; and it is a violence inflicted upon black women by the black community's patriarchal norms.

V

> We got a home in this rock.
>
> Toni Morrison, *Song of Solomon*

Baldwin's contributions to the migration narrative include a consideration of the consequences of violence on the black community and of the gender-based differences in reasons for leaving the South. Two black women, Toni Morrison and Gloria Naylor—both writing after the Civil Rights Movement of the 1960s and both profoundly influenced by Baldwin—complete the literary move from the individual to the collective community and from the power struggle between black and white men to the black family as a site of violence, respectively. Both women are historically and physically removed from the reality of lynching and castration.[54]

Toni Morrison's *Song of Solomon* (1977) was the first Book-of-the-Month Club selection by an African-American author since Wright's *Native Son*. It was on best seller lists for four months. The critical and commercial success of this, Morrison's third novel, solidified her stature as a major American literary presence. According to Henry Louis Gates,

> Toni Morrison along with her contemporaries, Black women novelists Alice Walker, Gloria Naylor, Jamaica Kincaid and Terry McMillan, are more widely read by a broader section of the American reading public than any other Black writers have ever been in this country. Morrison's devoted readers are found on every continent, representing both sexes and all colors, ages and creeds . . . a large cosmopolitan readership of women—including intellectuals, professionals, feminists—in addition to the more traditional, but smaller, Black reading audience than anyone could have imagined just two decades ago.[55]

With her ascendancy to literary prominence, Morrison strongly challenges Wright's perspective on the South.

In *Song of Solomon* the murder of a black person by a white mob is of major importance to the fate of all black people. The trend that starts with Baldwin is fulfilled here. Morrison spends little time graphically detailing the murder of the individual, Macon Dead I. However, the consequences of his murder are highly significant for his black neighbors and his progeny.

The murder of Macon Dead I forces the flight of his orphaned children and kills the spirit of the black boys who remain. Pilate, his daughter, goes farther South, where she knows she will find her history, her people; she will eventually become the elder of the text—the one who embodies the wisdom and history of the ancestor. Macon, his boy, goes to the city in an effort to escape the violence of his past and to search for a spiritually empty material comfort.

Macon Dead I was the model of what a hardworking, determined black man could accomplish if he owned land. He embodied that to which Toomer's Tom Burwell aspired. Unlike his son, who seeks to own property and people, to acquire money and status, the elder Dead wanted land to produce food for his family, to ensure stability and independence. He had a relationship with the land, and for the neighboring blacks his success was not reason to envy him but served as an inspiration and motivation:

> Head and shoulders above all of it was the tall, magnificent Macon Dead, whose death, it seemed to him, was the beginning of their own dying even though they were young boys at the time. Macon Dead was the farmer they wanted to be, the clever irrigator, the peach-tree grower, the hog slaughterer, the wild-turkey roaster, the man who could plow forty in no time flat and sang like an angel while he did it. He had come out of nowhere, as ignorant as a hammer and broke as a convict, with nothing but free papers, a Bible, and a pretty black-haired wife, and in one year he'd leased ten acres, the next ten more. Sixteen years later he had one of the best farms in Montour County. A farm that colored their lives like a paintbrush and spoke to them like a sermon. "You see?" the farm said to them. "See? See what you can do? Never mind you can't tell one letter from another, never mind you born a slave, never mind you lose your name, never mind your daddy dead, never mind nothing. Here, this here, is what a man can do if he puts his mind to it and his back in it. Stop sniveling," it said. "Stop picking around the edges of the world. Take advantage, and if you can't take advantage, take disadvantage. We live here. On this planet, in this nation, in this country right here. *No*where else! We got a home in this rock, don't you see! Nobody starving in my home; nobody crying in my home, and if I got a home you got one too! Grab it. Grab this land! Take it, hold it, my brothers, make it, my brothers, shake it, squeeze it, turn it, twist it, beat it, kick it, kiss it, whip it, stomp it, dig it, plow it, seed it, reap it, rent it, buy it, sell it, own it, build it, multiply it, and pass it on—can you hear me? Pass it on!"
>
> But they shot the top of his head off and ate his fine Georgia peaches. And even as boys these men began to die and were dying still.[56]

In this magnificent passage Morrison deconstructs the notion of Jefferson's pastoral agrarian vision of an America populated by independent yeoman farmers. The sermon, seemingly spoken in the voice of the land, at first preaches "cast your buckets where you stand," but the brief and powerful "They shot his head off" subverts that possibility for a black man in a racist land.

However, the land, which in the works of the previous authors has been portrayed as blood-drenched and keeper of the shameful secret, is here exposed as ally. "Stake your claim in me," it says, "You have a right." Macon Dead and the land become one in the commands to the black community, embracing them with the term "we." With the words "A farm that . . . spoke to them like a sermon,"

Morrison suggests the land preaches the sermon, yet the sermon is preached in the voice of Macon Dead. Here the land and the ancestor are conflated into one benevolent, protecting, and wise figure. Because of the orality of this passage, the text itself becomes the repository of the ancestor.[57] Melvin Dixon tells us that the land has a "voice full of the language and cadence of Negro spirituals."

At the same time, the land has a curious bisexual nature, for as it articulates Macon's sermon, it is described in very sensual, sexual, and at times violent terms. The sexualization of the land here resembles Toomer's construction of the land as sexual object. Yet it differs from his use in that for Toomer the land is always a woman. For Morrison, the land, like the notion of the ancestor, is bisexual or not bound by conventional gender definitions. The land as woman is possessed and controlled by the farmer. The land as farmer is provider of nourishment and stability. Together the two give birth to something to be passed on to continue the perpetuation of subsequent generations. The rock on which Lawrence's mourning figure sits becomes "home" in this sermon.

The sermon is about the promise that Macon Dead I represented, the promise that was murdered with him. It is also the promise that can be resurrected with the retelling of this tale. It establishes the African-American birthright. There is no time spent detailing the blood or the gore; instead Morrison opens and closes with the shot that killed their dreams. Although his children leave and the other children lose their dreams, the retelling of this story in the early 1970s to Milkman, his grandson, nourishes the younger man. Milkman knows of the brutal murder, but it is the other part of the story which nourishes and motivates him to continue his own quest. He knows that his grandfather possessed qualities of manhood quite different from those he has acquired and, like his aunt before him, he too seeks to acquire them by traveling farther south.

The first lynching we hear of in *Song of Solomon* is the historically accurate 1955 murder of Emmett Till. The actual lynching of Emmett Till is linked to a white woman. He allegedly whistles at a white woman and is lynched, castrated and burned. The fictional black men of the barbershop in *Song of Solomon* use Till's lynching to reflect on their own positions in the white man's world, just as Macon Dead's murder causes reflection on the part of the Southern men around the store stoop. However, when Macon Dead is murdered, there is no woman, no white woman for him to desire, no black woman for him to protect. There is land and the independence that comes with its ownership. When female imagery is used symbolically to signify issues of power and ownership it is the power and ownership of the black man and not the white. It is quite significant that in Morrison's text the pivotal murder of a black man is focused not on sexuality but on land ownership. This is what it is all about. The threatening black man is not a sexual threat; he is an economic threat. Manhood is not about the possession of a penis but about the possession of economic and spiritual independence. In stressing the link between black economic self-sufficiency and lynching, Morrison is following foremother Ida B. Wells, who at the turn of the century argued that lynching was "an excuse to get rid of Negroes who were acquiring wealth and property."[58]

Writing after the Black Power Movement and the spate of black urban male bildungsromans of that era, Morrison offers an alternative definition of black manhood, one which focuses not on the body but on the land, one which embraces the ancestor in its quest for new notions of black masculinity. In this way, Morrison initiates a project of imagining possibilities for black masculinity that allow for the spiritual and psychic wholeness of both black men and black women.[59] The publication of *Song of Solomon* marked Morrison's ascendancy into the dominant position that had been occupied by Richard Wright. Melvin Dixon claims that Morrison

> manipulates and enlarges the conventions of surrealism and the bildungsroman, which Ellison viewed as granting the writer freedom from the sociological predilections and realistic persuasions most readers impose upon black American fiction. This was Ellison's main criticism of Wright, but his injunction stops there. Morrison undercuts the hegemony of Ellison's preferred narrative strategy . . . by enlarging the structure to encompass multiple lives and points of view as her characters aim for motion. . . . The multiplicity of perspectives and situations in Morrison's fiction requires protagonists writ large; her novels are bildungsromans of entire communities and racial idioms rather than the voice of a single individual.[60]

Morrison's vision and her language take much more from the legacy left by Baldwin than that left by Wright or Ellison. She responds to Baldwin's call by shifting her emphasis from a single black victim of racial oppression to a community and a people. The consequences of that victimization take on historic proportions. Morrison has acknowledged her debt to Baldwin. Of Baldwin, she says, "[He] gave me a language to dwell in."[61]

VI

> I'll beat it out of you.
>
> Gloria Naylor, *Women of Brewster Place*

Morrison inherits and revises Baldwin's language, his moral vision, and his concern with the consequences of violence on history and community. Her contemporaries Gloria Naylor and Alice Walker begin to explore in greater detail Baldwin's depiction of Southern black families as patriarchal institutions. Unlike Morrison, these two authors have defined themselves as feminists and their texts participate in the black feminist literary movement of the seventies and eighties. Responding to the sexism of the Black Arts and Black Power movements, black feminist writers seek to give voice to the silenced black women of earlier texts. For our purposes Gloria Naylor's *The Women of Brewster Place* best represents these concerns because it is a more explicit migration narrative than Walker's *Third Life of Grange Copeland*.[62]

The Women of Brewster Place is a novel about poor and working-class women whose relationships with each other help them to endure the brutalities of urban life. Published in 1982, Naylor's first novel won the American Book Award. Upon publication, *The Women of Brewster Place* entered into a literary arena that had already heard black feminist voices like Alice Walker and Ntozake Shange. In 1989, *Brewster Place* was the basis for a television miniseries that became a regular show, running for one season. Both programs were produced by and starred Oprah Winfrey. No book by a black author had received such treatment since Alex Haley's *Roots* in the mid-seventies.

For Naylor the act of violence that finally causes her protagonist to leave the South is the physical abuse she incurs at the hand of her father. Mattie Michael first defies her father by dating a man of whom he does not approve. Then she further defies him by refusing to name this man as the father of her unborn child. In an effort to learn the name, her father "came towards her, grabbed her by the back of her hair and yanked her face upward to confront the blanket of rage in his eye" and then "she took the force of the two blows with her neck muscles and her eyes went dim as the blood dripped down her chin from her split lip."[63] Here the physical characteristic of the lynched body—the limp, hanging neck, the dim eyes, and the bloodied mouth—are imposed upon the body of the beaten black woman. If in the world of *Cane* the black community repeats the codes of violence enacted upon them by whites, here it is done more specifically on black women by black men: "Mattie's body contracted in a painful spasm each time the stick smashed down on her legs and back, and she curled into a tight knot, trying to protect her stomach" (p. 23).

This brutal beating by a man she loves and respects, serves as the primary catalyst for Mattie's migration north to a place that offers anonymity. In her short story "The Child Who Favored Daughter," Alice Walker shows us what might have been Mattie's fate had she not left home. In that story the protagonist pays for defying her father when he mutilates her body. In order to avoid further abuse, Mattie flees the abuse of her father. Economic restraints or threats of violence from a white community are not factors in her migration. In this way, Mattie shares much with Baldwin's Florence, in that for both women, black patriarchy is a significant factor in their decisions to leave the South. Once she is in the North, Mattie is met by her best friend, Etta, who is Florence's direct literary descendant. The strong-willed, sensual Etta leaves the South for reasons that are very similar to Florence's. "Rock Vale had no place for a black woman who was not only unwilling to play by the rules, but whose spirit challenged the very right of the game to exist" (p. 59). Naylor suggests that Etta's leaving is in some way linked to mob violence, but she never fully explores this. The failure to fully characterize Etta by providing a past for her appears to be a weakness of the text.

Nonetheless, Etta, Mattie, and Florence are representative of the hundreds of black women migrants ignored by history. Darlene Clark Hine urges historians to consider domestic abuse as another of the many "push" factors that contributed to migration. According to Hine, many black women migrants went north out of the "desire for freedom from sexual exploitation, especially rape by white men, and to escape from domestic abuse within their own families."[64]

Black woman novelists like Gloria Naylor anticipated Hines's call and are at the forefront of a revisionist project that reconsiders the role of sexual violence and abuse as a catalyst for migration.

VII

> I am fed up
> With Jim Crow laws
> People who are cruel
> And afraid,
> Who lynch and run,
> Who are scared of me
> And me of them.
>
> I pick up my life
> And take it away
> On a one-way ticket—
> Gone up North,
> Gone West,
> Gone !
>
> Langston Hughes, "One Way Ticket"

Violence as a catalyst to migration is a recurring theme in the migration narrative of African-American artists. Because historical and cultural interpretations are contested terrains, because they are influenced by a variety of social and political forces, the causes, victims, and victimizers are constantly shifting, but the tenet remains the same: In the creative imagination of black literary and visual artists, the systematic forms of violence enacted upon black bodies is a primary cause for their choosing to leave the South.

Trudier Harris notes that between 1853 and 1968 a literary tradition of portraying lynching emerged among black male writers. She suggests that after 1968, lynching had less symbolic significance for black writers and appears with less frequency than in previous years. Also, she asserts that black women are less concerned with the graphic depiction of rape and lynching because the former does not constitute death for them and they are not victims of the latter.

Harris is correct in her assertion that after 1968 we see fewer fictional lynchings and that black women writers seem less concerned with this type of violation of black people by whites. However, writers like Alice Walker and Gloria

Naylor choose instead to focus on the graphic details of the violence enacted upon black women. Changing political circumstances lead to greater attention to interpersonal and familial relationships. These writers give voice to abused women like Richard Wright's Sarah of "Long Dry Song." More important, however, we must not essentialize tendencies by attributing them to male and female writers only: Toni Morrison's lynching scene falls into another category of post-1968 works, and as we have seen James Baldwin participates in the trend toward exploring the black family as a site of oppression for black women.

Baldwin provides us with a critique of patriarchy which affects women and men who do not live up to the patriarchal ideal of manhood. His characters Florence, Elizabeth, and John are victims of patriarchy within their households. Walker and Naylor represent two emerging feminist voices, responding in many ways to the sexism of the Black Power Movement. Toni Morrison shares their concern with the destructive effects of black male sexism; however, she sees it as destructive to both black men and women.

In short, the shift that occurs in post-1960s writing takes two forms. On the one hand it focuses less on the details of the violent act and looks instead at the consequences for a people. Lawrence's lynching painting foreshadows this tendency. Morrison's text, like Lawrence's painting, absents the dead body, focusing on the land, the people, and the death of promise. The remains of the lynched ancestor accompany the living characters of the text; Pilate holds her father's bones in her home. There is one major difference, however, between Morrison and Lawrence. In Morrison's text there are redemptive possibilities in the telling of the tale, in the remembering of the history. For Lawrence the only hope is flight. The second shift that occurs in the portrayal of violence focuses no less intently on the act, but shifts the site from the lynching tree to the cabin. In this case, as with the earlier texts, the black body is central.

A distinct shift in narrative structure accompanies the shift from the lynched individual to the collective community. In both Morrison and Baldwin, the narrative is cyclical. Through the use of flashbacks and spirituality, both make the past live next to and affect and shape the present. In Morrison, as I have demonstrated, the text itself takes on the quality of the ancestor outlined in the introduction. History, as it is presented in these texts, is not linear. The actions of the fathers bear on the lives of the children. With this conception of the relationship between past and present, it is impossible to completely abandon the South. The other, more linear texts tend to see no possibility for black people in the South and therefore do not emphasize it as the site of the ancestor.

The creative texts, be they visual, literary, or musical, stress the migration of one character, who stands in as representative of the mass. The sociological and historical studies and the letters of migrants focus on the migration of a people, and in so doing they create a sort of epic narrative on the scale of Exodus. Because of this they tend to highlight a broader range of reasons for leaving the South.

If we consider "the lynching" a sign at work in our culture, then the texts discussed in this chapter illustrate the manner in which this sign is manipulated for different purposes. Initially the sign of lynching was used by the dominant white culture of the South to evoke fear in the hearts of African-Americans and in so doing to help maintain the social order. As Jacquelyn Dowd Hall has convincingly argued, this image had ramifications throughout the United States, because black communities were constantly aware of it; the South of their memory was a South painted with lynched bodies as well as natural beauty. By claiming it as part of their historical legacy, African-American artists were able to utilize the image in a variety of ways. When the image of lynching appears in the texts of African-American artists it is not used to inflict a sense of inactivity, but instead to provoke activity: either it is a catalyst to Northern migration or it provides the foundation for staking a racial claim on the South.

The differing ways that the image is utilized is evidence of the struggle for meaning and interpretation that characterizes all societies, traditions, and even individual artists. As significant as the choice to use the lynching sign is the choice not to use it. The near absence of lynching imagery in blues lyrics and migrant letters suggest two things. First, this image is one which constructs them as victims, a status they choose not to claim. Second, the absence might be evidence of a silence and hence a very present and real fear of violent repercussions which characterize black lives in the South.

In all instances, however, writers, scholars, and musical and visual artists have a similar understanding of power. They share this with the blues lyricists and the Southern letter writers. This is an unsophisticated, known power. We know the white men of the mob; we witness their crimes and work for them. (Reverend Cooper tells Milkman who conspired to kill his grandfather: "Circe worked for the people who killed him.") If we so desire, we can act against them. (Even surrealistically, as Morrison's Circe does to the white family for whom she works, the Butlers, and who she holds responsible for the death of Macon Dead.) The tormentors are our bosses, landlords, or their sons, our poor white neighbors, the mayor, the sheriff. Sometimes they are our fathers, husbands, and brothers. Power is negative, it is dismembering, it seeks constantly to repress us, and when it is white on black, it comes with spectacle and torture.

This configuration of power changes significantly when the migration narrative moves north. It begins to change on the train just as soon as we cross the Mason-Dixon Line. The memory of the South as land of racial horror and shame or as the land that houses the ancestor plays a significant role in the migrants' confrontation with this new experience of power in the North.

2

The South in the City:
The Initial Confrontation with
the Urban Landscape

In contrast to the bare, stagnant landscape of Jacob Lawrence's Southern paint-ing, panel 1 of *The Migration of the Negro* (Figure 2.1) possesses vibrancy and movement. Visually, the painting differs a great deal from panel 15, discussed in Chapter 1. In fact, it seems to be the binary opposite of the lynching painting: While the lines of the Southern painting are horizontal, these are primarily vertical. In contrast to the roundness of the noose, the figure, and the stone of panel 15, here the lines form triangles and diamonds. The human figures are capped and further add to the triangular formations.[1]

Unlike the Southern painting, panel 1 is crowded with black bodies. Instead of the lone anonymous figure of the lynching painting, who sits with back turned to the viewer, here the figures are standing upright and are marching. We can see their profiles. Among these figures there is diversity of age and gender. Finally, the two paintings differ in that the South is portrayed as an open landscape, while the city scene is crowded and enclosed.

This major difference between the two paintings—the open landscape of the South versus the enclosed space of the North—also suggests a commonality between the two. In both paintings, there is a sense of uncertainty and precar-iousness. While the vivid color and sense of movement (created by the use of vertical diagonals) in panel 1 suggest possibility and hope, there is also a sense of enclosure. The Northern figures are contained by lattice bars. Their vibrancy and movement are checked by the lattice fence, which narrows the crowd as it enters the city. These bars contain and control the flow of the migrants.

The uncertainty of this painting lies in the fact that it does not tell us what awaits the migrants on the other side. Those figures who are already beyond the walls have their backs turned to the viewer. While they press out into the different cities, with the largest number headed for Chicago, there is no sense of the impact they have on these Northern centers or of the impact of cities on them. This uncertainty is one that the migration narrative, as well as other sources documenting the black migration, seeks to clarify.

48

Figure 2.1 Jacob Lawrence, *The Migration of the Negro*, 1940–41. Panel 1. "During the World War there was a great migration North by Southern Negroes." Tempera on masonite, 12″ × 18″. (The Phillips Collection, Washington, D.C.)

As with the portrayal of their departure from the South, the portrayal of the migrants' arrival in and impact upon the city is still another area of contest. From the perspective of the observers—Northern whites and middle-class blacks—it seems that the migrants represent a black mass, changing the face of the city forever. Those artists who portray their arrival from the perspective of the migrant document the impact of urban modernism, dislocation, and confusion on them.

I

The Negroes are coming.

St. Clair Drake and Horace R. Cayton,
Black Metropolis: A Study of Life in a Northern City

From the beginning of the Great Migration, Northern newspapers noted the arrival of black migrants with horror, humor, and disdain. According to many newspaper accounts the black horde was changing the face of the city. Nowhere was this more evident than in Chicago, which gained over fifty thousand migrants between 1910 and 1920. One Chicago headline screamed: "HALF MILLION DARKIES FROM DIXIE SWARM TO THE NORTH TO BETTER THEMSELVES."[2] The accompanying map (Figure 2.2) portrays the migration as an ever-growing dark-

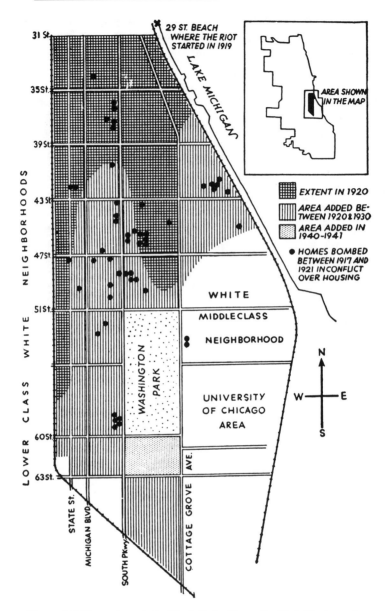

Figure 2.2 Expansion of the Black Belt. (From St. Clair Drake and
Horace Cayton, *Black Metropolis*)

ness expanding beyond borders into white territory.[3] The shaded area represents
two decades of black migration to Chicago's South Side. Black dots depict literal
explosions that were the immediate result of the influx; the most volatile and
significant effect of white response to the black migration was the eruption of
violence during the 1919 race riots, which tore the city apart. Commissions,

studies, boards, and institutions were created to explore the causes and conse-quences of the riots. Most cited the migration of blacks as the starting point.

This map and the headlines that blazed across Chicago's white-oriented news-papers are evidence of white response to black migration. Prior to the Great Migration, Northern cities were predominantly white, with small pocket commu-nities of Northern-born blacks who offered no viable threat to the dominant population. Although there had been occasional outbreaks of racial violence, these were usually of the "keep the Negroes in their place" variety. After the Great Migration, whites felt violence a necessity to stop and control the black hordes.[4]

F. Scott Fitzgerald's Nick Carraway, narrator of *The Great Gatsby*, articulates the response of the upper-middle class and wealthy whites: Spotting a limousine "driven by a white chauffeur, in which sat three modish negroes, two bucks and a girl . . . [whose] eyeballs rolled . . . in haughty rivalry," Carraway notes, "'Any-thing can happen now that we've slid over this bridge . . . anything at all. . . .' Even Gatsby could happen."[5] The growing number of blacks in America's urban centers was viewed as an omen of a dramatic change in Western society; as one example of the crisis of modernism: evidence that the natural order was in jeopardy. Their presence provoked fear, anxiety, and insecurity. Still, there is a weird sense of possibility implied by Carraway's comment. Under these circum-stances, "anything can happen"; a "nobody" like Gatsby can completely invent himself. For an artist like Fitzgerald, a marginalized black presence was a source of energy.

Whereas black and white Northerners believed the migrants to be an intru-sive presence, the migrants themselves present an alternative picture—one that portrays the urban assault on the migrant psyche. "My first glimpse of the flat black stretches of Chicago depressed and dismayed me, mocked all my fanta-sies. . . . The din of the city entered my consciousness, entered to remain for years to come."[6] So opens *American Hunger*, the second volume of Richard Wright's autobiography. Throughout much of his writing, Wright, along with other urban writers like Langston Hughes and Rudolph Fisher, documented the migrant's first confrontation with the urban landscape. These writers provide no evidence of their characters' membership in a black horde. Instead, fear and confusion consume the migrant psyche. In Rudolph Fisher's "City of Refuge" King Solomon Gillis, standing "dazed and blinking" upon his arrival in New York, is immediately set up by Northern hustlers.[7] The title proves to be an ironic one in that there is no earthly refuge for the black migrant.

In the context of the migration narratives the arrival of Southern blacks is marked by an immediate confrontation with a foreign place and time, with tech-nology and urban capitalism, with the crowd and the stranger.[8] Stephen Kern has demonstrated the ways in which changes in technology and culture between 1880 and World War I "created distinctive new modes of thinking about and experi-encing time and space."[9] Similarly, the African-American migrants of the migra-tion narrative confront changes in technology and culture that affect their way of experiencing time and space. The portrayal of the migrants' initial confrontation with urban modernity differs in the various migration narratives. While some artists and scholars focus on the degree to which migrants are transformed by the urban landscape, others portray the way they transform the city.

However, one aspect remains constant throughout most of the narratives: In the North the focus on the body, which is so prevalent in the Southern sections of the migration narrative, shifts to a focus on the migrant psyche. The effect on the psyche is an indication of the complexity of Northern power. The psyche is the realm where power is enforced and it is the ground on which the migrants seek first to resist objectification.

"The South in the city"[10] of this chapter describes the migrants' initial interaction with the urban landscape as well as those remnants of the South which are retained by them. Representations of the former illustrate the artists' emerging concern with the migrant psyche and how it is influenced by changes in the experience of time and space. In this context the "South in the city" is literally the South embodied in the migrant. The latter "South in the city" is embodied in spaces, rituals, and belief systems which act to either nurture or inhibit the urban protagonist.

The blues provides an excellent metaphor for what happens to the migrants when they arrive in the city. In terms of content, blues lyrics focus upon the impact of the city on the migrant. However, the form of the blues, the development of urban and city blues (as well as the development of gospel blues), and their subsequent impact on other forms of American music suggest that the migrants impacted upon the city as much as it impacted upon them.

This chapter provides an extended discussion of the blues as migrant. After this discussion there is a very brief description of the recorded sermons and gospel songs that also appealed to migrants. A more detailed reading of the various ways the migrants' arrival is represented in the literary texts of Jean Toomer, Richard Wright, Dorothy West, James Baldwin, and Gloria Naylor follows the discussion of music. Toomer's vision of the migrants' initial interaction with the urban landscape is continued and revised by Wright. However, West, Baldwin, and Naylor provide an alternative narrative, one that asserts the significance of Southern retention. Finally, a reading of Stevie Wonder's "Living for the City" closes the chapter where we begin—with the music.

II

What am I doin' up here?

Anonymous blues lyric

Both notions of the South in the city are evident in the changes, developments, and contributions of African-American music as it migrates north. Amiri Baraka notes that African-American music serves as a barometer of the experiences of black people in the United States.[11] The changes that occur in the music are intimately related to the experiences of the Southern migrant portrayed by the artists under consideration: Its confrontation with an unfamiliar environment, interaction with technology and capitalism, and resulting transformation and transformative activity all mirror the experience of the migrant. A review of these changes provides a map for reading the migration texts and suggests signs, concepts, and metaphors for understanding the story that literary artists seek to tell.

Amiri Baraka and Paul Oliver document the change in lyrics as the blues travel north. Prior to the development of a new and distinct urban blues, blues lyrics experience a transitional phase, a phase of confrontation and uncertainty.[12] This uncertainty often leads the singer to question the wisdom of the decision to migrate.

The South figures prominently in the early urban blues. When the bluesman sings: "I'm a poor ol' boy, a long, long ways from home / My home's in Texas, what am I doin' up here?"[13] he articulates the major tensions of a new migrant's psyche. First, the South is home, it is the place where "I" am from. Second, this place is so far, not only in space, but also consciously far from his own existence. "Here" signifies both time and place: Up here is the site from which he speaks, but the use of "here" also designates the present. "Here" is the present and home is a long way and time from "here." With the use of this word, the bluesman conflates time and space. "Here" is literally translated to mean here and now. In this context, home, no matter how horrifying it may have been, is seen through a lens tinted with nostalgia. Finally, the question, "What am I doin up here?" indicates the wonder of it all, the confusion, and the longing for purpose. The question is not "Who am I?" or "Am I?" It is not a question of identity but a question of purpose, direction, intent. It is not an inward question, but one that questions the "here" as much as it questions the "I." The worrying of the word "long" stresses the emotional, physical, and psychic distance from home. The conditions of migrancy are inherent in this lyric: dispossession, displacement, and the confrontation with new ways of understanding time and space.[14]

This song and others like it have serious implications for an understanding of African-American life that sees the primary quest of African-Americans as a quest for identity. A review of African-American song lyrics, folk practices, and some fiction suggests that the quest for identity is most often the quest of literate African-Americans or those who have biracial parentage. The question "Who am I?" is not as prevalent in African-American music.

Other bluesmen continue to question the here, but they do so in more concrete, material terms. In the "Bourgeoisie Blues" Huddie Ledbetter (Leadbelly) tells of the harsh racial and class discrimination the migrant meets:

> Me and Marthy we was standin' upstairs
> I heard a white man say: I don't want no niggers up there.

> Me and my wife we went all over town
> Everywhere we go the colored people would turn us down . . .
> Don't try to buy a house in Washington D.C.

Not only is the migrant victim to racial discrimination and segregation; he is also subject to the abuses of a Northern black middle class, who feel that their interests are threatened by any identification with him.[15]

Another artist, Jazz Gillum, illustrates poor housing conditions and cold weather as reasons for longing for the South:

> It's a sign on the building
> There's a sign on the building we all got to move right away,
> I ain't got no money, no rent that I can pay
> It soon will be cold, you hear me sing, yes I mean
> It soon will be cold, I ain't got no place to go
> I'm goin back down South, where the chilly winds don't blow.

In her autobiography, *Lady Sings the Blues*, Billie Holiday expresses a similar wonder about the practice of eviction in the North. She notes, "I didn't know they did things like that up North. Bad as it was down South, they never put out on the streets."[16] Similarly, the eviction scene in Ralph Ellison's *Invisible Man* further demonstrates the change in values experienced in the North.

While the lyrics offer significant evidence of this primary confrontation with the Northern landscape, the change in form, performance, and the influence of recording, distribution, and consumption of the blues most profoundly illustrates the immediate consequence of migration. As the blues migrate north, several formal changes occur. More instruments are added, each becoming more specialized. The technological addition of electric guitars and the amplification of microphones create larger volume and density.[17] In the North the performance venue changes from fields, juke joints, and tent shows to after-hours spots, rent parties, or, as in the case of classic blues, theaters. Moreover, the performance milieu instigates further formal changes. Charles Keil explains that songs become more standardized, defined; there is less improvisation, fewer deviations. The blues narrative becomes less fragmented, more condensed and consumable. Keil notes that in the North, there is an "increasing emphasis on lyrics that tell a story as opposed to the country practice of stringing together phrases linked only to a very general theme or emotional state."[18] In a social situation that is itself fragmented, the blues begins to provide some narrative coherence and order.

The blues performance fills a void in the migrants' urban existence. While lyrics may reflect a sense of fragmentation, performance provides order, stability, and community. As Baraka notes, the blues performance becomes a form of "acclimatization" to the North. It serves as a transitional space, making the transformation from migrant to urban dweller a little less harsh. It does this by providing the stability of "home," as well as offering a means to negotiate the "here." According to Keil:

54

Individual catharsis is still a sine qua non to successful performance, but in anemic, or bewildering urban situations, characterized by shifting values and interpersonal conflicts, people expect something more than personal lament from a singer. He must not only state common problems clearly and concisely, but must in some sense take steps towards their analysis and conclusion.[19]

In the South, where a sense of community exists, the bluesman can serve as the wandering stranger, but in the North, where the context in itself is the "stranger," the bluesman convenes the community and sets the atmosphere to invoke tradition. The blues performance therefore exists as a safe space where migrants are healed, informed, ministered, and entertained. When the pianist James P. Johnson recalled dances held for Southern migrants in New York City, he noted how they would sometimes call out "Let's go home." Johnson knew this to be a request for a more Southern style of music and he would oblige them. For those few hours that the migrants danced to a familiar Southern style of music, they recreated the South right in the middle of Manhattan.

Recent studies of the recordings and performances of "classic" blues singers like Bessie Smith reveal that these individual performers had very close relationships with their audiences.[20] Danny Barker, guitarist for Bessie Smith, recalled: "If you had any church background . . . you would recognize a similarity between what she was doin' and what those preachers and evangelists . . . did, and how they moved people. Bessie did the same thing on stage. . . . She could bring about mass hypnotism."[21] This description of Bessie Smith's performance reveals the element of ritual in the blues performance. As was the case with the preacher-centered migrant churches, the blues performance centers around a charismatic personality. Nevertheless, observers of these performances have noted that the relationship between the audience and the performer was a reciprocal one, with the same kind of call-and-response patterns that are evident in other aspects of African-American oral, musical, religious, and literary culture.

While the blues performance did not serve as a worship ritual, Smith's performance was more than mere entertainment. It acted as a means of convening community, of invoking common experiences and values. Though not necessarily a resistant space, it was a space where migrants could let their hair down, be themselves, and have a good time. As such, it was a healing space. It is quite significant that Barker's description of Smith's performance relies on descriptive terms borrowed from the church, which remains the model for a ritual and healing space. Along with preachers and gospel singers, blues artists provided their audiences with a scheme for survival that would allow them to locate a sense of integrity in their Southern pasts.[22]

Because Smith performed for diverse audiences—in black vaudeville theaters in New York, Chicago, and Philadelphia; cabarets in Atlantic City; and tent shows throughout North Carolina—she did not play the same roles each time she performed. In parts of the South she had a substantial white following. In Nashville, Smith had to add two special shows for the all-white Orpheum Theater.

According to Chris Albertson, Smith did not alter her shows for her white audiences. However, Albertson notes that "their enthusiasm was reserved for her artistry."[23] One can easily imagine that though the material remained similar, the performance and the interaction between audience and performer were quite different in the shows for white audiences and those for blacks.

In the North the performance of the blues split into two distinct arenas. On the one hand, there was the emergence of the classic blues singers—women like Bessie Smith, Alberta Hunter, and Victoria Spivey—who were the first to record. On the other hand, there was the urban blues, largely dominated by male performers like John Lee Hooker, Muddy Waters, and Big Bill Broonzy. While the classic blues was performed in tent shows and white-owned theaters, to black and white audiences, the developing urban blues was performed in after-hours joints and at rent parties—spaces less directly under the control of whites. As a result, the urban blues inherited from the country blues a direct connection to people's lives.

Both the classic and the urban blues had enormous influence on more popular forms of American music. As the first to be recorded, the classic blues was engaged in a process of stylistic exchange. While it infused American popular music, early recorded blues was formed and shaped by confrontations with capitalism and its developing technologies. Recording the blues led to standardization of the form. "Recorded performance meant that there was a certain limited space of time in which the singer could perform."[24] Recording also led to a four-stanza limit. In addition, the content of the lyrics reflect the change of the blues into an object of consumption. Sex becomes the dominant theme of the lyrics. Women become the primary performers. As these race records are distributed, they influence singers from various regions and begin the process of erasing regional differences. The classic blues singers also sang Tin Pan Alley tunes. However, even when Bessie Smith sang pop tunes or copyrighted blues, she inserted "a floating verse" from earlier country blues.[25] In doing so, she maintained a connection with her audience, who would recognize that verse as part of their own discourse. This floating verse became the "ancestor" of her blues narrative.

The blues is not a passive migrant. The blues-tinged jazz that migrates after the closing of Storyville in 1917 enters into the European-influenced ragtime.[26] Where ragtime strove toward a European "authenticity," the blues represented the ancestor of Southern black music. The meeting of the two conceived the new form of urban jazz. Eventually the blues mixing with other forms gave birth to the distinct urban forms of rhythm and blues and rock and roll. The blues infused urban music with the secret ingredient of the "blue note," which in this instance might be considered the repository of the "ancestor," of "home." William Barlow defines blue notes as the "melodic tendency to express rising emotions with falling pitch accomplished by bending or flattening certain notes on the diatonic scale, using one's voice or a musical instrument."[27] Technically, blue notes are the lowered third, fifth, and seventh degrees of a key. However, one might also speculate that at the level of content, the falling pitch of the blue note acts as the space where the absence, the terror, the fear, and the tragic moments of black life reside. In this sense the blue note is truly the site of history and memory.

In documenting the transition from country blues to an emerging urban blues both Amiri Baraka and Charles Keil focus on male artists. For Baraka the classic women blues singers were pop-influenced and commercial. However, he does credit the women blues singers with having formalized the blues. According to Baraka, "Classic blues differs a great deal from older blues forms in the content of its lyrics, its musical accompaniment, and in the fact that it was a music that moved into its most beautiful form as a public entertainment, but it is still a form of blues, and it is still a music that relates directly to the Negro experience."[28]

Keil, however, strikes a blatant sexist stance. Of the classic blues singers, he says: "A series of women, starting with Mamie Smith, turned out one standardized blues after another."[29] In his dismissal of the classic blues singers he denies their importance in providing some women with a scheme for survival in the city—a scheme tinged alternately with humor and pathos. I do not underestimate the importance of male performers in the development of the urban blues; however, the female singers provide us with a rare glimpse of the transition from the country blues to the urbane sophistication of Billie Holiday. They also reveal themselves as voices of one type of migrant female experience.

Bill Broonzy and Bessie Smith are two examples of the blues as it migrates north. Smith is the literal transition between the rural blues influence of Ma Rainey and the more stylized sophistication of Billie Holiday. Broonzy is interesting because throughout his career he was both a country and urban blues artist. Keil places the two singers under the rubric of "city blues," different from "urban blues" because of its use of piano accompaniment, the use of two or more instruments, and the standardized form. According to Keil, the urban blues is characterized by the addition of saxophones and by freer vocal phrasing.

With songs like "Pickpocket Blues" and "Dying Gambler Blues," Smith preached a secular sermon, lessons with which to negotiate the urban landscape and social relations. Other songs—"Washerwoman Blues," "Woman Trouble Blues," and "Anywoman's Blues," for example—were directed specifically at the women in her audience and articulated responses to their racial, gender, and class oppression.

The persona of "Woman Trouble Blues" sings of her unjustified incarceration: "When a woman gets in trouble, everybody throws her down. / When a woman gets in trouble, everybody throws her down. / Look for her friends and none can be found." The opening lyric, precursor to Billie Holiday's "God Bless the Child," is evidence of the alienation and fragmentation experienced in the city. Here social relations are fragile and the woman can depend on no one during her deepest hours of need. "I got to go to jail in a car. I got to do my time. / I got to go to jail in a car; I got to do my time. / Because the Judge is so cruel, he won't take no fine." Smith might very well have been singing of the plight of her young fan Billie Holiday, who was incarcerated on several occasions and given more severe punishments than her acts of prostitution and truancy warranted.

According to William Barlow, "the classic blues women were cultural rebels, ahead of the times artistically and in the forefront of resistance to all the various forms of domination they encounter."[30] While the blueswomen were models of sexual and economic independence, we must not romanticize their "feminism." For every defiant assertion of their independence and resistance, there is a song documenting domestic abuse and sexual oppression. For instance, there is a strain of streetwalker blues portraying abusive relationships between prostitutes and their pimps.

Smith's songs, however, were not directed only at women. Her most blatant protest song, "Poor Man's Blues," included a concern for both the men and women of her race.

> Mister rich man, rich man, open up your heart and mind,
> Mister rich man, rich man, open up your heart and mind,
> Give the poor man a chance, help stop these hard, hard times.
> While you're living in your mansion, you don't know what hard times mean,
> Poor working man's wife is starving, your wife is living like a queen.
>
> Please listen to my pleadin', 'cause I can't stand these hard times long,
> Please listen to my pleadin', 'cause I can't stand these hard times long,
> They'll make an honest man do things that you know is wrong.
>
> Now the war is over, poor man must live the same as you,
> Now the war is over, poor man must live the same as you,
> If it wasn't for the poor man, mister rich man, what would you do?[31]

Smith disguises a harsh critique as a plea in this blues. The juxtaposition of images of rich women who live like queens and poor women who starve asserts that women are linked more closely to the men of their class than to each other in any bond of sisterhood. Smith goes on to assert the connection between crime and poverty. The empathy with the jailed woman of "Woman Trouble Blues" is explained here, because Smith knows that the poor are often forced into lives of crime in order to sustain themselves. The final stanza articulates a sophisticated analysis of the link between the wealthy and the poor. The wealth of Mr. Rich Man is gained by the labor of Poor Man. Here Smith voices the concerns of her constituency and she provides them with an analysis and critique of the conditions responsible for their poverty.[32]

The sentiments of Smith's "Poor Man's Blues" are echoed in Bill Broonzy's "Unemployment Stomp." Like Smith, Broonzy also articulated the concerns of the working-class migrant. His "Unemployment Stomp," recorded in 1938, embodies, in both form and content, the changes in blues styles in the North. "Unemployment Stomp" is a rare recording of the boogie-woogie blues. Along with the harsh bass-defined urban blues, the boogie-woogie blues was developed in the urban arena of after-hours joints and rent parties. Like the classic blues, boogie-woogie blues was characterized by "standardized forms, regular beginnings and endings, [and] usually two or more instruments."[33] Also, like the classic blues, the boogie-woogie blues utilized the piano. According to Baraka, boogie-woogie blues

> seemed to be a fusion of vocal blues and the earlier guitar techniques of the country singers, adapted for the piano. . . . Ragtime was the first appropriation of white pianistic techniques by Negro musicians, boogie woogie was the second, but in such a blatantly percussive and blueslike manner as to separate it immediately from any more Europeanized music. In keeping with the traditional styles of Negro music, boogie woogie also was predominantly a music of rhythmic contrasts rather than melodic or harmonic variations.[34]

In light of this, the boogie-woogie blues exemplifies the manner in which urban black music brought elements of a black Southern past into contact with a "white pianistic technique" in order to create a unique urban art form. Also, boogie-woogie blues provides a foundation upon which later rock and roll piano players would build. Listening closely to "Unemployment Stomp" one can hear a precursor to Jerry Lee Lewis's piano. The trumpet sounds very much like the trumpet of "Boogie-Woogie Bugle Boy," recorded almost a decade later. These two instruments, accompanied by a bass drum, provide a very danceable rhythm. Boogie-Woogie blues was clearly a dance music. The rhythm is perfect for the lindy hop—yet another art form developed by migrants that was appropriated by mainstream society and renamed the jitterbug.[35]

The instruments and Broonzy's voice give us a faster tempo with more notes to a measure than we have heard up to this point. There are no moans or hollers but a clearly articulated lyric. What remains of his earlier country style is the rhythm and the call-and-response form of his aab line structure. Finally, the lyrics of "Unemployment Stomp" are clearly directed to the migrant audience. Topical and humorous, "Unemployment Stomp" voices the fear and frustration of the migrant community during the Great Depression:

(Boogie-Woogie trumpet and drum opening. Drum keeps 4/4 beat and trumpet responds to call of the singer, piano in background.)

> I'm a law abidin' citizen, my debts I sure will pay.
> I'm a law abidin' citizen, my debts I sure will pay.
> I hope war don't start and Uncle Sam don't have to send me away.
>
> I have never been in jail and I've never had to pay no fines.
> I have never been in jail and I've never had to pay no fines.
> I wants a job to make my living cause stealing ain't on my mine.
>
> I know a time when I raised my own meat and meal.
> I know a time when I raised my own meat and meal.
> My meat was in my smoke house and my meal was in my field.

Oh When Mr. Roosevelt sent out them unemployment cards.
Yes when Mr. Roosevelt sent out them unemployment cards.
I just know'd for sure that the work was goin' to start.

Broke up my home 'cause I didn't have no work to do.
Broke up my home 'cause I didn't have no work to do.
My wife had to leave me 'cause she was starvin' too.

In the first stanzas the persona establishes himself as a model, hardworking, taxpaying citizen; he expresses concern over the entrance of the United States into World War II. The third stanza appeals to a migrant's sense of nostalgia for the Southern home where he might at least keep his family from starvation. In the South, he was able to grow and raise his own food. The emphasis in this stanza is on the possessive pronoun "my." What little he had—meat, smokehouse, meal, and field—belonged to him. Here he resembles Morrison's Macon Dead I. Yet now he is dependent on government-issued jobs, which are not reliable. Like the persona in "Poor Man's Blues," he is unable to provide for his family. Consequently, his marriage is destroyed. The breakup of his marriage is further evidence of the disruption of urban life.

Throughout the song, the trumpet and piano respond to the vocalist in a traditional call-and-response pattern, but there are far more notes to the 4/4 measure. This almost reflects the quickened pace and fragmentation of the urban landscape as it is experienced by the migrants. According to Richard Wright: "Our nervousness and exhaustion are pounded out in the swift tempo of boogie-woogie."[36] However, the coherence of Broonzy's narrative provides a strand of stability and order.

The boogie-woogie rhythm became a mainstay of American popular music during the 1940s. For Baraka, this appropriation of the blues tradition was a caricature of the original. White musicians were not the only ones to appropriate elements of the boogie-woogie blues. Black middle-class performers and audiences also made use of them. Hazel Scott gained fame and a large following with her boogie-woogie interpretations of classical music. The boogie-woogie blues, like the classic blues and the harsher forms of urban blues, was both influenced by and did much to shape mainstream American popular music. Like the migrants who created it, the blues responded to the confrontation with the urban landscape, technology, and industrial capitalism in a process of give and take, a sense of adaptation, necessary for its survival.

The migrant blues was immediately confronted with a change in the way time and speed were experienced as well as with the machinations of new recording technologies and capitalist means of production and distribution. These factors all contributed to the "here" the blues sought to describe and to negotiate. At the same time, because of the unfamiliarity of this "here," the blues also reflects a nostalgia for the South and those aspects of it that stood for "home." The performance of the blues often offered a type of safe space in the North which allowed for community and regrouping as well as providing a transitional space where migrants could make the transition from Southern migrant to urban dweller. Finally, the blues was both influenced by and capable of influencing the forms of music and performance with which it began to interact. It was not only shaped by new technology and new music but it helped to lay the foundation for brand new types of American popular music like gospel, rhythm and blues, and rock and roll.

III

> The devil should not be allowed to keep all this good rhythm.
>
> Anonymous church elder

In the Northern churches migrants founded and in those established churches they influenced, they also nurtured a music that became the sacred sister of the blues. Although far fewer scholars have focused their attention on black gospel, this musical form also sought to address migrant concerns. However, unlike the blues and the spirituals that preceded them, early urban gospel or gospel-blues "recognized and discussed the troubles, sorrows, and burdens of everyday existence" but it also asserted that one had to take comfort from the blessings one had and "from the assurances of the Almighty."[37] Gospel music seeks to spread the "good news" of salvation through Christ, and its infectious rhythm suggests true Christians can experience joy through Christ in this life as well. Together gospel music and preaching provided an alternative to blues.

Church culture offered another means of navigating the urban landscape. A number of migrants found blues lyrics vulgar and worldly. However, they often claimed the rhythm and form of the blues while rejecting the lyrics and performance venue. Gospel traveled from the South into established black Protestant churches and migrant-founded storefront churches in the North. It fused with the blues to create a distinct black sound. Like the blues, it was first rejected by Northern black congregations for the sensuality of its rhythms and the emotional form of worship it inspired.[38] As a result of this, the Northern black church became a site of contestation between migrants and Northern-born members. In some instances, the migrants left the larger established churches to found their own storefront congregations.

While scholars disagree about the significance of storefront churches to migrant lives, almost all assert that the Great Migration had an enormous impact on church culture. According to Allan Spear:

> Of all aspects of [black] community life, religious activities were most profoundly influenced by the migration. Before the war, the large, middle-class Baptist and Methodist churches had dominated Negro religious life. . . . Al-

though they had not completely discarded the emotionalism of the traditional Negro religion, these churches had moved toward a more decorous order of worship and a program of broad social concern. The migration brought to the city thousands of Negroes accustomed to the informal, demonstrative, preacher-oriented churches of the rural south.[39]

Spear, along with other scholars who focused their attention on Chicago—St. Clair Drake, Horace Cayton, and James R. Grossman—note that with the arrival of large numbers of black migrants, Chicago's established black Baptist and Methodist churches grew dramatically. Mount Olivet Baptist Church in Chicago grew by more than five thousand members between 1916 and 1919.[40]

According to Drake and Cayton, Spears, and Grossman, many of the larger established churches welcomed the migrants, but others did not offer the style of preaching and music that the migrants sought. Consequently, dissatisfied migrants often founded storefront Baptist, Pentecostal, and Holiness churches.[41] These churches were characterized by fundamentalist interpretations of the Bible, shouting, glossolalia (speaking in tongues), healing, and gospel music.[42]

Michael Harris's recent study of the life and work of gospel pioneer Thomas Dorsey challenges the notion that migrants fled established churches for the storefronts. Instead, he argues, migrants saw the larger churches as a means of upward mobility. According to Harris, Southern migrants remained in the established black Protestant churches and offered a formidable challenge to worship practices. Nowhere was this more evident than in the struggle over the kind of music performed during services.[43]

Whatever the case, for the most part both the storefronts and the larger churches, like rent parties and juke joints, operated free of white control. One migrant exemplified the significance of this freedom when she said: "I goes every Sunday and Wednesday nights to prayer meeting just to thank God that he let me live to go to a place of worship like that, a place where my people worship and ain't pestered by the white men."[44] Black churches provided another arena where migrants were able to convene community; in some instances, church was a place where migrants could invoke the South as a means of sustaining them in the city. They were spaces that provided information about the South, assisted migrants upon their arrival, and helped to smooth their transition into the city. Most important, however, they were spaces where the South was invoked through music, preaching, and worship. According to Grossman, because of these churches migrants had the "chance to adjust to the urban North, while still retaining aspects of one's Southern cultural heritage."[45] This was not always an easy task, as is evident in the resistance that early migrants met in the older churches. The rise of the storefront church and the ascendancy of gospel music within the established churches is an indication of the intraracial conflict that was intensified when large numbers of poor blacks migrated to Northern cities. The popularity of gospel music among working-class migrants suggests an interclass conflict as well. Consideration of gospel music complicates our current understanding of working-class migrant culture as having been characterized only by the blues.[46]

Paul Oliver documents the existence of the "other half" of the race records industry: the religious vocal tradition of recorded sermons and gospel songs. These records were produced by the same companies that produced the classic blues singers: Okeh, Columbia, Paramount. They were advertised in newspapers like the *Chicago Defender* alongside advertisements for blues recordings.[47] Although it is not possible to determine sales figures for these records, it is significant that the companies continued to record and release sermons and gospel songs for over a decade, suggesting that there was indeed a buying public for them.[48] It is quite possible that many of the people who purchased these religious records also purchased blues records.

Just as the blues was influenced by technologies of production and distribution, so too was gospel music. It is evident that the recorded sermons were staged for the purpose of recording them. Most are marked by their canned "congregational" responses to the minister's admonitions. Usually the sermon is cut to three minutes and a "congregation" of two women and a man responds to the preacher with amens, hallelujahs, and punchlines. So-called sermons like the popular and much-recorded "Dead Cat on the Line" were clearly for entertainment purposes only. However, the gospel songs were for both entertainment and inspiration.

When Blind Willie Johnson sang "I'm gonna run, I'm gonna run, I'm gonna run to the City of Refuge" where the "Holy Ghost will set you free," he continued a migration theme originating with the spirituals. The recent migrants in his listening audience knew that the cities to which they fled were not the one about which he sang. In the early parts of the record, Johnson's guitar playing and his voice greatly resemble the performance of the rural bluesman. In fact, the song has a blues structure. However, by the end of the track, the refrain, "I'm gonna run to the City of Refuge," is sung in the rough, coarse manner of a straining preacher. At this point the performer sounds like a man who has been running— his breath is short, his voice strained yet determined.[49] Johnson becomes a surrogate for the black migrant — part of a legacy of black people who from slavery on fled hostile places in search of freedom. Within the context of the song itself he seems to change from a bluesman to minister. He is literally transformed, "set free" by the "Holy Ghost." In this song, its lyrics and its performance, the message is clear. One cannot simply move from place to place, from the South to the city, in search of freedom. Freedom can be granted only by the Holy Ghost; it is fully achieved only in the sacred "City of Refuge."[50]

Blind Willie Johnson was one of the most important gospel performers of his day. Between 1927 and 1930 the Texas-born Johnson made approximately thirty recordings for Columbia Records. Mark Humphrey says:

More than any other sacred singer of his era, Blind Willie Johnson left a palpable imprint on American music. What came to him from folk tradition went back to it molded in his likeness. Such disparate artists as the Rev. Blind Gary Davis, Fred McDowell, and [Pops] Staple listened, bringing traces of Johnson's repertoire and style to the 1960's folk/blues revival.[51]

The blues and gospel were influenced by and served to influence the culture of the cities to which the migrants fled. In this way, the music shares a great deal with the migrants who produced it and who were its primary audience. Written migration narratives revolve around two different understandings of the migrant's confrontation with the urban landscape and the place and importance of the South in "safe spaces" of nurturing, transition, or resistance. Some artists paint portraits of a city transformed by the arrival of migrants; others paint portraits of migrants transformed by the city. Some assert the possibilities inherent in Southern retention in safe spaces within the city; others see them as limiting and provincial. Still others doubt that the South is capable of survival in the city.

IV

> Money burns the pocket, pocket hurts,
> Bootleggers in silken shirts,
> Ballooned, zooming Cadillacs,
> Whizzing, whizzing down the street-car tracks.
>
> Seventh Street is a bastard of Prohibition and the War. A crude-boned, soft-skinned wedge of Nigger life breathing its loafer air, jazz songs and love, thrusting unconscious rhythms, black-reddish blood into the white and whitewashed wood of Washington. Wedges rust in soggy wood. . . . Split it! In two! Again! Shred it! . . . the sun. Wedges are brilliant in the sun; ribbons of wet wood dry and blow away. Black reddish blood. Pouring for crude-boned soft-skinned life, who set you flowing? Blood suckers of the War would spin in a frenzy of dizziness if they drank your blood. Prohibition would put a stop to it. Who set you flowing? White and whitewash disappear in blood. Flowing down the smooth asphalt of Seventh Street, in shanties, brick office buildings, theaters, drug stores, restaurants, and cabarets? Eddying on the corners? Swirling like a blood-red smoke up where the buzzards fly in heaven? God would not dare to suck black red blood. A Nigger God! He would duck his head in shame and call for the Judgment Day. Who set you flowing?
>
> Money burns the pocket, pocket hurts,
> Bootleggers in silken shirts,
> Ballooned, zooming Cadillacs,
> Whizzing, whizzing down the street-car track.

Jean Toomer, "Seventh Street"

The migrants of Jean Toomer's *Cane* are not unlike those of the map with which we opened the chapter. Toomer's migrants transform the urban landscape with their active vibrancy. The distanced narrator observes them from afar and records their impact on the city. In the Southern section Toomer says "time and space have no meaning in a canefield."[52] The language of that section is slow, sonorous, and cyclical; it is the language of the spirituals. In contrast, the first piece of the second section, "Seventh Street"—an eighteen-line, one-paragraph-long prose poem framed on either side by verse—is marked by an immediate change in rhythm, pace, and content. In this respect, it is like the urban blues.

As mentioned earlier, there is no single migrant from the Southern section who emerges on this new landscape; instead, we the readers are the migrants of this text. It is our consciousness which immediately confronts the Northern metropolis. The verse section speeds us quickly to Seventh Street, where we are confronted with a whir of excitement and almost as quickly as we arrive we are rushed away again by the repeated verse.

The verbs of the verse section are harsh and quick verbs of movement. Assonance and consonance further enhance the sense of motion, but the repetition of the harsh double consonants *gg* and *zz* in the words nigger and whizzing speed the passage toward a swift conclusion. The imagery is distinctly urban: Fast money, hustlers, and transportation technology contrast with the sunsets, swan songs, and beautiful, sensual women of the Southern section. The sounds are literally the sounds of cars and streetcars. Money is made illegally. The language itself is colloquial; the sentences are incomplete, as if there is no time to finish them. This is not a lyrical, smooth movement. The tongue is forced to stagger over words like jazz, Nigger, soggy, dizzy, creating a sense of fragmentation.

In the South, nature is personified; on Seventh Street money is personified. There is the suggestion that relationships are elements of commerce. Seventh Street is populated by fast men of the underworld. It is the product of an illegitimate sexual union between two disciplinary acts of government, one a legislative act, the other a declaration of war. Prohibition breeds a seedy area that lies waiting for migrants heading north because of World War I.

Toomer's migrants have black-red blood that is alive and vibrant—flowing forcefully into the white stale wood of Washington. It is blood as intoxicating as the brew made illegal by prohibition. The verbs are the verbs of sex and reproduction: breathing, thrusting, split, shred, pouring, flowing. It is a harsh, crude sex: "crude-boned" and "soft skinned." Migrant blood becomes a metaphor for the culture that the migrants bring. Washington is a white woman, a stale and stagnant being entered forcefully by the black male migrant blood. It is significant that Toomer's migrants are defined as masculine.

Like Nick Carraway when confronting the onslaught of blacks, white Washington must feel that this is the end of Western civilization, that surely God is dead. "God would not dare to suck black red blood. A Nigger God!" One can hear their indignant Humph! "He would duck his head in shame and call for the Judgment Day." However, there is no imagery of coming doom and death of culture; instead it is the infusion of a new, fresh, and colorful culture. Nellie McKay says of the Seventh Street migrants: "From the blood and ashes of so many Tom Burwells, phoenixlike, a new people have begun to rise."[53]

Within the context of the entire text, "Seventh Street" makes the reader a migrant. We arrive from the languorous, seductive language of the South and are immediately confronted with swiftness and technology. This change in language comes as a shock to our eyes, ears, and powers of comprehension. The language confuses us and we must shift our consciousness if we are to grasp it and read its signs.

There are four possibilities offered to the Seventh Street migrants of *Cane*: they can become completely transformed into materialistic automatons like Rhobert; they can become class-conscious social climbers like Muriel; they can hold on tightly to their Southern sensibility and in so doing not survive the city like Avey or Dan; or they can seek out a form of balance between Southern spirituality and Northern ingenuity as does the narrator of the entire volume. The last choice proves to be the most difficult, painful, and ultimately rewarding. Rhobert, who resembles the bourgeois blacks of Leadbelly's "Bourgeois Blues," wears a house that crushes him and drives the life force out of him. Though people see a strong man with material success, the cost of that success has been the loss of his own spirit. The "h" inserted in his name, otherwise spelled "Robert," seems to literally illustrate his wearing a "h"ouse; it has become that significant to his identity.

However, the fate of those who maintain a strong sense of the South is that of poetic tragedy. "Avey" and "Box Seat" illustrate the destiny of the migrant who is unable to negotiate the swiftly changing pace of Washington. "Avey" exists as a literal Southern space within the Northern section of *Cane*. The language, imagery, distanced male gaze, and impenetrable woman all invoke that of the Southern section. As migrating readers who have been thrust onto Seventh Street and then confronted with the house-wearing Rhobert, we breath a sigh of relief at "Avey" until we become aware of the consequences of maintaining the South. If we look closely enough, we will not be lulled to security, for here the young trees are in boxes which they will soon outgrow.

For the boys, Avey's presence invokes the easy sexuality of the South. She is possibly the only person who can "[swing] along lazy and easy as anything" (p. 44). The young male narrator who desires her is always fully engaged, fully active, in contrast to the indifferent Avey, who is an observer at best. When Avey is near, the very atmosphere is transformed. With her, the narrator notes, "The moon was brilliant. The air was sweet like clover." As with the canefield, with Avey "there is no set time to go home."[54]

However, for all of her sensual power, we learn that Avey will not survive the North; the narrator foreshadows her end in his description of a summer outing: "The next time I came close to her was the following summer at Harper's Ferry. We were sitting on a flat projecting rock they give the name of Lover's Leap. . . . A railroad track runs up the valley and curves out of sight where part of the mountain rock had to be blasted away to make room for it" (p. 46). Harper's

Ferry is the site of a failed slave revolt, Lover's Leap connotes death, and the phallic railroad track running through a mountain whose rock had been blasted indicates technological destruction of the natural landscape. Failure, death, and violent destruction are metaphors for the options that lie ahead for Avey.

The narrator's final encounter with her is marked by the refrain from the Southern section: "One evening in early June, just at the time when dusk is most lovely on the Eastern horizon, I saw Avey" (p. 47). Just as it did in the South, dusk on the eastern horizon connotes death and demise. He takes her to a place where he tries to invoke the pastoral serenity of the South, in hope that her languorous presence will complete the picture: "And when the wind is from the South, soil of my homeland falls like a fertile shower upon the lean streets of the city. . . . I started to hum a folk tune" (p. 46). However, with the sleeping Avey he is unable to consummate his passion. There is no possibility for sexual connection, for regenerating life when the South remains Southern in the city of *Cane*. It cannot survive as a live being, but only as a spiritual source to nurture the imagination of the artist. Avey, "who is dusk," does "not have the gray-crimson splashed beauty of dawn."

If the feminine South as Avey slips quietly away into a dusklike slumber, the masculine South as Dan of "Box Seat" fights all the way down. In "Box Seat," the town is dominated by images of houses. Like Rhobert, the town dwellers of "Box Seat" are chained and bound to their houses. In keeping with "Seventh Street" the houses (metaphors for the town) are likened to women, and the crude Southern migrant is likened to trees and men. "Shake your curled wool blossoms Nigger. . . . Stir the root-life of a withered people. Call them from their houses, and teach them to dream. . . . Dark swaying forms of Negroes are street songs that woo virginal houses" (p. 46). Women are civilized, tamed, enclosed spaces. Men are natural, wild, and open.

Dan, the awkward male migrant, fumbles at the gate of the house he visits. He has "wool blossoms for hair," which are like the "chestnut buds and blossoms of wool" on the trees. In this way Dan is linked to nature. However, despite his resemblance to these trees, he does not fit in with the loveliness of the houses. They represent a different kind of beauty. "He strains to produce tones in keeping with the houses' loveliness. Cant be done. He whistles. His notes are shrill" (p. 56).

Throughout the story Dan does not fit in, and it is for this reason Muriel, the woman he loves, rejects him. Muriel aspires to be like Mrs. Pribby, the home-owner with whom she lives. While Mrs. Pribby and Muriel click metallically into their chairs, Dan sinks softly into a sofa. Muriel, who is also of the South, tries to wash Southern soil from her skin. Just as she rids herself of her Southern ways, her sensuality embodied in her dancing with dress hiked above her thighs, so too she must rid herself of Dan. "Pity about Dan. He doesn't fit in," she thinks. She loves him, but she knows that the town "will not let her."

Though she responds with a heart-wrenching honesty in her thoughts, her dialogue with Dan is short, witty, and ultimately uncommunicative. Muriel seeks happiness and beauty. Dan informs her that life is a balance between the two, between suffering and laughter, beauty and ugliness. "There is no such thing as happiness. Life bends joy and pain, beauty and ugliness, in such a way that no one may isolate them. No one should want to. Perfect joy, or perfect pain, with no contrasting element to define them, would mean a monotomy of consciousness, would mean death. Not happy, Muriel. Say that you have tried to make them create" (p. 59). Dan recognizes that the balance of the two is necessary. Muriel and other urbanized individuals strive for only one dimension of the human experience: happiness. Like the black middle-class described by St. Clair Drake and Horace Cayton in *Black Metropolis*, Muriel and her peers seek to acquire, to become and own houses. This inhibits their creativity and prohibits them from ever really experiencing any happiness at all.

Although Muriel is busy trying to fit in, she is too conscious of the ways in which she doesn't fit to ever truly be happy. When finally it seems as though she and Dan might communicate and consummate their love for each other, they are stopped by the rattle of a newspaper and the chime of a clock: "A sharp rap on the newspaper in the rear room cuts between them. The rap is like cool thick glass between them. Dan is hot on one side. Muriel, hot on the other. . . . A clock strikes eight." (pp. 60–61) The clock and the newspaper both represent a different, more modern conception of time. Stephen Kern notes that the clock, which measures time in hours, minutes, and seconds, fragments and itemizes our days. The newspaper, as a result of changing printing technologies and the news wire, rearranges our conception of the past and the present. Suddenly, the newspaper transforms what happened yesterday or before the evening edition into the past. The wall that these two put between Muriel and Dan is a wall separating the past from the present, the South from the North—a distance measured by different notions of time. In stark contrast to bluespeople, although both Muriel and Dan are hot on either side of the glass wall, they can see but will never touch each other.

The final alternative offered to *Cane*'s migrants, that of seeking a balance between Southern spirituality and Northern ingenuity, seems like a remote possibility for the majority of the characters in the text. For the most part the characters of this section suffer from a sense of alienation from those aspects of Southern culture that might sustain them. As Houston Baker points out, "The whole of part 2 [of *Cane*] might justifiably be called a portrait of the artist who has been removed from a primitive and participatory culture to suffer the alienation of modern life."[55] Only Kabnis, protagonist of the final section, attempts to pursue the alternative of finding the balance between the spiritual sustenance of Southern culture and the ingenuity of the modern North. The consequences of his search are explored in the final chapter.

V

I felt lonely.

Richard Wright, *American Hunger*

Cane's migrants infuse the city with their culture, but they are destined to die if they do not incorporate the swift changes that confront them upon their arrival. Though Richard Wright continues the male-defined thrust of Toomer, his migrants arrive confused, afraid, and uncertain of which masks to wear in the city. They are transformed or killed by the city but there is no evidence that they affect it in any real way. Those rare few who are transformed and who attain a critical consciousness are able to march into modernity, demanding their rights with other modern men. This requires a full separation from any folk sensibility or remnant of the South. Those who are not transformed are destined to remain unenlightened and premodern. In the world of Richard Wright, women are relegated to this latter group by the mere fact of their gender. Men are offered alternatives and choices. However, few of them acquire the necessary critical consciousness to resist the negative effects of urbanization.

Wright explores the consciousness and psyche of the black migrant in greater depth than any other artist. He is therefore central to any discussion of the migration narrative. In his autobiography *American Hunger*, the documentary text, *12 Million Black Voices*, and two of his novels, *Lawd Today* and *Native Son*, Wright illustrates the varying ways the experience of migration affects black men. His migrants are not only thrown into an unfamiliar space, but they are also in an unfamiliar time.

In his second autobiography, Wright is the migrant who enters Chicago, confused and uncertain. As with Jacob Lawrence's panel 1, so with Wright's Chicago: "There were no curves here, no trees, only angles, lines, squares, bricks and copper wires" (p. 2). The Chicago of *American Hunger* is colorless, flat; it contrasts with the catalog of natural beauty found in *Uncle Tom's Children* and *Black Boy*:

> My first glimpse of the flat black stretches of Chicago depressed and dismayed me, mocked all my fantasies. Chicago seemed an unreal city whose mythical houses were built on slabs of black coal wreathed in palls of gray smoke, houses whose foundations were sinking slowly into the dank prairie. Flashes of steam showed intermittently on the wide horizon, gleaming translucently in the winter sun. The din of the city entered my consciousness, entered to remain for years to come.[56]

The depressing tone of this opening paragraph echoes the tone of the "What am I doing up here?" blues lyrics. The city, like Rhobert, is sinking; it is described in supernatural tones—a kind of twilight zone–purgatory. The environment is an unfamiliar planet, resembling the image of the day after doomsday in a science fiction novel. It induces a druglike stupor on Wright's consciousness. Urban power manifests itself in the very atmosphere, it is as translucent and as effective as the steam; it is in the very air he breathes and affects first and foremost not his physical or economic self, but his consciousness.[57]

Each of his senses is in turn affected by this change in atmosphere. As with "Seventh Street" in Toomer's Washington, in Chicago, "Streetcars screeched past over steel tracks. Cars honked their horns. Clipped speech sounded about me" (p. 2). The sounds of the city confuse and engulf him. Language is not a means of communication but another aspect of the urban landscape that baffles him. The pace of the city is evidenced in its sound. Sound attacks his Southern sensibility with a violent staccato. It is the staccato that begins to be reflected in the electrification and quickened pace of the urban blues.

Wright, the confused migrant, looks for the familiar signs of segregation in public accommodations and transportation as well as in the actions and attitudes of the people, but he finds none. What he does find is slightly more disarming in its unfamiliarity. Although there is no threat of physical violence from the white people, there is the dehumanizing effect of indifference. "Each person acted as though no one existed but himself." From this point on Wright experiences the alienation that characterizes urban life.

Immediately, he begins to wonder if he will ever fit into the urban environment. His cultural illiteracy is apparent in his inability to read and negotiate the signs of the urban landscape: "I began to grow tense again, although it was a different sort of tension than I had known before. I knew that this machine city was governed by strange laws and I wondered if I could ever know them" (p. 2). He becomes further alienated from himself by the unfamiliar laws of the new society. No longer are the "ethics of living Jim Crow" adequate. In many ways *American Hunger* documents Wright's journey from alienation to dealienation through a growing critical consciousness of the factors that alienate him.

Initially power affects him without spectacle and torture. Instead it affects his consciousness because he cannot immediately identify it. The city is likened to a machine. It seeks to reconstruct him as an urban subject. His first lesson in the construction of the urban subject occurs when he looks at his aunt: "I was learning already from the frantic light in [Aunt Maggie's] eyes the strains that the city imposed upon its people" (p. 2). Here is the first lesson in the construction of an urban subject.

Like the bluesman, Wright asks himself: "Should I have come here? But going back was impossible. I had fled a known terror, and perhaps I could cope with this unknown terror that lay ahead" (p. 2). The South is a place to which he cannot return; the city is a land not of opportunity but of unknown terror. Wright's description of his arrival is filled with the conditions of migrancy— displacement, disruption, and transience:

> Everything seemed makeshift, temporary. I caught an abiding sense of insecu-
> rity in the personalities of the people around me. . . . Wherever my eyes

> turned they saw stricken, frightened black faces trying vainly to cope with a
> civilization that they did not understand. I felt lonely. I had fled one insecurity
> and had embraced another. [p. 3]

Insecurity, fear, and loneliness—these are traits Wright shares with the characters he creates: Bigger and Jake. In this paragraph the single most dominant
theme in all of Wright's migration narratives emerges: the inability of the majority
of black people to understand and enter "civilization." Their alienation from
themselves and all the forces that surround them is only intensified in the North.

Of his aunt, he says, "She was beaten by her life in the city" (p. 3). She was
not beaten by a white man, but by the city, which here takes on enormous and
omniscient proportions. Like Ann Petry's "street," the city silently and invisibly
operates on its inhabitants. Even the room in which he lives is as "cold as the
Southern street had been in the winter." Like Frances Harper before him,
Wright suggests that the climate in the South was friendlier and more conducive
to life than that in the North.

Wright knows that his major problem in the city is his reluctance to forget the
signs of his old world: "I was persisting in reading my present environment in the
light of my old one." He needs new conceptual tools to explore and understand
his new conditions.

While there is no evidence of literal safe spaces—spaces that might ease his
transition—for Wright to retreat to and resist his objectification, he does identify
such a space within himself. Ironically, it is a space that will be fed and nurtured,
not by an ancestor, but by a growing critical awareness that moves him closer to
the position of stranger than of ancestor:

> Slowly I began to forge in the depths of my mind a mechanism that repressed
> all the dreams and desires that the Chicago streets, the newspapers, the movies
> were evoking in me. . . . A dim notion of what life meant to a Negro in
> America was coming to consciousness in me, not in terms of external events,
> lynchings, Jim Crow and the endless brutalities, but in terms of crossed-up
> feeling, of psychic pain. [p. 7]

He places a critical distance between himself and the attempts to manipulate his
desire. Whereas in the South his perception of power was one of exploitation and
oppression, here he is conscious of its effects on his psyche, on its attempts to
construct his subjectivity.

The sentiments expressed in *American Hunger* are echoed in Wright's fiction
and in his documentary text, *12 Million Black Voices*. Black migrants enter the
modern city ill-prepared for the civilization that awaits them. They suffer an
immediate attack on their consciousness and experience the effects of domination on psychic and spiritual levels. Those who, like Bigger's mother, cling to
their Southern folkways are doomed to complacency. Those who, like Bigger,
reject the folkways without acquiring a critical consciousness of their oppression
are destined to act out in nihilistic rebellion. Those rare few, like Wright, who

acquire a critical consciousness may overcome and emerge into the modern world. Even this latter possibility is characterized by the loneliness and marginality of the stranger.

This sense of the marginality of the stranger in Richard Wright is greatly influenced by the work of the Chicago school of sociology, especially the work of Louis Wirth and Robert Park.[58] Park further developed Simmel's notion of the stranger and marginal man to fit the context of urban America and its black and Jewish inhabitants. The stranger becomes the marginal man in the context of the United States. According to Park, the marginal man is

> a cultural hybrid, a man living and sharing intimately in the cultural life and traditions of two distinct peoples; never quite willing to break, even if he were permitted to do so, with his past and his traditions, and not quite accepted, because of racial prejudice, in the new society in which he now sought to find a place. . . . He is par excellence, the "stranger," whom Simmel . . . has described with such profound insight and understanding. [p. 355][59]

For Park, the marginal man provided the best source for studying the changes and fusion of culture and the "processes of civilization and of progress." He "invariably becomes in a certain sense and to a certain degree a cosmopolitan. He learns to look upon the world in which he was born and bred with something of the detachment of the stranger. He acquires, in short, an intellectual bias."[60] Wright seeks to acquire the status of stranger or marginal man. *American Hunger* documents this process of search and discovery. It is the voice of Wright as stranger which informs and articulates *12 Million Black Voices*. Wright even acknowledged, "It was from the scientific findings of men like the late Robert E. Park, Robert Redfield, and Louis Wirth that I drew the meanings for my documentary book, *12,000,000 Black Voices*; for my novel, *Native Son*."[61]

Of the nonfiction documentary texts that focus on African-Americans, Wright's *12 Million Black Voices* is the only one written from the perspective of the migrant. Southern blacks migrate into James Weldon Johnson's *Black Manhattan* (1930), Claude McKay's *Harlem: Negro Metropolis* (1940), St. Clair Drake and Horace Cayton's *Black Metropolis* (1945), and Arna Bontemps's *They Seek a City* (1945) and *Anyplace but Here* (1968). These other texts provide general histories of the cities to which the migrants come. The migrants play minor roles in the histories provided by Johnson and Bontemps.

In Wright's text we follow the migrants as they enter the city. The Chicago of *12 Million Black Voices* is bustling, the pace many times quicker than that of the South from which the migrants come. Again, the landscape is gray and the people indifferent. In place of cabins and fields, there are the black-belt tenements with many families in rooms meant for one. In place of blue skies and pastoral lands there are gray clouds and concrete buildings. There are no visible "colored only" signs, no Jim Crow buses. In Wright's written text, all the characters in the urban setting resemble the figures of an Edward Hopper painting: Blank faces stare into nowhere with little or no regard for the persons in front, in back, or next to them. The photographs that accompany this section feature families and individuals in impoverished interior settings and abandoned, dirty exterior lots. As noted in the previous chapter, there is a tension between the photographic and the written narrative. This is still the case in the Northern section of the text.

Interestingly, although Richard Wright wrote the preface to *Black Metropolis*, and though he was greatly influenced by the work of Drake and Cayton, his portrayal of the migrants' arrival in Chicago differs a great deal from theirs. In *Native Son*, Wright seems to lift the map with which we opened this chapter directly from the pages of the Drake and Cayton text. Here, however, the growing blackness of the map connotes state power closing in on the "fugitive" Bigger. The white portion of the map is the portion that is yet to be searched, and therefore still "free" like Bigger. The shaded section is controlled and contained by the search, as are its residents, who must suffer harassment and abuse as long as Bigger remains uncaptured. This use of the map differs from that in Drake and Cayton, for it does not portray the black migrant as an out-of-control mass.

As indicated by his use of the map, Wright focuses on the city's immediate impact on the migrants in his description of their initial confrontation with the urban landscape. Again, power takes on a different face. It is more nearly omniscient and less identifiable. Housing conditions are terrible, but the landlord is an absentee. There are hordes of foreign immigrants and white migrants, who progress at the expense of the black migrant. Yet these whites do not directly possess power over the blacks. There are the "gangster politicians," who both exploit and protect their black constituency. There is conflict between the races, sometimes erupting in vicious race riots. Significantly, there are various avenues open to the new migrant to act out his rebellion. These come in the form of organizations, institutions, and urban chaos.

For the first time the migrant is confronted with options for a resisting discourse in the form of nationalism and communism. Should he find neither of these entirely desirable or suitable, he may choose the individual, solitary intellectual route of Wright, a choice supported by free access to institutions like libraries, or like the mass of Wright's migrants, he may act out his frustrations through violence, liquor, religion, or sex.

To understand the world of Wright's migrants it is necessary to understand the ways in which power functions as domination *and* exploitation. It functions on them not just as economic subjects but also as racial subjects. These men are poor and black. They are cyclical in a world of linear time. They are often confused and motivated by fear. Most lack an understanding of the forces that act upon them. Only Wright himself claims any enlightenment in this sphere, and with understanding comes further alienation and dissatisfaction.

The complexity of urban power is evident when contrasted with Southern power. The earlier section of *12 Million Black Voices*, "Our Strange Birth," documents slavery, and the effects of oppression on the black body is of central concern. The second section, "Death on the City Pavements," focuses on the effect of oppression on the black migrant psyche. Now for the first time there is death, not in a field, not by a lynch mob, but "on the city pavement." There is no visible murderer; the living conditions themselves serve as the lynch mob. The black migrants leave the South unprepared for what awaits them. The train or bus ride serves as a transition, Southern swamps turn into roads, but the most evasive change occurs in the language: "The slow Southern drawl, which in legend is so sweet and hospitable but which in fact has brought down on our black bodies suffering untold, is superseded by clipped Yankee phrases, phrases spoken with such rapidity and neutrality that we, with our slow ears, have difficulty in understanding" (p. 98). Note the shift from "our black bodies" to "our slow ears" and "[our] difficulty in understanding." As was the case with *Cane* and *American Hunger*, language is the medium through which the migrant is first alienated. The migrant cannot enter it, cannot yet steal it and forge it into something new, as was the case in the South. The "rapidity," the "clipped" phrases, indicate fragmentation of the modernist experience. It is through the medium of language that the migrant immediately becomes an alienated individual, alienated from the context in which he lives and from other human beings. The quest will be to find meaning which transcends this alienation—to grasp the language which gives meaning. But in many cases this understanding will lead only to further alienation.

Language marks a temporal, spatial, and psychic change. The slowness of the Southern drawl is directly related to the pace of Southern life, slow and melodic. Yankees speak in clipped phrases, which represent a change in time and consciousness. The migrants, a people of the land, are overwhelmed by this new way of speaking. "Our" consciousness is a slow one; "our" understanding is limited. Even "our" feet are "awkward" on the pavements (p. 93). This alienation leads to alienation from human possibility. Wright asserts: "It is the beginning of living on a new and terrifying plane of consciousness" (p. 99). Again, here is evidence that the change in the way black people experience power is not simply a temporal change but primarily a spatial one. In this text, it seems all of "our" beginnings are terrifying ones. However, this passage also reveals one of Wright's many blindnesses about the wealth of possibilities offered by black culture. He is unable to see the migrant as an agent in language. Black migrants, like their African forebears, also display linguistic innovation and agency in the creation of new hybrid forms of language on the urban landscape. This language, in the form of slang, urban blues, and other forms of black English, best articulates their experience on the urban landscape.[62]

In the North, white men "seem impersonal . . . indifferent." The black migrant is anonymous in the crowd where everyone, like Mrs. Dalton of *Native Son*, is blind to his existence. Though there are many more people here, it is impossible to know them. Everyone lives in a state of anonymity. This anonymity does not signal freedom, for the migrants are seeking to be seen, to be known, to be recognized.

Soon the migrants begin to penetrate the workings of this strange environment:

> The bosses of the Buildings are not indifferent. They are deeply concerned about us, but in a new way. It seems as though we are now living inside a machine; days and events move with a hard reasoning of their own. We live amid swarms of people, yet there is a vast distance between people, a distance that words cannot bridge. No longer do our lives depend upon the soil, the sun, the rain, or the wind, we live by grace of jobs and the brutal logic of jobs. We do not know this world, or what makes it move. In the South life was different; men spoke to you, cursed you, yelled at you, or killed you. The world moved by signs we knew. But here in the North, cold forces hit you and push you. It is a world of things. [p. 100]

Again, the modes of existence resemble the functioning of a machine. The industrial imagery which we first saw in *American Hunger* provides a way of understanding the urban attack on the migrant's psyche. Time is transformed by the market economy of which the migrants are pawns.

The kitchenette is the dominant visual and literary image in the "Death on the City Pavements" section. It serves as a synecdoche for all the forces that act in the construction of a black urban dweller and it is the domain of the bosses of the buildings: "The kitchenette is our prison, our death sentence without a trial, the new form of mob violence that assaults not only the lone individual, but all of us, in its ceaseless attacks" (p. 106). In the written text, the kitchenette is a metaphor for the intricate way that power in the North omnisciently infiltrates every aspect of a black man's being. It kills black babies, creates disease, and "scatters death so widely among us that our death rate exceeds our birth rate" (p. 107). Its effect is that of genocide. Most significantly, however, the kitchenette acts to form and shape black personalities:

> The kitchenette injects pressure and tension into our individual personalities, making many of us give up the struggle, walk off and leave wives, husbands and even children to shift as best they can. . . .
>
> The kitchenette blights the personalities of our growing children, disorganizes them, blinds them to hope, creates problems whose effects can be traced in the characters of its child victims for years afterward. [pp. 109–110]

The kitchenette differs from the tyrants of *Uncle Tom's Children*—tyrants who are known, confronted, and with whom characters interact. Instead, the kitchenette shields our oppressors from us. Bigger Thomas's life is shaped by the South Side tenement, yet he does not know that the absentee landlord, Mr. Dalton, is the executor of his oppression.

Here power is exercised not just to exploit but also to dominate. It creates urban subjects who are resigned, irresponsible, and lacking hope. Yet they cannot easily point their fingers to the source of their demise. It seems as if they alone are responsible for their fate, and yet they know that it is beyond their control. The kitchenette acts as one of Foucault's institutions. Like the prison, the mental institution and the school, it serves to create the migrants' subjectivity.

Wright's fellow Chicagoan Gwendolyn Brooks also portrays the role of the kitchenette as a space shaping and inhibiting the black psyche. Writing almost a decade later, Brooks portrays the kitchenette as both a place of despair and a place of community. In the poem "Kitchenette Building" and the "Kitchenette" chapter of her novel *Maud Martha*, the kitchenette is the birthplace and deathbed of dreams as well as the site of communal activity. Brooks provides a feminine sense of neighborhood that is absent in Wright but that reemerges later in the work of Gloria Naylor. However, in both Wright and Brooks the kitchenette provides an image of the overcrowded living space of the Northern ghetto.

Like Lawrence's panel 1, the visual images of the "Death on the City Pavements" section of *12 Million Black Voices* are dominated by photographs of crowds: crowded living conditions, churches, dance floors, and dilapidated concrete building structures. Human figures are engulfed by brick walls, smoke stacks, and signs. Inside, everything is broken: walls are cracked, sofas sit on one leg, the porcelain of the toilet is cracked and dirty. Outdoors, children play amid garbage, dirt, and debris. In the workplace black people are servants or manual laborers. The vast majority of the photographs in this section were taken by FSA photographer Russell Lee. According to Nicholas Natanson, the literary sensation sparked by the publication of *Native Son* in 1940 was one of the developments that led to the FSA's "massive Chicago series."[63] Though the photographs were not taken specifically for *12 Million Black Voices*, they were certainly informed by Wright's sensibility.

While the migrants of Wright's written text seem initially to be filled with resignation and hopelessness, the faces in the photographs give an appearance of optimism. There is the closeness of the family of ten in Russell Lee's *Negro Family* (Figure 2.3, also called *Family on Relief*). Dressed in their best clothing, they sit around the table, surrounding their one possession—an alarm clock. It is a symbol of their urban existence.[64] Though the wallpaper is ripping, the tablecloth tattered and torn, the dwelling is clean, its inhabitants pleasant and dignified.[65]

In this way there is a tension between the written narrative and the photographic one. The visual countenances suggest possibility and hope. A change in circumstances seems to await them. The man in Arthur Rothstein's *Interior* (Figure 2.4) simply seems to be waiting for his ship to come in, for a change of luck that will better his condition. Again, there is a kind of serene dignity in his countenance.

The two photographs of this section that seem to resist the visual narrative illustrate the violence and brutality of the North. Interestingly, neither of these comes from the FSA files. Figures 2.5 and 2.6 show battered black men, engulfed

Figure 2.3 Russell Lee, *Negro Family.* Chicago, Illinois, (Farm Securities Administration).

by police. Like the lynching photograph discussed in the previous chapter, Figure 2.6 stands out for the grainy quality of the photograph, the brutality of the act, and the clothing of the actors. The police seem to be of another era, not the late thirties or early forties of the other photographs. The urban crowd, made up predominantly of black men, stands by, daring not to enter the action. Just as lynching kept the black community in its place in the South, so too does this display of police brutality in the North. These two photographs tell a story quite different from the rest of the visual narrative. There is no sentimentalizing physical violence here. These two photographs agree with Wright's written narrative. As Gramsci teaches us, sophisticated power is not unwilling to resort to coercion and force when necessary.[66] Interestingly, the two photographs that immediately follow these portray black dances, laughter-filled faces, and bodies controlled and manipulated not by white policemen but by their owners. These lindy-hopping scenes suggests that the dance is an act of healing.

Figure 2.4 Arthur Rothstein, *Interior*. Washington, D.C., Farm Securities Administration.

However, in the written text the acquisition of a critical consciousness that demands the death of folk sensibilities is the only way to free these subjects from the reins of sophisticated power. Wright acts as a narrator who is of the people but beyond them. He occupies a space of critical distance which allows him to describe as well as analyze the migrant ordeal.[67] He occupies the space of the stranger in relation to them. Georg Simmel's stranger stands on the outside with an objective view of the community. Though Wright consciously identifies himself with the group through the use of the word "we," he nonetheless establishes the necessary distance to present their case to his white readers.

In the world of *12 Million Black Voices*, there are safe spaces where black people act and speak freely, but Wright does not see any revolutionary potential in these spaces because they fail to offer an analysis of the oppression that has created their necessity. "After working all day in one civilization, we go home to our black belts and live, within the orbit of the surviving remnants of the culture of the South, our naive, casual, verbal, fluid folk life" (p. 127). The two safe spaces he identifies are churches and dances. Both mark sites where elements of the South are retained.

Of churches he notes, "it is only when we are within the walls of our churches that we are wholly ourselves, that we keep alive a sense of our personalities in relation to the total world in which we live. . . . Our churches are where we dip our tired bodies in cool springs of hope, where we retain our wholeness and humanity despite the blows of death from the Bosses of the Buildings" (p. 131). His words echo those of the migrant cited earlier: "I goes every Sunday and Wednesday nights to prayer meeting just to thank God that he let me live to go to

Figure 2.5 *Harlem Looters*. New York, New York. (UPI/Bettmann Newsphotos)

79

Figure 2.6 *Race Riots*. Detroit, Michigan. (AP/Wide World Photos)

a place of worship like that, a place where my people worship and ain't pestered by the white men."[68] In Wright's view the church nurtures and sustains; it helps to maintain humanity and dignity and it ensures survival. However, there is no evidence that it provides the foundation for resistance to the social order.

While Wright acknowledges the healing powers of the black church, he goes on to criticize it for its provinciality. According to Wright, those churches which most retain a Southern style of worship offer the least possibility for resistance to the dominant social order. Instead, by preaching a doctrine of "our time will come," they help to create complacent black subjects. Perhaps the greatest sin of the church in Wright's eyes is the fact that it is the domain of black women. Wright's women migrants, like Bigger's mother and Jake's wife, are even more premodern than the men: "The consciousness of vast sections of our black women lies beyond the boundaries of the modern world, though they live and work in that world daily" (p. 135). Black women walk through the pages of his text like creatures from another time, unable to grasp the rings of urban civilization.

While black women retain the culture and values of the South and in so doing ensure some type of historical continuity, for Wright they are the chains which bind black people to a premodern world. There is no hope for them to enter the modern age. And this is ultimately what the migrants must do if they are to survive. Wright advocates the migrants' joining the struggles of other oppressed groups as they march into the future. As Houston Baker points out, "There is little doubt that the strongest accents of black women's characterization [in *12 Million Black Voices*] fall on what might be called their essential inessentiality in the progress of black males."[69]

In seeming contrast to the church, the second space, the dance hall, is slightly more promising, but it still does not offer the analytical tools needed for resistance. Black music is significant in that it offers itself to the world as a means of expressing the angst of modern man. In this way it moves beyond the provincial stance of Southern styles of religious worship. Wright says, "Our music appeals because all modern men feel deep down as we do" (p. 128). In this way, the migrants contribute to modernity.

Black dance, like black music, also moves beyond the provinciality of black religion. According to Wright, black dancing, especially the lindy hop—one of the first dances created by migrants in Northern dance halls—holds "a sense of what our bodies want, a hint of our hope of a life lived without fear, a whisper of the natural dignity we feel life can have, a cry of hunger for something new to fill our souls, to reconcile the ecstasy of living with the terror of dying" (p. 126). Again, the dance takes on the qualities of the blues: It provides an opportunity for the expression of black humanity.

For Wright, the intricacies and complexities of black dance are indicative of the possibilities for black creativity. With no access to art, industry, finance, education, or aviation, black migrants fill their "hunger for expression" with dance, music, slang, and colorful dress. All of these elements are present on the dance floor. Malcolm X, whose migration narrative we will discuss in the next chapter, was one of the frustrated lindy-hoppers described by Wright. In addition to crime, X also poured his energies into dancing at Harlem's famous Savoy and its Boston namesake:

> With most girls, you kind of work opposite them, circling, side-stepping, leading. Whichever arm you lead with is half-bent out there, your hands are giving that little pull, that push, touching her waist, her shoulders, her arms. She's in, out, turning, whirling, wherever you guide her. With poor partners, you feel their weight. They're slow and heavy. But with really good partners, all you need is just the push-pull suggestion. They guide nearly effortlessly, . . . maneuver is done on the floor before they land, when they join you, whirling, right in step.[70]

Delilah Jackson, a famous Harlem lindy-hopper, best expressed the role of dancing for the migrant community: "[It] was therapy . . . kept you from dope and drinking."[71] Wright agrees; for him, the dance hall is a place where migrants "plunged into pleasure to obliterate the memory of the slow death on city pavements."[72]

When viewed closely, these two spaces, the church and the dance hall, reveal a crucial dialectic in African-American identity: Black people are at once modern and premodern. According to Wright, black religion is characterized by a premodern primitiveness; however, because black people have been denied civilization, they experience the ruptures of modernity more intensely than do other groups. At the same time, black people are model men, as is evident in their music—music that speaks most effectively to the conditions of modernity:

> Our blues, jazz, swing, and boogie woogie are our "spirituals" of the city pavement, our longing for freedom and opportunity, an expression of our bewilderment and despair in a world whose meaning eludes us . . . Our thirst for the sensual is poured out in jazz; the tension of our brittle lives is given forth in swing; and our nervousness and exhaustion are pounded out in the swift tempo of boogie woogie.
> We lose ourselves in violent forms of dance.[73]

It is quite significant that Wright conveniently leaves out the role played by women in the creation and perpetuation of black musical traditions.

Pockets of the South in the city offer no real possibility for resistance in *12 Million Black Voices*: Any attempt to maintain contact with the ancestor ensures that black people will not emerge into the modern world. The only possibility for resistance is a shift of consciousness, and this is possible only through a critically distanced understanding of the forces that oppress. While the women of the storefront churches remain premodern, those men who possess a critical consciousness are able to emerge into the modern world. "As our consciousness changes, as we come of age, as we shed our folk swaddling-clothes, so run our lives in a hundred directions." Again, "The seasons of the plantation no longer dictate the lives of many of us; hundreds of thousands of us are moving into the sphere of conscious history."[74]

VI

> Sometimes you hankered to pick a bone and talk with your mouth full.
>
> Dorothy West, *The Living Is Easy*

Wright's view of the South in the city would emerge as the dominant African-American literary perspective during the 1940s. While Wright's *Native Son* became a Book-of-the-Month Club selection and won a wide popular reading audience, women writers like Dorothy West, and later Gwendolyn Brooks, were creating alternative visions of the "South in the city." Dorothy West's *The Living Is Easy* (1948) began to lay the foundation for this alternative view, and it would eventually be picked up by Gloria Naylor and other black women.

When Richard Wright moved to New York in 1946 he helped to edit a new post–Harlem Renaissance journal called the *New Challenge*. The journal had been founded, edited, and financed by a young black woman from Boston, Dorothy West. In 1948, West published her first novel, *The Living Is Easy*—a novel so strikingly different from any ever written by Wright that it is of no surprise that there were tensions between the two at the *New Challenge*. In fact the conflict over the editorial direction of the journal is in and of itself evidence of the different ways the two writers would approach the migration narrative.

In West's version the South not only survives in the city but is necessary for the sustenance and survival of the migrant. However, West's novel did not receive the popular or critical attention that greeted Wright's work. The lack of attention given to West's novel cannot be attributed entirely to sexism, for Ann Petry's *The Street*, published just two years before *The Living Is Easy*, did quite well commercially.[75] However, the success of Petry's novel is evidence of Wright's hegemony. Petry's novel shared much with Wright's vision of a bleak urban landscape. Although Petry departs from Wright in her sense of possibility offered by black culture, her novel's similarities with Wright ensured it an audience and a more receptive critical establishment than West. After all, Lutie Johnson, working-class protagonist of *The Street*, falls victim to the harsh realities of the urban North because she ignores the sustaining elements of her culture. These are the same elements that West's protagonist, Cleo Judson, craves.

West's novel differs from Wright's work because it is concerned with a black middle-class protagonist. It also differs because it stresses the importance of the South for the survival of the Northern protagonist and it demonstrates new migrants changing the landscape of Boston. However, this latter difference is closely linked with the first. *The Living Is Easy* is a novel that parodies middle-class black life in the tradition of Jessie Fauset. Lawrence Rodgers, who sees the novel's satiric element as a distinct effort to "revise the (male) Great Migration novel," claims that West is "the only woman to fictionalize the migration experience."[76] While West's novel is an especially significant migration narrative, it is not the first woman-authored migration narrative. It is preceded by Nella Larsen's *Quicksand* and by several of Marita Bonner's short stories.

The Living Is Easy records the impact of the migrants from the perspective of a middle-class protagonist for whom their presence is a constant source of anxiety. West's protagonist, Cleo Judson, the strong-willed, fair-skinned wife of a black entrepreneur, is a migrant to Boston. She, however, does not identify with the mass of migrants who burst onto the city during the war years. Instead, she stands disdainfully on the sidelines, and it is through her piercing critical commentary that we get a glimpse into their interactions with the New England metropolis.

Interestingly enough, though Cleo holds the Southern blacks in contempt, she nonetheless tries to recreate the warmth, comfort, and security of her Southern childhood by bringing her three sisters to Boston to live with her. While seeking the acceptance by white Bostonians and attempting to lay the foundations for a black elite, she also tries to create a safe space where the memory of her mother can be evoked by the melodic laugh and sensual drawl of her three younger sisters. The narrative also seeks this balance; sprinkled throughout the text are Southern chapters, which often serve as chapters from Cleo's memory. They serve much the same function to the narrative that Southern memories serve for Cleo. Cleo's husband and daughter emerge as the most balanced characters of the text because they are able to tap into the South which exists within them for sustenance.

In the hands of Dorothy West, Cleo Judson becomes a fiercely determined, competitive, and highly motivated black middle-class woman, seeking some balance between that from which she comes and that to which she aspires. In the process she ruins her husband's financial empire and her sisters' marriages, but unlike so many migrants she stands at the end of the novel as determined and forceful as she is when we first find her. Like a sepia Scarlett O'Hara, she promises to move beyond her momentary troubles and to rebuild her life.

Early in the novel the reader glimpses the newly arrived Southern migrants through the class-conscious hazel eyes of Cleo. Passing by a schoolyard in Boston's South End with her daughter, Cleo notes:

> These midget comedians made Cleo feel that she was back in the Deep South. Their accents prickled her scalp. Their raucous laughter soured the sweet New England air. Their games were reminiscent of all the whooping and hollering she had indulged in before her emancipation. These r'aring-tearing young ones had brought the folkways of the South to the classrooms of the North. . . . Those among them who were born in Boston fell into the customs of their Southern-bred kin before they were old enough to know that a Bostonian, black or white, should consider himself a special species of fish.[77]

This first image of the migrant children, though derogatory, fills them with power and transformative possibility. The first two sentences open with racial stereotypes. However, the movement of the paragraph portrays the children as energetic, capable of affecting the staid Boston atmosphere. With their Southern folk-

84

ways, they even transform Boston-born black children. Furthermore, because the migrants of this passage are children, it seems their folkways will continue in the city for quite some time.

Most important, Cleo sees herself in the children, and this is why she harbors such resentment toward them. She sees the Cleo of her youth in their games and she fears that her fellow Bostonians will see it as well. The little migrants take her back to a place she felt she long escaped. Yet they remind her that the place never left her. Cleo knows that not too far beneath the surface of her very proper exterior lies the South. "Sometimes you felt like cutting the fool for the hell of it. Sometimes you hankered to pick a bone and talk with your mouth full."

This odd combination of disdain, identification, and need leads Cleo into a highly complex scheme which will allow her access to the South as well as the power to contain it. After convincing her husband to rent a huge Brookline house, Cleo sends for each of her Southern sisters and their children. Through them the other side of the South—the communal, gentle, nurturing side—emerges.

Cleo manipulates her siblings so that they provide her with a sense of consistency and balance. While they suffer a great deal, their presence creates a safe space for Cleo and ensures her continued strength. Cleo Judson represents the Northern black middle class at its worst: Materialistic and competitive, she seeks to manage the lives of her Southern sisters for her own benefit and social advancement. In her contradictory need and disdain for Southern migrants she also embodies the contradictions of the bourgeoisie. Like the black middle class described by Drake and Cayton in *Black Metropolis*, Cleo's class status is defined not by income, but by "a pattern of behavior . . . a great concern with 'front' and 'respectability' and a drive for getting ahead."[78] According to Drake and Cayton, the middle-class migrants resent the lower class among them: "[The middle class is] unable to keep their communities 'middle-class' because the Black Ghetto is too small to accommodate its population and the less well-to-do must filter into these 'best' areas."[79]

Cleo Judson feels both nurtured and inhibited by her poorer Southern siblings. Through Cleo, West suggests that a Southern retention—here represented by the family—is necessary to provide balance and stability for black migrants. Cleo is willing to concede that the warmth and community provided by her sisters are necessary to her own sustenance. Like everything else, Cleo wants to manipulate the degree and kind of "South in the city" that enters her life. She wants only that which reminds her of the positive aspects of the South. When confronted with the continued racial terrorism of that region, Cleo vehemently throws it out.

Cleo hosts a dinner party where the guest of honor, Dean Galloway, dean of a Southern black college, gives a talk on the injustice of Southern courts: "Something has happened in my city that happens every day in the South. A Negro is going on trial for his life before a lily-white jury." Galloway then seeks to recruit the black Bostonians gathered at Cleo's house, in the service of his cause, "a committee for the defense of Robert Jones." Throughout Galloway's talk, Cleo had been engaged in a trite conversation with one of her female guests. When Galloway seeks affirmation from her as a fellow Southerner, she "felt slightly embarrassed. Robert Jones. The same old nigger name as [her sister's husband]. Every poor darkey in the world was named Jackson or Johnson or Jones. . . . Just because she was from the South didn't make Robert Jones any nearer or dearer to her than to anyone else in the room" (p. 260).

If Cleo isn't moved by his plea, her reluctant guest are: "They had been moved by Dean Galloway against their will. He had brought the dehumanized South to their doors. They had felt their oneness with Robert Jones. Through the soft iridescence of tear-filled eyes they saw their Southern brothers as themselves" (p. 263). This is a very different kind of South in the city. These Northern blacks are compelled toward action as a result of having "the dehumanized South" brought to their doors. This sense of the South in the city is linked to the acquisition of a critical consciousness and a sense of racial identification that Wright had not anticipated.

In response Cleo, "her voice . . . beautiful and compelling," says

> Dean Galloway, I am sorry to say I do not see what benefit will be derived from making the name of Robert Jones a household word. He had a reason for killing. But when one colored man commits a crime, the whole race is condemned. Tell Robert Jones' story to the world, and the world will be stirred by the drama and tragedy of the killing. But the rest of the race will be the real martyrs. Wherever white people see them, they will watch them for danger signs. They will be frightened by a dark face, or a slow answer, or a quick step. They will think that all Negroes are armed. . . .
>
> [Colored men] feel mean and low at every slight, at every setback, and want to weep on the world's shoulder. But colored women can't afford self-pity. They're the ones that raise the children. What kind of children would they raise if they let them see their grief and despair? They'd raise humble dogs or mad dogs. They wouldn't raise human beings. [pp. 263–64]

Cleo falls into a discourse of good images and bad images. She is so convincing that her female guests side with her and refuse to support Galloway's endeavors. In this way, West's black middle-class women are susceptible to the critique launched by Wright. They stifle the political progress of the race with their concern over good and bad images, their unwillingness to rock the boat.

At the end of the evening, the triumphant hostess sits alone in her parlor, haunted by the image of "the drowned face of her father," a victim of the South's racial violence. "She moaned softly. . . . But the tears refused to fall" (p. 266). Cleo Judson fights back the horror of her past with the same conviction that she climbs the social ladder.

Lawrence Rodgers asserts: "In Cleo's act of denial, West locates the primary flaw of both her protagonist and black Boston. To be an accepted part of this society, she must outwardly cut all social and psychological ties to her Southern roots, 'disclaim' her past, even though she inwardly needs to be fortified by her recollections of its effect on her."[80] In fact, Cleo is very conscious of that which she will "disclaim" and that which she will allow to fortify her. For Cleo, as with many migrants, the only part of the South worth retaining in the city are "the happy days of [her] childhood." Unlike Wright's migrants, Cleo refuses to be haunted by the horrors of her Southern past.

West begins the project of providing an alternative to Wright's absolute dismissal of the black Southern past; she also provides another source of possibility of the South in the city—it can be a source of inspiring resistance. Although this possibility is not realized on the pages of her narrative, by introducing it, she makes a significant departure from Wright.

VII

> The city was real.
>
> James Baldwin, *Go Tell It on the Mountain*

While Cleo Judson feels nurtured and inhibited by her black Southern family, the protagonist of *Go Tell It on the Mountain*, John Grimes, expresses these contradictory feelings toward the black church. James Baldwin follows West by providing a full-scale rewriting of the relationship between Southern retention and black urban migrants and their progeny.

Once again, in *Go Tell It on the Mountain*, Baldwin (along with Ralph Ellison in *Invisible Man*) acts as a transition between the dominance of Wright's view of migration and that which emerges as dominant following the Civil Rights Movement. He does so by focusing on the institution Wright dismisses: the storefront church.

Charles Scruggs notes that unlike Wright, for Baldwin "there are possibilities [for black people in Northern cities] and that some of these possibilities exist within African-American culture."[81] While Baldwin shares Wright's belief that black culture, as it is manifested in the black church, can be both provincial and anti-intellectual, he also notes that it holds potential for black life and redemption as well. For Baldwin, a place that affirms black humanity, that provides possibilities for redemption, is as necessary for black liberation as the acquisition of a critical consciousness is for Wright.

Go Tell It on the Mountain challenges Wright's view of the importance of Southern folk retention in both its form and content.[82] Just as John vacillates between the larger white world of the stranger and the insular black world of Temple of the Fire Baptized, so too does the very language in which his story is told vacillate between that of the Western literary tradition and that of the black church. Those moments when the language is embedded with the spirituals and the rhythms of a black sermonic tradition act as the ancestors of the text.

John's points of reference come from the world of Western literature (especially Henry James and Charles Dickens) and the world of the black church.[83] Describing a morning when he wakes up late, he says, "He could believe, almost, that he had awakened late on that great-getting up morning."[84] Here he invokes the black spiritual "In That Great Getting Up Morning." Though the song itself is a joyful one, reveling in the coming of Judgment Day, John fears that he has missed it, slept right through it, and is left on earth with the damned. As was the case with Wright's characters, John's life is dominated by fear. Yet, unlike them, John does not fear white people nearly as much as he fears the wrath of God.[85]

Just as his daily life is relayed in terms born of the church and its culture, the life he wants to live is colored by images from literature and popular culture. As he walks the streets of midtown Manhattan, he compares the white people to those he has seen in the movies or those about whom he has read in books. He imagines his life in a narrative from Hollywood: "He thought of what it would be like to have one day a horse of his own. He would call it Rider, and mount it at morning when the grass was wet. . . . Behind him stood his house, great and rambling and very new, and in the kitchen his wife, a beautiful woman, made breakfast" (p. 35). John compares his own life with that of white New Yorkers and he says, "These glories [of eternity] were unimaginable—but the city was real" (p. 34). What he fails to notice is that the glories of the city are not real either. He imposes a life on the people he sees walking the streets of New York, for in reality he knows little of them.[86]

For John, life beyond Harlem, beyond the church, holds limitless possibilities. Yet he is aware that he must come through Harlem, come through the church, before he can attain these possibilities. On approaching the New York Public Library he thinks:

> The Public Library, a building filled with books and unimaginably vast, and which he had never yet dared to enter. He might, he knew, for he was a member of the branch in Harlem and was entitled to take books from any library in the city. But he had never gone in because the building was so big that it must be full of corridors and marble steps, in the maze of which he would be lost and never find the book he wanted. And then everyone, all the white people inside, would know that he was not used to great buildings, or to many books and they would look at him with pity. He would enter on another day, when he had read all the books uptown, an achievement that would, he felt, lend him the poise to enter any building in the world. [p. 37]

The library becomes a metaphor for the life John wishes to lead: a huge, complex world filled with intricate mazes. However, he is not yet able to navigate such a life. A passage through his own world, through his own culture—here the Harlem branch—will provide him with the foundation and the map for navigating this larger white one. His own world will provide him with "the poise to enter any building in the world." It is hard to imagine that Wright's protagonists could find anything in a black neighborhood that would give them such poise.

Although John believes that the love he seeks is available only in this world of white strangers, his experience suggests that it exists uptown as well. In the essay "Down at the Cross: Letter from a Region in My Mind," Baldwin notes:

> Perhaps we were, all of us—pimps, whores, racketeers, church members, and children—bound together by the nature of our oppression, the specific and peculiar complex of risks we had to run; if so, within these limits we sometimes achieved with each other a freedom that was close to love. I remember, anyway, church suppers and outings, and later, after I left the church, rent and waist-line parties where rage and sorrow sat in the darkness and did not stir, and we ate and drank and talked and laughed and danced and forgot all about "the man."[87]

Here Baldwin list those aspects of black life denied by Wright in his discussion of the black church and black night life. For Baldwin, oppression has not completely robbed black people of their ability to give and receive love; instead he seems to suggest that it has helped to create a beloved community of sorts. Also significant is his listing of church members and children with pimps, whores, and racketeers. He makes no distinction between these various communities—all are capable of creating community free of the white gaze. Here is the connection between the blues club and the church. Both are places where black humanity is affirmed, where black creativity is nurtured. Though Baldwin makes no claims that these are resisting spaces, spaces from which to launch revolutions, they are nonetheless necessary preconditions to any type of agency, in that they affirm and uphold black subjects above and against a world that tries to destroy them. Baldwin is no romantic; he shares many of Wright's complaints about the provincial nature of the black church, yet Baldwin knows that black life is far more complex than Wright seems to allow.

John Grimes experiences both the best and the worst that the church has to offer. On the one hand, there is the self-righteous, hypocritical Christianity of his father, Gabriel. On the other hand, there is the brotherly/sensual love that is manifested in his relationship with another of the text's migrants, Elisha. As was the case in Baldwin's earlier linking of migration with the Old Testament flight from Egypt, it seems that the hope of the city will be realized by the younger generation represented by John and Elisha.

The church is a place where the older generation—Florence, Gabriel, and Elizabeth—must come face to face with the sins of their pasts. It is also the place where the generation that follows them, those first-generation urban dwellers, are separated from the sins of their fathers and allowed finally to come into their own. In "Down at the Cross," James Baldwin tells us that his own youthful conversion provided him the means of "breaking [his father's] hold" on him (p. 48). By the end of *Go Tell It on the Mountain*, this is also the case for John. Contemplating his salvation, John thinks:

He, John, who having lain in darkness would no longer be himself but some other man. He would have been changed, as they said, forever; sown in dishonor, he would be raised in honor: he would have been born again.

Then he would no longer be the son of his father, but the son of his heavenly Father, the King. Then he need no longer fear his father, for he could take, as it were, their quarrel over his father's head to Heaven—to the Father who loved him, who had come down in the flesh to die for him. Then he and his father would be equals, in the sight and the sound and the love of God. Then his father could not beat him any more, or despise him any more, or mock him any more—he, John, the Lord's anointed. He could speak to his father then as men spoke to one another—as sons spoke to their fathers, not in trembling but in sweet confidence, not in hatred but in love. His father could not cast him out, whom God had gathered in. [p. 145]

John's conversion is not an end in and of itself. It is part of a process, a process that allows him to come into his own with his father. As is the case with Baldwin, salvation is a great equalizer. Interestingly, the language of this passage greatly resembles language used by abolitionists when arguing for the equality and humanity of slaves and former slaves. Baldwin has cast John in the role of the oppressed and Gabriel the father in the role of oppressor. The Southern past, in the form of the older migrant, is oppressive, but one must confront and come through it.

John has another model of Christian love, one that is also Southern but not oppressive, in Elisha. The young migrant Elisha embodies all John aspires to become as well as all John desires. Elisha is a playful, guiding older brother, but he is also the object of John's first major crush. It is with Elisha that John has his only lasting moments of affection and genuine love.

On the morning following his conversion, John turns to Elisha for comfort and explanation:

"Elisha. . . . You pray for me? Please pray for me?"

"I been praying, little brother, " Elisha said, "and I sure ain't going to stop praying now."

"For me," persisted John, his tears falling, "for *me*."

"You know right well, " said Elisha, looking at him, "I ain't going to stop praying for the brother what the Lord done give me." [p. 219]

This simple exchange carries great significance for John because it is one of only two places in the entire novel where he is affirmed just for being himself. The first occurs when his mother gives him extra change for his birthday. During earlier moments of apparent affirmation that come from his white teachers, he is encouraged for his talent, for what he might become; but here, Elisha affirms him . . . just because. In the black Southern Christianity of their ancestors, there is a place for this kind of affirmation, a place where all human beings who might otherwise be invisible are seen and noticed and valued. Thus the significance of John's repeated statement "For me," and Elisha's reassurance that yes, John will be the continued benefactor of his prayers.

As Elisha departs,

> John stood still, watching him walk away. The sun had come full awake. It was waking the streets, and the houses, and crying at the windows. It fell over Elisha like a golden robe, and struck John's forehead, where Elisha had kissed him, like a seal ineffaceable forever. [p. 221]

The rising sun, literally a new day, drapes Elisha in a sacred way and joins him and John in a brotherhood sanctioned by God. Again, the strength that John receives from this relationship, one that is based in a black Southern tradition, gives him poise to enter any building in the world, even his father's house. "He turned to face his father—he found himself smiling, but his father did not smile. They looked at each other a moment. His mother stood in the doorway, in the long shadow of the hall. 'I'm ready,' John said, 'I'm coming. I'm on my way.'" John is now prepared to enter a new phase of his life—one that might eventually lead him away from the church. However, his involvement in the church provides him with the love and sustenance that is a necessary prerequisite to his moving on beyond the world of his father and to his resisting the tendencies of the larger white world to dehumanize him.

For Baldwin, the church is an ambiguous space: a space that affirms black life, but also suppresses sexuality and secular forms of creativity. In his fiction and his essays he attempts to wrestle the best of the values espoused by the church from its more provincial inhibiting practices. For him African-American culture in general and those retentions of Southern black culture that exist on the urban landscape are fundamental to an expression of black humanity. Following the Civil Rights Movement several writers would begin to pick up his lead. In these later works there is little possibility of remaining whole in the context of urbanization without a safe space. As Baldwin demonstrates, an author's gender is not the basis for determining whether his or her characters will benefit from Southern retention. However, black women writers have been especially vigilant in stressing the importance of the South in the city.[88]

VIII

> Brewster Place became especially fond of its colored daughters as they milled like determined spirits among its decay, trying to make it a home.
>
> Gloria Naylor, *The Women of Brewster's Place*

Gloria Naylor's *The Women of Brewster Place* enhances the visions of Dorothy West and James Baldwin. The novel revises many of the tropes of the migration narratives already discussed.

Naylor's opening description of Brewster Place echoes Toomer,[89] for Brewster Place, like Toomer's Seventh Street, is the product of an illegitimate union:

"Brewster Place was the bastard child of several clandestine meetings between the alderman of the sixth district and the managing director of the Unico Realty Company."[90] By the time the "Afric" migrants come to Brewster Place it has already served as a steppingstone for Irish immigrants and their swarthy Mediterranean cousins. These southern European immigrants infused it with their own foods, smells, and colors. The black Southern migrants do not enter a stale "white washed wood" neighborhood but one already seasoned with the spice of difference. They cling to the street with a sense of desperation and some hope of carving a slice of choice out of their choicelessness, for unlike those who preceded them, the black migrants will not leave Brewster Place:

> They clung to the street with a desperate acceptance that whatever was there was better than the starving South from which they had fled. Brewster Place knew that unlike its other children, the few who would leave forever were to be the exception rather than the rule, since they came because they had no choice and would remain for the same reason. [p. 4]

Interestingly, in contrast to the quickening pace of Seventh Street, the pace of Brewster Place is one of urban lyricism. Instead of the colorful modernist painting described in Toomer's "Seventh Street," the black daughters of Brewster Place are portrayed like an Impressionist canvas. They create the softly blurred boundaries of a Gauguin rather than the sharp harsh edges of a Picasso:

> Brewster Place became especially fond of its colored daughters as they milled like determined spirits among its decay, trying to make it a home. Nutmeg arms leaned over windowsills, gnarled ebony legs carried groceries up double flights of steps, and saffron hands strung out laundry on back-yard lines. Their perspiration mingled with the steam from boiling pots of smoked pork and greens, and it curled on the edges of the aroma of vinegar douches and Evening in Paris cologne that drifted through the street where they stood together—hands on hips, straight-backed, round-bellied, high-behinded women who threw their heads back when they laughed. . . . They were hard-edged, soft-centered, brutally demanding and easily pleased, these women of Brewster Place. They came, they went, grew up and grew old beyond their years. [pp. 44–45]

Different from the consciously thrusting, throbbing, male-defined migrants of Seventh Street, these are migrant daughters engulfed and welcomed by a maternal Brewster Place. While Toomer portrays the initial confrontation of the migrant with the urban landscape as that of a masculine presence forcing itself into a staid white woman that is Washington, D.C., here the daughters come to a final home of the mother. There are no harsh, verbs. They mill like spirits and seep, not like blood into wood, but like ghosts into the atmosphere. These are the daughters of Brewster Place's December-days. The language is consciously feminine; it rolls sensually over the reader's tongue. The passage is round and even in its violent moments it is cyclical. The migrant daughters literally color Brewster Place in shades of nutmeg, ebony, and saffron.

This maternal imagery and the roundness of the syntax characterize all of Naylor's descriptions of the South in the city: not just the migrants who enter Brewster Place, but those spaces in the context of the narrative where she presents safe spaces of nurturing and healing as well.

Mattie Michael arrives on Brewster Place on the last leg of her life's journey. "She refused to pity herself and to think that she, too, would have to die here on this crowded street because there just wasn't enough life left for her to do it all again." This sense of resignation is not unlike that of the urban dwellers of Ann Petry's *The Street*, yet Mattie's existence on Brewster Place is significantly different from that of Lutie, because Mattie survives to act as a maternal source of nurturing for the other female inhabitants of Brewster Place. She both benefits from and provides safe space on Brewster Place. The home of Miss Eva, which she shares shortly after her arrival, the laying on of hands ritual she performs on the young Ciel, her friendship with Etta—each serves as safe space in the context of Brewster Place. While these spaces are not enough to alter the social circumstances that act upon Mattie and the other women, they do provide a space, however temporary, for healing and wholeness.

As a young mother, Mattie is nurtured in the home of Miss Eva. The older woman becomes a surrogate mother for her. In *Brewster Place* all visits to safe spaces are represented by a return to the mother. Nowhere is this more evident than in the laying on of hands ritual in the text. We will explore this extensively in the next chapter. However, for our purposes here, Mattie's friendship with Etta, like John's friendship with Elisha, serves as the best example of the way that the South in the city ensures the nurturing and survival of the migrant.

When Etta arrives at or returns to Brewster Place, it is as a woman clinging "to a body that had finished a close second in its race with time" (p. 56). She is tired and frustrated from having left yet another failed relationship. For her, a return to Brewster Place is a return home to Mattie. Their friendship, not the physical structure of Brewster Place, is the space that equals home in Etta's life. Upon seeing her, Mattie calls her "Tut," a nickname that immediately says "I knew you when." It invokes pride in the way she used to be, and a tired middle-aged lady once again becomes a defiant, proud young girl who "always had her shoulders flung behind her collarbone and her chin thrust toward the horizon" like "the wife of King Tut." It was this very proud defiance that had her leave Rock Vale, Tennessee, years ago.

The depth of the friendship between Mattie and Etta is apparent in its sense of timelessness:

> [Etta] breathed deeply of the freedom she found in Mattie's presence. Here she had no choice but to be herself. The carefully erected decoys she was constantly shuffling and changing to fit the situation were of no use to her. Etta and Mattie went way back, a singular term that claimed co-knowledge of all the important events in their lives and almost all of the unimportant ones, and by rights of this possession, it tolerated no secrets. [p. 58]

Like John's relationship with Elisha, the friendship between Mattie and Etta is a safe space, a space where they can shed all pretensions, a healing space. As Nel tells Sula in Toni Morrison's novel *Sula*, "[They] was girls together." These two women, looking beyond the horizons of their youth, have shared the passage of time. This simple fact makes their friendship, one in which the mere mention of a nickname invokes the pain and warmth of a Southern past, a necessary prerequisite to survival in the city.

Later that evening, when Etta returns from a disappointing rendezvous with a minister, she finds Mattie waiting for her. "Someone was waiting up for her . . . Etta laughed softly to herself as she climbed the steps towards the light and the love and the comfort that awaited her" (p. 74). Mattie provides Etta with grounding and stability in simple gestures like name calling, teasing, concern for physical and spiritual well-being, a space that shares the foundation of a common past, and common origin minus the negative aspects of patriarchal and racial oppression. Brewster Place, like Gwendolyn Brooks's kitchenette, represents for its inhabitants both their low social status and their sense of community—of home.

IX

Wow—New York, jus like I picture it. Skyscrapers and Everythang!

Stevie Wonder, "Living for the City"

In 1973, Stevie Wonder's hard-driving funk-induced "Living for the City" hit the airwaves. One of several hits off of the introspective *Innervisions* album, "Living for the City" is the quintessential rhythm and blues–pop migration narrative. While the form is different, the story is a very familiar one:

> A boy is born in hard time Mississippi
> Surrounded by four walls that ain't so pretty.
> His parents give him love and affection
> To keep him strong, moving in the right direction.
> They give him jus enuff, jus enuff for the city.
>
> His father works some days for fourteen hours
> And you can bet he barely makes a dollar.
> His mother goes to scrub the floors for many
> And you best believe, she hardly gets a penny.
> Livin' jus enuff, jus enuff for the city.
>
> His sister's black, but she is sure nuf pretty.
> Her skirt is short, but lord her legs are sturdy.
> To walk to school, she has to get up early.
> Her clothes are old, but never are they dirty.
> Her brother's smart, he's got more sense than many.

His patience's long, but soon he won't have any.
To find a job, is like the haystack needle.
'Cause where he lives, they don't use colored people.
Livin' jus enuff, jus enuff for the city.[91]

Wonder's unnamed protagonist leaves the South because of the lack of economic opportunity for an ambitious black man. The South of this narrative is characterized by economic poverty and racial segregation but most significantly it is also characterized by a loving, supportive, and sacrificing nuclear family. The major goal of the family is to provide the son with "just enough for the city." The city takes on mythic proportions not unlike that sacred city of Blind Willie Johnson's "City of Refuge." From the beginning, Wonder sets the tone of a sermon, by invoking biblical imagery and narrative. The tale thus far is almost like that of a Southern black prodigal son. The line "His sister's black, but she is sure nuf pretty," echoes the "I am black, but comely" of the Old Testament "Song of Solomon." It also reflects a tendency in African-American life to qualify the description of someone who is dark with "but pretty," because so often dark is synonymous with ugly, as in the phrases "black and ugly" and "ugly black thang." So Wonder at once invokes a biblical past as well as a racially coded present. In so doing, he aligns his text with the sermons of black ministers who use biblical text as metaphors for black experience.

The first and second part of the lyric are bridged by a musical interlude made up of a gospel piano, a hard bass drum, female vocals, churchlike hand clapping, and the distorting screeching of a computerized synthesizer. The music provides the journey north. The clapping and background female vocals are retentions of the warmth and community of the Southern church as well as the rhythmic backbone of the musical text. Upon arrival in the city, the clapping gives way to the a "tic-toc" sound, a synthesizer, and street sounds of car and bus engines and police and ambulance sirens. The music provides us with the sounds described earlier by Toomer and Wright. The sound of the ticking clock also mirrors Toomer and Wright in the assertion of industrial time in the city. Beneath it all, however, remains the rhythm of the drums and the gospel piano/organ.

The narrator's sermon song gives way to a polyphony of spoken voices in the second section:

Bus driver: The Bus for New York City
   Migrant: Hey bus driver! I'm gettin on there. Hold it. Thanks a lot.
         Wow—New York, Jus like I pictured it. Skyscraperers and Everythang!!!
(sounds of him leaving the bus, sirens, street cars and then:)
   Hustler: (in a hip whisper) Hey, hey brother, come here slick You look hip man. Look
         her, you wanna make yourself five bucks man. Look here, run
         thisacrossthestreetforme!!! Right, Quick!
   Migrant: Yeah . . . I
(Sirens grow closer)

Policemen: Get your hands up punk! Let's go.
  Migrant: What, I didn't know. I'm jus' goin across the street. What did I do?
Policemen: Shut your mouth. Turn around, put your hands behind your back.
     Judge: A JURY OF YOUR PEERS HAVING FOUND YOU GUILTY. TEN YEARS.
Prison guard: COME ON, GET IN THAT CELL NIGGER! GOD!
   Migrant: Lawd! Lawd!

Wonder's text greatly resembles Rudolph Fisher's 1925 short story "City of Refuge." In both instances, naive, unsophisticated migrants arrive in New York and are immediately greeted and framed by slick drug-dealing strangers. The urban hustlers appeal to each migrant's ego by addressing them as fellow hipsters. Both Wonder's migrant and King Solomon Gillis are confused and in awe of the pace and complexity of the city. Both are arrested for drug possession. It is clear that Wonder's city is that of Fisher and not of Blind Willie Johnson.

The migrant's slow Southern drawl stands in stark contrast to the surrounding quick, urban sounds of cars, buses, and sirens. The various discourses of the city—that of the urban hustler, the police, the judicial system, and the prison—assault his slow Southern ears in an endless series of directives and admonitions.

The variety of voices that enter the dialogue in the second part of "Living for the City" provide a cast of characters for the urban landscape. Several plays are made upon the different meanings of words. The hustler addresses the migrant as a brother. The migrant's understanding of the term as one used in the South to signify kinship in the lord makes him immediately trust the hustler. He is a victim because, like Wright, he "persists in reading his new environment in light of his old one." The white police officers attack his Southern sensibility and, like the migrants of *12 Million Black Voices*, he has difficulty understanding them. The authoritative voice of the judge, spoken from on high, articulates his fate in a clear, precise, and removed manner. Finally, for the first time, we hear the word "Nigger" from a Northern white prison guard. Again, meaning is contested in both the guard's use of the word "God" and the migrant's use of "Lawd." The guard calls out God in vain. It is a curse. The migrant calls upon the Lord as savior and master to get him out of his present situation.

The minister-narrator returns in the third section. Not only do the words sound like a sermon, but Wonder's singing voice also resembles the voice of a black Baptist minister in the final parts of his sermon, the portion which most rouses his congregation. He sings in a heavy, guttural tone:

> His hair is long. His feet are hard and gritty
> He spends his nights walkin' the streets of New York City.
> He's almost dead from breathin' in air pollution
> He tried to vote, but to him there is no solution.
> Livin' jus enuff, jus enuff for the city.
>
> I hope you hear inside my voice of sorrow,
> And that it motivates you to make a better tomorrow.
> This place is cruel. No place could be much colder.

> If we don't change, the world will soon be over.
> Livin' jus enuff, Stop givin' jus enuff for the city.
>
> *(voice trails up to a sacred humming)*

The image of the migrant with long hair and gritty feet resembles an urban Christ, who again cannot find shelter. In contrast to his Southern sister, whose clothes were old but never dirty, he is unkempt, his feet grimy. This urban Christ figure is close to death because of the city's assault on the environment. Unlike the blues persona of "Unemployment Stomp," he no longer tries to act the good citizen, because hope has died. The refrain "Living jus enuff for the city" takes on a different meaning here. In the South, it meant living for the possibility offered by the city. Here it means living just enough to get by in the city, just enough to make it from day to day.

In the last stanza, Wonder's prophetic voice speaks in the tradition of the blues singer and the sanctified preacher. His moralizing voice warns, "This place is cruel. No world could be much colder . . . Stop givin' jus enuff for the city." These final lines assert that the tremendous drive for the city, the great hope of Southern blacks, was a misdirected goal. The lyrics stress the loss of values and humanity in the process of migration. "If we don't change, the world will soon be over" is the final powerful statement in the sermon. Like the preacher who warns of coming doom, Wonder asserts that prolonging Armageddon is within our control. If we stop "livin' jus for the city," to begin living for the Christian values of the migrant's Southern family, we might be able to delay doom. Wonder embodies both the sacred and the profane ministers of the black experience: the preacher and the blues performer. The final music and the choirlike humming takes on a sacred tone, at the end of the song, further asserting the song's sermonlike quality.

Stevie Wonder brought many of the elements of the African-American musical and oratorical tradition into the pop mainstream. He emerged as social critic, preacher, and prophet. Ellen Willis, in an article titled "The Importance of Stevie Wonder," noted that Wonder presided over his audience, reminding them of the pathos and possibilities of life.[92] Similarly, a *Newsweek* article by Maureen Orth asserted, "Stevie's songs don't just entertain, they inspire."[93]

"Living for the City" stayed on *Billboard*'s rhythm and blues chart for sixteen weeks. It peaked at number one—a position it held for two weeks. These figures suggests its popularity in the black community. The record peaked at number eight on the overall pop charts and by the end of the year it was designated number twenty-two for the entire year. The song emerged during an era of socially conscious songs. Of these only Marvin Gaye's "What's Going On," "Mercy, Mercy Me," and "Inner City Blues," all released in 1971, rival Wonder's in their passionate portrayal of urban chaos.[94]

During his 1974 tour, Wonder ended many of his concerts with "Living for the City." The text with which he chose to leave his "congregation" has become one of the most influential migration narratives of the late twentieth century. In its documentation of the problems and the plight of the post-1960s city, Wonder's prophetic "Living for the City" warns of the conditions out of which exploded the violent, almost nihilistic urban rap of the 1980s. The dominance of Wonder's song, again rivaled only by Gaye's "What's Going On?" is evident not only in sales but also in influence. It has been recorded by artists as diverse as Ray Charles and the New Jack group Troop. The original recording is still used in African-American pop culture (especially in the films *Jungle Fever* and *New Jack City*) to evoke a sense of urban despair.

Significantly, that which is absent in Wonder's powerful narrative is any of his migrant's maintenance of ties with a Southern family. Many of the literary narratives explore the migrants' attempts to sustain themselves in the face of the urban chaos documented by Wonder. The maintenance of an alternative community in both domestic sites and sites of a street culture prove to be alternately nurturing and detrimental to them.

Wonder's refusal to document such spaces links him with Richard Wright, who blatantly denies them. However, Wonder departs from Wright in his moralizing tone, which links him more closely with James Baldwin. Like Baldwin's essays of the 1960s, Wonder's sermon is an American jeremiad.

The impact of migration on the migrants and on the cities to which they flee is multifaceted. As we have seen, individual migrants are influenced by their confrontation with the urban landscape, and as a group they begin the process of changing the sights and sounds of the cities they inhabit. The portrayal of the migrants' initial confrontation with the urban landscape is divided and contested along several axes: race, gender, class, generation, and genre.

For white urbanites and for much of the black middle class, the migrants constituted a black mass changing the face of the city. The result was the explosion of race riots and the rising anxieties of the black bourgeoisie. In recording the impact of migration on the city of Boston and the impact of Southern black migrants on her heroine, Dorothy West is one of the few fiction writers to provide us with a black middle-class perspective on black migration. (In the texts of Nella Larsen and Jessie Fauset, the migrant women who appear briefly have names like Zulena and are contrasted to their cream-colored employers by virtue of their dark skin.)

For the most part, the artists upon whom this chapter focuses are primarily concerned with the impact of the city on the minds and lives of black migrants. These narratives portray the city as a harsh, cold, and indifferent space of exploitation and domination. In the North the forces of oppression are less visible and act more severely on the migrant psyche than those that existed in the South.

Once in the North, migrants attempted to counter the isolation of the urban landscape in their creation of community. Nowhere is this sense of community better reflected than in the creations of the migrants themselves—the blues and the storefront church. Both blues and gospel performances embody the significance and continuity of the South in providing community and nurturing for dislocated migrants. Blues lyrics resonate the impact of the city on the migrant. The form reflects the manner in which migrants adapt through a process of exchange with the dominant culture as well as advances in technology. Gospel lyrics and music reflect the migrants' desire for refuge and hope in the face of the unfamiliar. The spread, adoption, and in some cases appropriation of the music embodies the influence migrants have on American popular culture.

This influence is especially evident in the movement of the musical migration narrative into the popular mainstream. One of the primary vehicles for accomplishing this task was Motown. The financially and culturally astute Berry Gordy founded Motown in 1959 in the city of Detroit (center of the auto industry, the employer of many migrants, and home of a thriving blues culture as well as blues great and migrant John Lee Hooker). Motown brought the textures and rhythms of black rhythm and blues to the attention of mainstream white America with a string of hits and stars who embodied the vibrancy of the sixties. Among the most gifted on Motown's list of great talents was the young Stevie Wonder.

Wonder's contribution to the tradition of African-American migration narratives not only signaled the emergence of the form into the mainstream of American popular music, but also continued the project of Toomer and Wright in its denial of possibilities for resistance and of safe space in the city.

Each of the artists considered in this chapter recognizes the complexity of urban power. Each of them also recognizes a need to confront this power with a degree of intellectual and/or spiritual consciousness. For some, this consciousness can be acquired only in migrant-defined safe spaces.

3

Safe Spaces and Other Places: Navigating the Urban Landscape

Jean Lacy's *Welcome to My Ghetto Land* (Figure 3.1) depicts the facade of an urban kitchenette building. As with *The Women of Brewster Place*, a variety of black women, alternately sensual and sacred, lean from the windows of the tenement, each seeming to possess her own tale. The small 6″ × 3″ rectangular wooden panel is divided into smaller rectangles that become the bricks, windows, and doorways of the building. The dominant rectangular shape is softened by the addition of curved arches, which top the windows and doorway. Intense primary colors along with the architectural elements—columns and arches—lend a stained-glass quality to the painting. Together, these forms and colors align the building with a cathedral. The cathedral motif is furthered by the gold leaf outlining and the female figures, who in this context become religious icons. The technique of gold leafing, the medium of wood panel, and the iconic figures are all elements of medieval illuminated manuscripts, Renaissance gold leaf panels, and Russian religious icons. Outside, Lacy incorporates elements drawn from various West African traditions: sculpture-textured drums, turtles, and twins are situated on the outside pavement and at the foot of the building as if to protect the house from the outside world. In other contexts Lacy uses the turtle motif to signify the historic migrations that have characterized black life throughout the African diaspora.

The combination of European religious motifs with those from West Africa indicate that the inhabitants of the building are inheritors of both legacies. In Lacy's painting, the kitchenette building becomes a sacred space that is the domain of black women. The women are softly curved, echoing the roundness of the arches and countering the harsh rectangular form of the painting. The arches and their curved bodies evoke both the secular and the sacred. Such a combination is one that seems like a paradox in the Western tradition, but in the West African tradition it is not as rare. Light emanates from the women like spiritual auras. The two sets of figures on the first floor are madonna and child images. The sensuous women of the second and third stories are more like saints than madonnas. However, unlike saints of the Western tradition, Lacy's women are

100

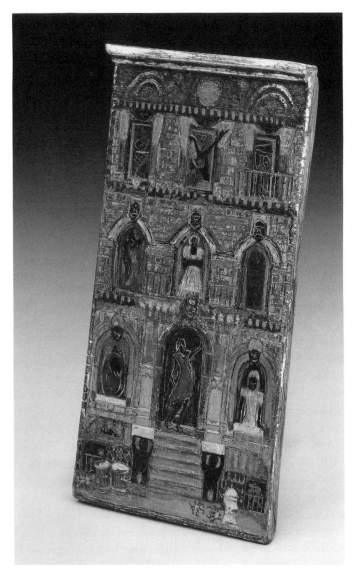

Figure 3.1 Jean Lacy, *Welcome to My Ghetto Land.* Paint, gesso, gold
leaf on wood panel, 6″ × 3″. (Dallas Museum of Art, Metropolitan
Life Foundation Purchase Grant)

both sacred and sexual. In this sense they share more with West African ancestors.

Lacy turns the kitchenette, the hell hole of Wright's *12 Million Black Voices*,
into a sacred space of black women. The difference between Wright's kitchenette
and Lacy's embodies the contest over migrant spaces on the urban landscape.
Lacy's tenement as sacred and Wright's as hell represent two extreme interpreta-

tions. In the context of the migration narrative, urban spaces—kitchenettes, workplaces, street corners, prisons, and theaters—are some of the sites where migrants, white powerholders, and the Northern black middle class vie for control.

All these spaces are created by a sophisticated urban power, yet this very power is engaged in a constant struggle to maintain control over them. The contest over space is symbolic of the larger contest over black bodies. Within these spaces, a struggle ensues in which the migrant tries to resist efforts to dominate him or her.

Evidence of the subtleties and sophistication of modern urban power fill the pages of the migration narrative: the opening alarm clock of *Native Son*;[1] the discipline and surveillance of Jake's workplace in *Lawd Today*; the discourses on race, sex, and violence that confront Bigger and Lutie; the invocation of desire in popular culture forms like movies and advertisements that affect Bigger in *Native Son*, Lutie in *The Street*, and Pauline Breedlove in *The Bluest Eye*; the desire for white women documented by Wright and Malcolm X; the desire to meet white standards of beauty represented by Morrison's Pecola and Hagar. This power controls the migrant body not only by inflicting violence upon it, but also by controlling its experience of time and space, by regulating it, and by creating desire.

Urban power separates and categorizes individuals. The ghetto dwellers are enclosed within neighborhoods and kitchenettes. They are not allowed beyond certain borders. Urban power sustains a discourse around race, sex, and desire which confines the black migrant. This power also seeks to educate migrants and to create in them a desire for those things available in the dominant society. Education is the task of a segment within the black middle class who quell dissatisfaction and help to transform the migrants into efficient workers and citizens. Finally, urban power will also resort to the use of force and repression when necessary.

At times, the migrants themselves engage in acts of self-discipline. Often in their very attempts to resist they have so internalized the effects of the power that represses them that they become complicit in their own subjugation. Nevertheless, this is not always the case. Migrants are not passive victims, subjected to the whims of urban power. They are also agents who sometimes are capable of resisting. Often they can use the very structures and ideologies that repress them as means of enabling their agency.

Whatever the case, in the city, black migrants come to the realization that their search for a freer space has led to a space where they are confined in ways they had never imagined. Houston Baker describes the paradox the migrants confront in their search: "For place to be recognized by one as actually PLACE, as a personally valued locale, one must set and maintain the boundaries. If one, however, is constituted and maintained by and within boundaries set by a dominating authority, then one is not a setter of place, but a prisoner of another's desire."[2] Even migrant-defined "safe spaces" fall under the authority of the dominant society. This severely circumscribes the resisting possibilities of these spaces, but it does not prohibit them altogether. Consequently, safe spaces may play an important role in assisting migrants to resist dominant constructions of them. In other cases, they serve only to create a sense of complacency.

I

> He watched the clock
> He was always behind
> He asked too many questions
> He wasn't ready for the next step
> He did not put his heart in his work
> He learned nothing from his blunders
> He was contented to be a second-rater
> He didn't learn that the best part of his salary was not in his pay envelope.

Young Negroes' Progressive Association handbill

This poem, printed on pocket-sized cards, was proffered to newly arrived industrial workers by the Young Negroes' Progressive Association of Detroit.[3] The organization obviously sought to help the migrant make the transition from the rural South to his new urban industrial workplace. This poem seeks to assert a degree of control over the migrant workspace by regulating time, movement, and attitude. Significantly, these new habits are habits of punctuality and thrift. As outlined in the previous chapter, the migrants' initial confrontation with the urban landscape is often portrayed as a confrontation with a new way of experiencing time and speed. The unfit worker of this poem is guilty of several crimes against modern industry. He refuses to incorporate the measure of time by the time clock, he is slow, too inquisitive, unprepared, not eager to work, and, worst of all, he places too much value on his salary. Thus the poem suggests that anyone who falls into this category is destined to failure in the urban North.

This fraternal organization sought to ease the transition of the migrant as well as discipline him into an efficient and productive worker. It is significant that the organization uses this written statement as a means of accomplishing its disciplinary work. Black middle-class fraternal and civic organizations as well as the black press all served as disciplinary agents in the process of creating new urban subjects.

The role of the Northern black middle class is especially evident in the work of the Urban League. The Chicago chapter of that organization issued the following flyer to newly arrived Southern migrants as part of its Education of the Migrants project:

I AM AN AMERICAN CITIZEN

I AM PROUD of our boys "over there" who have contributed soldier service.

I DESIRE to render CITIZEN SERVICE.

I REALIZE that our soldiers have learned NEW HABITS of SELF-RESPECT AND CLEANLINESS.

I DESIRE to help bring about a NEW ORDER OF LIVING in this community.

I WILL ATTEND to the neatness of my personal appearance on the street or when sitting in front doorways.

I WILL REFRAIN from wearing dust caps, bungalow aprons, house clothing and bedroom shoes out of doors.

I WILL ARRANGE MY TOILET within doors and not on the front porch.

I WILL INSIST upon the use of rear entrances for coal dealers, hucksters, etc.

I WILL REFRAIN from loud talking and objectionable deportment on street cars and in public places.

I WILL DO MY BEST to prevent defacement of property either by children or adults.[4]

The "schoolbook" affirmations enforce notions of citizenship and patriotism. There is no scheme for resistance here; instead migrants are encouraged to shun all their Southern mannerisms and make themselves useful workers and citizens. While the first affirmations focus on the creation of citizens, the remainder seek to accomplish the literal transformation of the migrants in terms of deportment and appearance. The goal is that they adopt a Northern middle-class outward appearance. It is as if their citizenship is directly related to these external features and not to any real notions of democracy or service to country and community. The final line asserts a necessary respect for personal property which every good citizen must possess.

As meditations, these rules are embedded in the migrant psyche. There is no separation from his will and that imposed upon him. Note especially those lines that are rendered in capital letters: I AM A PROUD AMERICAN CITIZEN; I DESIRE; I WILL REFRAIN; I WILL ATTEND; I WILL DO MY BEST.

In a special issue of the *Survey Graphic*, "Harlem Mecca of the New Negro," published in March 1925, the Urban League announced the establishment of the National Industrial Department. Among its stated goals were the following:

1. To assure industrial employers "a more efficient group of employees."
2. To help develop a social program by which Negro families may more easily become adjusted to the requirements for good living in the districts to which they go.

The link between industrial capitalism and the Urban League is evident in these goals. A segment of the black middle class sought to ease the transition by which migrants could function in factories run by Taylorism. In his prison notebooks, Antonio Gramsci explores the way highly rationalized systems of production like

Fordism (associated with the Ford Motor Company) and Taylorism (a system of scientific management founded by Frederic Taylor) characterize advanced capitalist societies. Under such systems of mass production, division of labor, and the "reduction of the worker's movements and tasks to a simple routine," workers are further alienated from their labor. These systems are also characterized by "the surveillance of workers lives outside working hours."[5]

By providing a detailed description of the post office—the workspace of his protagonist Jake in *Lawd Today*—Richard Wright documents the regimen for which migrants were trained. Jake's supervisors not only keep a running record of how often he beats his wife outside of work, but also subject him to "a high degree of division of labor and the reduction of [his] movements and tasks to a simple routine":

> Bentbacked and with their eyes on the dirty steel, they shuffled in the direction of the small letter racks. There were six rows, each row some forty feet long with letter racks on both sides of the row. Each took his place in front of a case. Above their eyes swung an electric bulb with a green shade which deflected a circle of light over the fronts of honeycomblike pigeon-holes. To all four sides were suspended catwalks in which were slits for spying. Midway between their loins and knees was a wooden ledge about twelve inches wide upon which rested their trays of mail. . . .
>
> [Jake] held his left arm stiff and straight, pointing floorward, about a foot from his body with the open palm of his hand extended upward. From each Illinois hole he took a handful of mail and stacked it in his left hand until it reached his chin, walking slowly from case to case. When he could take no more, he went to the tray station where he dumped the mail into a large tray, set the metal notch which would guide it to its section, and placed it upon a moving belt. . . . Jake turned on his heel mechanically and started another cleanout.[6]

In this model of a migrant workplace, the workers' bodies become one with the workplace apparatus. The wooden ledge between their loins and knees is like a third limb, located near their genitalia. This placement of the ledge suggest that the tools of the workplace compromise or threaten their manhood. Jake's body is no longer human, but automated like a machine—stiff, rigid, and mechanical. Human movement is regulated by a highly structured work environment.

The postal work described by Wright was probably the best job available to a black migrant. Wright himself worked in the post office. Urban post offices were filled with highly educated men unable to find work. For many, the post office served as a kind of safe, communal space that was an intellectual center. However, the post office was also evidence of the limitations placed on black professional mobility. In addition, the post office was illustrative of a workspace dominated by the efficiency of modern power. The control of this space ensures the control of workers' movements and imagination. Here modern power, as embodied in this institution of surveillance, acts to create automatized, efficient workers.

The vast majority of male migrants were forced into even more menial labor than that just described. Many migrant men found work on the assembly lines of the Ford Motor Company in the Detroit area. The number of blues lyrics about the Ford Company are evidence of the centrality of this workplace in the lives of many migrants. In Pittsburgh they worked in the steel industry; in Chicago migrant men often worked for packing houses. Most often, migrant women found work as domestics; a rare few worked in garment factories.

For the most part, this type of factory work is the employment for which the black middle-class organizations sought to prepare the migrant. Even the otherwise militant *Chicago Defender*, which had incited many migrants to move north as an act of defiance, also published articles that aided their transformation: "Quit calling the foreman boss. Leave that word dropped in the Ohio River. Also captain, general and major. We call people up here Mr. This and Mr. That. Keep your hand off of your hat when you pass men. There is no law that requires you to tip your hat to a man because he is white."[7] The established black middle class began to do the work of Southern black colleges as outlined by Booker T. Washington in his autobiography and as parodied by Ralph Ellison and Nella Larsen in their novels. However, the tone of the *Defender* article is slightly different from the Urban League publication in that it encourages migrants to give up the submissive habits that characterized their behavior in the South.

Earlier in the century this work of social management had primarily been the domain of middle-class black women's organizations like the White Rose Mission and the National Association of Colored Women (NACW). As the functions of these organizations began to be absorbed by organizations like the Urban League, they turned their attention to the migrants' homes. In a 1929 issue of the National Notes of the NACW, President Sallie Stewart wrote: "We want the mothers to take the children's wearing apparel out of trunks where they are stored, and allow the children to wear them . . . and give their children the right attitude of life and to help them in the formation of their characters in the formative period of their lives."[8] Because these organizations were often founded in response to attacks on black womanhood in the dominant society, they sought to redefine migrant women according to Victorian standards. The culmination was an image of an idealized notion of motherhood and home.[9] It is the failure to meet these standards of motherhood as well as the confining nature of discourse on black women and sexuality with which urban female protagonists are confronted in the migration narrative.

In addition to attempting to regulate migrant women's homes, black middle-class women's clubs, along with white agencies, also perceived "the need to police and discipline the behavior of black women in cities." According to Hazel Carby, these efforts marked an attempt to transform the "behavior of migrant working-class black women to conform to middle-class norms of acceptable sexual behavior while actually . . . [confirming] . . . their working class status as female domestics."[10] While Carby's observation is an important one, it should also be clear that many of the black women's organizations were sensitive to the kinds of sexual exploitation experienced by women migrants in both the South and the North and hence some of their efforts were attempts to protect the newly arrived migrants as much as they were attempts to "transform" their behavior to conform to middle-class standards.

Organizations like the Urban League, the Young Negroes' Progressive Association of Detroit, the National Association of Colored Women, and the White Rose Mission represent the service tradition within the black middle class. In seeking to make the migrant into a certain kind of urban dweller, they also sought to ease the transition to city life. There is a long tradition of service within the black middle class. In contrast to the service work of this segment of the black middle class, there is also the kind of distanced disdain of another segment of that class. E. Franklin Frazier provides the most scathing critique of this segment of the black middle class, who are also the subjects of panel 53 in Jacob Lawrence's Migration series: "The Negroes who had been North for quite some time met their fellowmen with disgust and aloofness."

Black migrants were not passive victims of white power or objects of black middle-class paternalism. They actively created spaces and cultures where they sought to sustain themselves and where they sometimes attempted to resist the negative impact of urbanization. These spaces might be identified as the pockets of resistance created by modern power.[11] A whole street and domestic culture provided migrants with an alternative means to counter efforts to discipline them. These alternatives were housed in various forms from parties, dance halls, pool halls, and barber shops to kitchens, churches, families, and friendships. Some of these were sites of the ancestor.

The degree to which the migrant is successfully disciplined by the efforts of a dominant white society and the Northern black middle class, as well as the degree to which he or she resists, is of major concern in the migration narrative. Representations of migration suggest that forces which serve to transform the Southern migrant include the disciplinary work of institutions and their accompanying discourses and the balancing and nurturing work of migrant-defined safe spaces. The relationship of the migrant to any or all of these factors determines his or her fate in the city. This experience is portrayed differently for male and female protagonists and the success of the resisting spaces is portrayed differently over time. In the later narratives, the migrant-defined safe spaces emerge as more powerful in offering the migrant possibilities for resistance.

The writers discussed in this chapter focus on the migrants' efforts to resist the detrimental effects of urbanization. Two spaces are crucial to these efforts—a domestic "homespace"[12] of women and the street culture space of men. However, because these spaces are created by the power which migrants seek to resist, they are sometimes complicit in oppressing them.

II

It was there on the inside, in that "homeplace" most often created and kept by black women, that we had the opportunity to grow and develop, to nurture our spirits.

bell hooks, *Yearning*

That corner became our operations center . . . our school, our home away from home, our starting point and checking point.

Nathan McCall, *Make Me Wanna Holler*

Gwendolyn Brooks documents the existence of both domestic and street spaces in two of her most significant poems. The first, "Kitchenette Building," portrays the domestic space described by Wright, a space where dreams are born, nurtured, and sometimes lost to more immediate, basic needs. The second, "We Real Cool," portrays young black men who inhabit street corners and pool halls in an effort to create community and who knowingly accept their fate—a quick, early death.

Brooks's poems give complexity and humanity to the lives that haunt the pages of *12 Million Black Voices*. Through her, we know that the inhabitants of Richard Wright's kitchenettes dare to dream in spite of the overwhelming weight of their oppression:

> We are things of dry hours and the involuntary plan,
> Grayed in, and gray. "Dream" makes a giddy sound, not
>   strong
> Like "rent," "feeding a wife," "satisfying a man."
>
> But could a dream send up through onion fumes
> Its white and violet, fight with fried potatoes
> And yesterday's garbage ripening in the hall,
> Flutter, or sing an aria down these rooms
>
> Even if we were willing to let it in,
> Had time to warm it, keep it very clean,
> Anticipate a message, let it begin?
>
> We wonder. But not well! not for a minute!
> Since Number Five is out of the bathroom now,
> We think of lukewarm water, hope to get in it.[13]

In some ways this poem represents a marriage between Eliot's "The Love Song of J. Alfred Prufrock" and "The Hollow Men" and Hughes's "Dream Variation" and "Harlem." In one strike, Brooks both documents the failed dreams of black ghetto dwellers and links their frustrations with those of millions of modern people. Like Wright's gray Chicago, here the inhabitants of the kitchenettes themselves are gray. The act of dreaming seems a waste of time in light of the realities confronting them, realities of providing shelter, food, and some degree of sensual pleasure; but they dream nonetheless. The remainder of the poem is a beautiful meditation of the dream's attempt to escape, its struggle with the reality of the tenement, the smells and sounds. The second and third stanza echo Prufrock's "would it have been worth it, after all" queries. There is a building, mounting tension that leads to an anticlimactic intrusion of reality: "We wonder. But not well! not for a minute! / Since Number Five is out of the bathroom now."

Gwendolyn Brooks's women attempt to make "homespace" out of their dilapidated kitchenettes. They attempt to nurture and sustain dreams and to create community with the others who share their station in life. More often than not, their efforts fail—the dreams die—but Brooks records the humanity of these attempts with grace and beauty.

A reading of Brooks's entire corpus reveals that the kitchenette dreamers are women. Annie Allen and Maud Martha are keepers of the dream, even though the reality of their lives often intrudes. Because they seek to make "homespace" out of their dilapidated living conditions and because they give birth to and nurture "the children of the poor," they continue to dream and their dreams are at best spaces of resistance and at least spaces of sustenance and survival as necessary as food, clothing, and shelter. In fact, Annie Allen tells her "children of the poor" to "First fight. Then fiddle." She sees a place for dreaming and for the creation of art, but it is a hard-won place.[14]

A closer reading of "Kitchenette Building" reveals a connection between "the dream" and "the work of art," or "the poem." "Poetry" itself seems giddy and weak in light of the harsh lives of kitchenette dwellers. Art and poetry require the time and nurturance that seem like unnecessary luxuries to poor people. However, though the content of the poem suggests that it is impossible to create poetry in the context of urban reality, its very existence asserts otherwise. Brooks herself was a kitchenette dweller, a wife and mother, who had to attend to the life needs of her husband and children, and yet she was able to turn the elements of her reality into poetry.[15] That reality is not just a domestic one, but a less optimistic street reality as well.

The male personae of "We Real Cool" seem to laugh in the face of dreams and homespace. They create an identity out of the urban despair in which they live, participating in a male-defined street culture that demands "cool" action and acceptance of death:

> We real cool. We
> Left school. We
>
> Lurk late. We
> Strike straight. We
>
> Sing sin. We
> Thin gin. We
>
> Jazz June. We
> Die soon.[16]

The poem—quick, spare, and tense—echoes the patterns of the lives it documents. As in Toomer's "Seventh Street," the verbs are abrupt and hard-edged, urging the reader to speed through them as the collective persona speeds through life. Hortense Spillers notes that the three-beat lines encourage a quick reading that causes the reader to "run out of breath, or [trip] her tongue, but it seems that such [breathlessness] is exactly required of dudes hastening toward their death."[17]

"We Real Cool" is a portrait of young men attempting to own their fates. They seem to say "If, as young men, we must die quick and violent deaths, then we shall live our lives in resistance to all that is *right* and *proper.*" There are no dreams here, simply harsh reality described by monosyllabic, action-oriented verbs. As is the case with Bigger Thomas and his friends, these young men are active and energetic but possess no outlet for the positive exploration of these attributes.

The two gender-based perspectives recorded in these poems also dominate the migration narrative's portrayals of the migrants' attempts to negotiate the urban landscape. For the most part, female protagonists attempt to create "home" in hope of providing a space where dreams are possible. It seems that male protagonists give up any hope of dreaming and seek instead to carve out some degree of manhood in a male-defined street culture and its accompanying spaces. Men and women respond to each other's spaces in opposing ways: Male characters find domestic space stifling; female characters find streetspace threatening.

III

> But could a dream send up through onion fumes
> Its white and violet, fight with fried potatoes
> And yesterday's garbage ripening in the hall,
> Flutter, or sing an aria down these rooms
>
> Even if we were willing to let it in,
> Had time to warm it, keep it very clean,
> Anticipate a message, let it begin?
>
> Gwendolyn Brooks, "Kitchenette Building"

Gwendolyn Brooks shows us that oppression does not hinder the birth of dreams but it does thwart their realization. In her poetry, black women provide the space where these dreams are nurtured and sent forth. Other black women writers concerned with the urban experience share her perspective.

However, as is the case with other aspects of the narratives, the degree to which these sites serve as "safe spaces" or "spaces of resistance" differs from author to author. Those authors who stress their importance portray them as sites where the South is evoked. In this context, the writers are not concerned with Southern exploitation and racial domination, but with the South as the site of African-American culture, community, and history.

"Safe space" takes shape in song, oral culture, memory, dreams, and spirituality. For purposes of this study I use the term "safe spaces" to designate all such sites. They exist as places where ritual evokes a Southern or African ancestor. In many ways they are spaces of "safe time" as well, for they evoke history and memory, and their pace is often slower than that of the city. In these spaces linear notions of time are challenged. The past exists alongside the present. The protagonist's relationship to these domains determines his or her fate.

At their most progressive, safe spaces are nurturing, healing, and resisting; at their most reactionary, they are provincial sites which discourage resistance and bind the protagonist to an oppressive past. The latter portrayal tends to emerge in the narratives of male authors; this is by no means a hard-and-fast rule; we need only recall Helga Crane's various experiences with homespace in *Quicksand*. Often, black women writers represent home–safe spaces as necessary to their characters' survival. On the pages of their migration narratives, these spaces distinguish themselves from the rest of the text in language, rhythm, and notions of temporality. They often disrupt the otherwise straightforward linearity of the narrative. Literary safe spaces fit Michael Awkward's definition of "historically determined tropological refigurations." In other words they exist as figures of language revised according to the historical moment in which they are used.

Marita Bonner's "The Whipping" (1940), Ann Petry's *The Street* (1946) and Gloria Naylor's *The Women of Brewster Place* (1982) all portray poor, black, single, working mothers, who live in Northern urban ghettos and who seek to provide for their sons. The women in the two earlier texts attempt to resist their construction or objectification by a dominant white discourse on black women, which constructs them as lascivious, lazy, and immoral. This discourse emerges in the words and images of white authority as well as in popular culture. The women of Brewster Place try to resist the psychic and physical violence and economic poverty inflicted on them by white society and black men. In all three works, each woman has varying degrees of access to safe space. Only Mattie Michael of Brewster Place takes advantage of that space. As a result, only Mattie survives to act as a creator of safe space for other women of Brewster Place. Each author exploits the literary possibility of "narrative" safe spaces differently.

Until recently, Marita Bonner's fiction, drama, and essays have received little critical attention. Fortunately, critic Joyce Flynn and Bonner's daughter, Joyce Occomy Strickland, have brought her work to the reading public. Bonner's corpus of plays and short stories call for a reevaluation of received notions of a black women's literary tradition. Her fiction depicts the lives of Chicago's migrant community.

Consideration of Bonner's writing reveals the foundation of a black women's literary tradition of urban fiction. Unlike Zora Neale Hurston, who was primarily concerned with rural blacks, or Jessie Fauset and Nella Larsen, who focused their creative attention on the lives and experiences of upper-middle-class black women, Bonner was among the first to find the lives of working-class and poor urban women worthy of literary consideration. Her protagonists do not attend endless rounds of parties; instead they often work difficult jobs. They are more likely to have a hard time putting food on the table than they are to host elaborate dinner parties. And always they meet head-on daily confrontations with racism and sexism; they live under the constant threat of incarceration, rape, and death. On the pages of Bonner's stories violent interracial confrontations and intraracial class and color conflicts come to life. The rediscovery of Bonner signals a new source for the urban fictions of Gwendolyn Brooks, Ann Petry, Toni Morrison, Gayl Jones, and Gloria Naylor. She also serves as a literary ancestor to Richard Wright, whose *Native Son* shares much with Bonner's short story "Tin Can," published in 1934 in *Opportunity*.

Marita Bonner's "The Whipping," is the tale of a Southern sharecropping family—Ma and her three adult children, Lizabeth, Bella, and John—who migrate north. The story demonstrates the disintegration of the family structure. Frustrated by her inability to feed her mother and child, Lizabeth, the eldest daughter and the story's protagonist, strikes her son. He falls from the force of the blow, strikes his head on the bed frame, and dies. Lizabeth is charged with his murder and sentenced to a jail described like the opening description of the South from which she fled. In the South, Bonner tells us, "Everything had been grey around Lizabeth most all of her life. The two-room hut with a ragged lean-to down on Mr. Davey's place in Mississippi where she had lived before she came North had been grey." At the close of the story Lizabeth sits in the prison's commissary and reflects, "the same grey hopeless drudge—the same long unending row to hoe lay before her."[18] The real whipping in the story is not Lizabeth's fatal slap of her child, but her own mental beating by urban poverty and the state bureaucracy which oversees it. Bonner deconstructs the "difference" between the North and the South by using a title which suggests the oppression of the South exists in the North in different but no less substantive ways.

"The Whipping" depicts the movement toward urbanization as a movement from the "mother" and "motherhood." First, the Southern-born children move away from their mother's values, and second, Lizabeth's final "unmotherly" act of striking her child leads to her institutionalization. The younger generation moves further and further away from Southern styles. While Ma "screams and shouts and gets happy in robust leather-lunged style of her storefront church run in the down-home tempo," her daughters "[loop] wider and wider in circles of joy." These wider circles of joy lead to the departure of one daughter; Bonner measures her distance in degrees of her changing appearance: "Straightened her hair first. Then curled her hair. Sassed Ma." Movement away from physical signs of her race and away from her mother signify her movement away from the South.

This daughter moves into her own apartment; she eventually becomes a prostitute.

The death of Lizabeth's brother provides the second departure. Although his mother recommends Southern home remedies to battle his illness, the Northern-born doctor immediately dismisses them. Instead, the doctor asserts that the young man will die and does not attempt to aid him.

In the North, the biological family fails to provide a homespace for its members. There is no sense of an extended family to fill the void left by the disintegration of the nuclear family. The community of Frye Street forms a gossip chorus, which only serves to advance Lizabeth's demise. First, her neighbors harass her about her husband's disappearance. Second, they inform her that her marriage is illegal. Third, they spread rumors that insinuate she earns extra income through prostitution. Finally, a member of her community tells a social service worker that Lizabeth is a violent drunk.

The white social service worker believes this because she has already established Lizabeth as a social deviant. "Her books had all told her that colored women carried knives." The received understanding of black women constitutes Lizabeth as crazed and violent; the social service worker acts upon the subject of this discourse, not the individual. The powerful bureaucratic system that legitimated this written discourse has the authority to feed the poor as well as institutionalize them. Driven to violence by hunger, poverty, and the inability to provide for her son, Lizabeth has no safe space from which to resist her demise.

In her introduction to Bonner's collected works, Joyce Flynn notes that the author refuses to romanticize the South. Though she portrays the breakup of the family upon their arrival in the North, Bonner does not present black Southern culture as a way of navigating the harshness of the urban landscape.[19]

Bonner's story illustrates the connections between Lizabeth's downfall and her construction in the dominant discourse on black women. The author dismisses three potential safe spaces—the family, the church, and the community—as viable alternatives to the brutality of Northern oppression. While the potential safe spaces are denied any power, the dominant discourse on black women acts upon them in powerful and destructive ways. By the end of the text, Lizabeth, like the persona of Gwendolyn Brooks's "Kitchenette Building," is destined to a life of grayness and debt: "The same grey hopeless drudge—the same long unending row to hoe—lay before her."

Not only does Bonner deny the power of material homespaces; she does not exploit the narrative possibilities of safe spaces either. Bonner shares with Richard Wright a tendency to dismiss the resisting potential of safe spaces, but she differs from him in that she does not portray these sites as stifling or detrimental. The harsh realism of her work precedes that of Wright. Writing on the heels of the Great Migration and the Great Depression, Bonner only documents the devastating effects of urbanization on her migrant character. Her omniscient narrator has the distanced gaze of the stranger. It is not insignificant that Bonner was a black New Englander, Boston-born and Radcliffe-educated. Her first contact with large numbers of poor and working-class African-Americans came after her graduation from college when she moved to Washington, D.C. Her experiences there are documented in her powerful piece "On Being Young—a Woman—and Colored." Bonner's New England upbringing and education provided her with the critical distance from which she explored the devastating effects of the city on ordinary black people.

Inheriting Bonner's concern with working-class black women, Ann Petry, another New Englander, experiments with the possibilities of safe spaces in both the content and the form of her urban narrative, the best-selling *The Street* (1946). Petry was featured in an *Ebony* article following the publication of her first novel, and the book was widely reviewed by both the black and white press. Unlike Bonner's work, which received little national recognition, Petry's novel, the first by a black woman to sell over a million copies, received a warm and enthusiastic reception upon publication. Much of her success resulted from her novel's resemblance to Wright's realist classic *Native Son*. Surely, Petry captured some of the audience created by Richard Wright's text. However, her novel also suffered from this connection to Wright, because male literary critics deemed it lacking in the realism of Wright and Chester Himes.[20]

Upon reconsideration, this comparison proves unfair. In its departure from the naturalism of Wright and the realism of Bonner, Petry's novel expands the means of representing the black, urban female experience. By providing viable safe spaces that are rooted in Southern culture, she marks a shift from Wright's view. By utilizing memory and dreams as a means of informing her protagonist, Petry distinguishes herself from Bonner. However, she shares with both of them the refusal to romanticize the South and a sense of urgency in asserting the negative impact of the city.

Petry makes a few safe spaces available to her protagonist, Lutie: community, family, and the voice of her grandmother.[21] Lutie dismisses all of them. I will focus on the grandmother's voice and Lutie's relationship to it, because as the ancestor of that text, the grandmother not only has the most potential for Lutie's resistance, but she serves as a resisting narrative device as well. Karla Holloway notes that texts privileging the ancestor's spoken word "dissemble EuroAmerican traditions that privilege writing."[22] In *The Street,* Petry privileges the Grandmother's voice over the written words of Benjamin Franklin. However, her protagonist, Lutie, does not. The urban fiction of Rudolph Fisher and Marita Bonner[23] precedes Petry's assertion of the resisting potential of Southern ancestors. However, of the three, Ann Petry provides the most profound exploration of the ancestor's possibilities. Petry's use of an ancestor figure joins Hurston's to lay the foundation built upon by Gloria Naylor and Gayl Jones in their fiction and Toni Morrison in her fiction and criticism.

Lutie's psyche embodies the ground upon which her best safe space exists;

here resides the ancestor of the text—Granny. However, Lutie's memory of her grandmother engages in a tug of war with her retention of Benjamin Franklin's autobiography. While her grandmother's spoken voice tries to guide her through the psychic maze of the street, the written text of Benjamin Franklin, espousing an ethic of hard work and success, influences her more. Lutie usually ignores the spoken voice of her grandmother while taking heed of the written words of Franklin. She fails to read the silences and the absences which undergird his manual for success. While he provides her with an ethic of hard work and thrift, she fails to see how Franklin's notion of success, grounded on a system of chattel slavery and on a discourse whose subtext constructs her as inferior, acts to her detriment. Even though she continues to suffer from and be defined by definitions of black women that first emerge in Franklin's day, she does not make the connection. Her failure to make the connection between Junto, the white owner of the building in which she lives and of the nightclub in which she seeks employment, and the factors that serve to oppress her is an outgrowth of her blindness in relation to Franklin.[24]

The safe space provided by Lutie's grandmother exists as an ongoing oral dialogue in Lutie's memory. In the urban North, the South—the ancestor—must live in the psyche because sophisticated, fragmented Northern power most effectively oppresses the urban dweller on this plane. Northern power constructs desire and a means of self-disciplining that precedes its need for physical force and coercion.[25] The grandmother always arrives when Lutie's well-being is threatened.

The reader first encounters the grandmother when the text's villain, Jones, the superintendent, shows Lutie an apartment. Here, Lutie makes a conscious effort to dissociate herself from her grandmother's influence. Throughout her first encounter with the super, her grandmother warns her of the danger he represents to her. "Granny would have said, 'Nothin' but evil, child. Some folks so full of it, you can feel it comin' at you oozin' right out of their skins.' She didn't believe things like that." Lutie justifies her rationalization of her grandmother's warning by juxtaposing her own rational understanding against Granny's more instinctual one:

> He probably wanted to hear his favorite program and she had thought he was filled with the desire to leap upon her. She was as bad as Granny. Which just went on to prove you couldn't be brought up by someone like Granny without absorbing a lot of nonsense that would spring at you out of nowhere, so to speak, when you least expected it. All those tales about things that people sensed before they actually happened. Tales that had been handed down and down, until if you tried to trace them back, you'd end up God knows where— probably Africa. And Granny had them all at the tip of her tongue.[26]

Here, in fearing and dismissing her grandmother, she dismisses the safe space embodied in the ancestor—a space grounded in the oral tradition and emerging from an African past. This early dismissal of her grandmother's advice will prove fatal for her. Not unlike the blues singers discussed earlier, Lutie's grandmother gives her a map for her own survival.

Still, subconsciously, Lutie knows that her grandmother's voice provides protection and guidance: Immediately after dismissing her grandmother's warning about the super, she begins to sing a song to soothe her discomfort. "She started humming under her breath, not realizing she was doing it. It was an old song that Granny used to sing." Her grandmother provides her with a song in the night to ease her fear and discomfort. The grandmother exists so deeply in her psyche that Lutie uses her, unaware of her presence—a presence which emerges even as she attempts to dismiss it.

When Lutie heeds her grandmother's advice, it strengthens her against the attempts of white people to objectify her. Considered a whore by the wealthy white women friends and relatives who visit her employer, she turns to Granny's voice to give her a sense of dignity in the midst of their constant accusing attack: "[Mrs. Chandler's mother] took one look at Lutie . . . and [said] in a clipped voice . . . 'Now I wonder if you're being wise dear. That girl is unusually attractive and men are weak. Besides, she's colored and you know how they are.'" Her employer's friends invoke similar stereotypes in relation to her:

> Whenever she entered a room where they were, they stared at her with a queer, speculative look. Sometimes she caught snatches of their conversation about her. "Sure she's a wonderful cook. But I wouldn't have any good-looking colored wench in my house. . . . You know they're always making passes at men. Especially white men." [p. 41]

Instead of becoming defeated by their construction of her as whore, she turns to her memory of her grandmother's voice:

> Of course, none of them could know about your grandmother who had brought you up, she said to herself. And ever since you were big enough to remember . . . had said over and over just like a clock ticking "Lutie, baby, don't you never let no white man put his hands on you. They ain't never willin' to let a black woman alone. Seems like they all got a itch and a urge to sleep with 'em. Don't you never let any of 'em touch you."
> Something that was said so often and with such gravity it had become part of you, just like breathing and you would have preferred crawling into bed with a rattlesnake to getting in bed with a white man. [pp. 45–46]

Here, Lutie is able to resist the white women's construction of her because she has been prepared by her grandmother and as a result she possesses an alternative definition of black womanhood. Her grandmother's voice is a part of her very being, not something removed which she can rationalize away. The grandmother's voice is inseparable from her own heartbeat.

This voice also helps her to avoid the economic exploitation that takes place in Harlem grocery shops. Again, even though she seemingly dismisses the advice of the ancestor, it nonetheless informs her choices. While glancing over the offerings at the local butcher, Lutie recalls:

> Someone had told Granny once that the butchers in Harlem used embalming fluid on the beef they sold in order to give it a nice fresh color. Lutie didn't believe it, but like a lot of things she didn't believe, it cropped up suddenly out of nowhere to leave her wondering and staring at the brilliant scarlet color of the meat. It made her examine the contents of the case with care in order to determine whether there was something else that would do for dinner. [p. 61]

Granny's advice serves to ensure Lutie's survival on the street. However, Lutie, not satisfied with merely getting by, eluding the danger of evil men like the superintendent, resisting her objectification by whites as whore, or avoiding exploitation by Harlem merchants, wants large game plans to ensure success. Her grandmother's advice provides small day-to-day measures for survival. Like the daydreaming persona of Brooks's kitchenette poem, Lutie thinks that retreating to her grandmother's voice wastes time in the face of harsh realities of urban living. She does not realize that she needs small, local, day-to-day resistances; she needs these safe spaces to act as foundation for her to make the big changes in her life.

The literate Lutie reads and grasps the written advice of Benjamin Franklin; the illiterate Lutie denies her grandmother's voice. For her it is "nonsense." She fails to see that the ancestor does not spring at her out of nowhere, when she least expects it, but instead it emerges just when she needs it most.

While the words of Benjamin Franklin provide her with steps to success for white men, they fail to inform her of the foundation upon which those steps stand—a foundation where white men have equal access because black men and women, Native Americans, and white women do not. His recipe for success depends upon denial of access to people like her. She does not realize that with the foundation provided by her grandmother, she has a much better chance of achieving a larger success; without it, she is destined to fail.

Marjorie Pryse's "'Pattern Against the Sky': Deism and Motherhood in Ann Petry's *The Street*" delineates all the references to Franklin's autobiography and illustrates Lutie's fatal, blind faith in his text. According to Pryse, "She fails to recognize the stigma of her race and sex and her consequent disqualification for achieving her particular version of the American dream."[27] Throughout the text Lutie unquestioningly follows Franklin's advice. Instead of listening to her grandmother's voice, she thinks, "Now that she had this apartment, she was just one step farther up on the ladder of success." Her blindness prohibits her from seeing that the apartment signals the beginning of her demise.

Lutie gains self-confidence from her dialogue with Franklin. Walking down 116th Street:

> She thought immediately of Ben Franklin and his loaf of bread. And grinned thinking, You and Ben Franklin. You ought to take one out and start eating it as

you walk along 116th Street. Only you ought to remember while you eat that you're in Harlem and he was in Philadelphia a pretty long number of years ago. Yet she couldn't get rid of the feeling of self-confidence and she went on thinking that if Ben Franklin could live on a little bit of money and prosper, so could she. [pp. 63–64]

Again, here she dismisses what she knows to be a crucial difference between her and Franklin. At this point in the text, Lutie does not yet realize the degree of difference between the streets of Philadelphia in the eighteenth century and the streets of Harlem in the twentieth. She fails to make a distinction between herself as a poor black woman and Franklin as a wealthy white man.

These are realizations that she stumbles upon only after she is faced with an endless web of exploitation and domination. Seeking vengeance for her failure to return his attentions, the super, Jones, involves her son in a scheme of mail fraud. It is significant that the same institution that surveys and controls Richard Wright's Jake ultimately captures Bub as well. The child is arrested and Lutie is unknowingly led to believe she needs a two-hundred-dollar lawyer's fee to free him. She seeks the money from another black male who desires her, Boots, only to have him attempt to rape her and then turn her over to his white boss, Junto.

Her recognition comes in three critical steps. First, she realizes that the street to which she moved provides no possibility for her. Lutie notes that "streets like the ones she lived on [and like Wright's kitchenette] were no accident. They were the North's lynch mobs. . . . The method the big cities used to keep Negroes in their place" (p. 323). Again, like those before her, Lutie realizes that Northern power appears in a different, more omniscient form than in the South. Nonetheless, it acts toward the same ends.

Second, she realizes the consequences of her failure to create community. She cannot turn to her co-workers to borrow the necessary money to free her son: "She didn't know any of them intimately. She didn't really have time to get to know them well, because she went right home after work . . . and she always took a sandwich along for lunch, and when the weather was good she ate on a park bench." Pondering her son's situation, she realizes that Granny had always provided a sense of security, a homespace for her as a child.

Her final realization of her failure to utilize safe space comes when she recognizes: "From the time she was born, she had been hemmed into an ever-narrowing space, until now she was nearly walled in and the wall had been built brick by brick by eager white hands." One hundred pages later, when she meets Junto in Boots's apartment, she has a face to place with those eager white hands: "And all the time she was thinking, Junto has a brick in his hand. Just one brick. The final one needed to complete the wall that had been building up around her for years, and when that one last brick was shoved in place, she would be completely walled in." The tone of this passage reeks with the resignation Lutie has sought to avoid. She makes no attempt to resist Junto, to prevent him from laying that last brick. The bricks of this wall are as fatal to Lutie as Bigger's brick is to Bessie in *Native Son*.[28]

While *The Street* ends with Lutie's confinement by this psychic brick wall, Gloria Naylor's *The Women of Brewster Place* ends with a vision of the destruction of the wall by those it seeks to confine. While the characters of "The Whipping" move further and further from "the mother," the women of Brewster Place return time and again to a maternal safe space whether it exists as the neighborhood itself, as ritual, or in friendships between the women. Unlike either earlier writer, Naylor explores the possibility of "neighborhood" first suggested in Gwendolyn Brooks's *Maud Martha*.

As I have demonstrated, Naylor's first novel belongs to a group of black feminist texts that emerged after the Black Power Movement of the sixties. Along with Ntozake Shange's *For Colored Girls Who Have Considered Suicide When the Rainbow Is Enuf* and the works of Alice Walker, Naylor's work asserts the vital necessity of women-centered ritual and community for black women. More than either Petry or Bonner, Naylor exploits the possibilities of safe spaces for her characters and her narrative strategy. Naylor's safe spaces challenge realism as an adequate form for portraying the lived experience of black women. However, like Bonner and Petry before her, she does not retreat from portraying the harshness of their urban existence.

The last chapter illustrated Naylor's opening of her text with a description of a maternal Brewster Place: a street that births several generations of immigrant children and in her old age grows fond of her colored daughters. The women of Brewster Place play a similar role in each other's lives. Mattie Michael, the protagonist, acts as a maternal healing space to the younger generation of women. Her role as healer and nurturer is most apparent in Naylor's portrayal of the laying on of hands ritual between Mattie and the younger Ciel.

When Lucielle almost dies from the grief of losing her toddler daughter, Mattie refuses to let her go. The oppression of racism and poverty lead to the kitchenettelike living conditions, which in turn lead to the death of the child and to Ciel's death-filled stare. Witnessing this, Mattie yells, "Merciful Father, no!" Naylor says, "There was no prayer, no bended knee or sackcloth supplication in those words, but a blasphemous fireball that shot forth and went smashing against the gates of heaven, raging and kicking, demanding to be heard." This is no passive spirituality, but a demanding, active one. It is the ultimate act of defiance for the very religious Mattie, for it resists the highest authority of all—God. "No, No, No." Safe spaces are spaces where black women find voice; here, Mattie finds voice, as will Ciel.

Although these women find voice, the ritual that provides them with it is conducted in silence: "She approached the bed with her lips clamped shut in such a force that the muscles in her jaw and the back of her neck began to ache."

The silence with which she speaks marks this as a very significant space within this narrative. Here, Mattie speaks with her hands. The laying on of hands ritual serves not only as a safe space where Ciel is healed, but also as a discursive retreat within the text itself:

> She sat on the edge of the bed and enfolded the tissue-thin body in her huge ebony arms. And she rocked. Ciel's body was so hot it burned Mattie when she first touched her, but she held on and rocked. Back and forth, back and forth—she had Ciel so tightly she could feel her young breasts flatten against the buttons of her dress. The black mammoth gripped so firmly that the slightest increase of pressure would have cracked the girl's spine. But she rocked.
>
> And somewhere from the bowels of her being came a moan from Ciel, so high at first it couldn't be heard by anyone there, but the yard dogs began an unholy howling. And Mattie rocked. And then, agonizingly slow, it broke its way through the parched lips in a spaghetti-thin column of air that could be faintly heard in the frozen room.
>
> Ciel moaned. Mattie rocked. Propelled by the sound, Mattie rocked her out of that bed, out of that room, into a blue vastness just underneath the sun and above time. She rocked her over the Aegean seas so clean they shone like crystal, so clear the fresh blood of sacrificed babies torn from their mothers and given to Neptune could be seen like pink froth on the water. She rocked her on and on, past Dachau where soul-gutted Jewish mothers swept their children's entrails off laboratory floors. They flew past the spilled brains of Senegalese infants whose mothers had dashed them on the wooden sides of slave ships. And she rocked on.
>
> She rocked her into childhood and let her see murdered dreams. And she rocked her back, back into the womb, to the nadir of her hurt, and they found it—a slight silver splinter, embedded just below the surface of the skin. And Mattie rocked and pulled and the splinter gave way, but its roots were deep, gigantic, ragged, and they tore up the flesh with bits of fat and muscle tissue clinging to them. They left a huge hole, which was already starting to pus over, but Mattie was satisfied. It would heal. . . .
>
> And slowly she bathed her . . . slowly, reverently as if handling a new-born. . . .
>
> All of this had been done without either woman saying a word. . . . Ciel stood there, naked, and felt the cool air play against the clean surface of her skin. She had the sensation of fresh mint coursing through her pores. She closed her eyes and the fire was gone. . . . So Ciel began to cry—there, naked, in the center of the bathroom floor. . . .
>
> And Ciel lay down and cried. But Mattie knew the tears would end. And she would sleep. And morning would come.[29]

There are so many dimensions of safe space here. First, Ciel's healing takes place in the space of the ritual. Second, Mattie's very body serves as a safe space as she holds and rocks Ciel. Her body constitutes the vessel in which Ciel travels over the seas of history and through which Ciel is reborn. Finally, the passage exists as a safe space. The phrase "back and forth, back and forth" provides the curve on which the paragraph itself rocks. Here spoken words and dialogue give way to silence. Naylor's portrayal of the ritual resists the straight linearity of the rest of the narrative, taking both Ciel and reader back through space and time.

The ritual occupies a realm—a women's sphere—where Ciel meets and melds her sorrow with the historical sorrow of other women who have lost their children to the violence of racial, ethnic, religious, and class oppression. Mattie rocks her back to her ancestral mothers—women forced to lose their children. She takes Ciel through and beyond historical time, and only then, when her sorrow and pain are merged with those of other women, only then does she return to that timeless place of origin—the womb. She must travel through collective history before she can return to personal history.[30]

The ancient laying on of hands ritual abounds in modern black women's fiction. Maya Angelou, Ntozake Shange, Toni Morrison, Toni Cade Bambara, and Paule Marshall utilize this ritual as a central element of their narrative strategy.[31] It exists as a womanist reclamation of divine healing and resurrecting powers. Some critics claim that the ritual's ability to lead to a "reborn self" is in and of itself an act of resistance. Ann Rosalind Jones credits French feminists like Julia Kristeva, Luce Irigaray, and Helene Cixous with identifying the "direct re-experience of the physical pleasures of infancy and sexuality," and the "return to the pre-verbal identification with the mother" as a means of resisting the oppression of patriarchal society. Kristeva charges that women write in a style which often involves "repetitive spasmodic separations from the dominant discourse."[32] Although Naylor's passage differs from Kristeva's description in that it remains linear and is not totally disrupting, Kristeva does provide some insight into the passage's portrayal of a return to the mother. In the foregoing passage, Ciel returns to a preverbal identification with the mother; however, in this case she is not resisting but healing from patriarchal oppression. Naylor does depict this healing process in a style much like that described by Kristeva.

In the narrative safe space of the ritual, Mattie enacts a biblical rite revised and maintained by New World Africans. Before she can be reborn the woman must be led back to the womb. Naylor portrays this ritual in language which separates itself from the dominant language of the narrative. Ciel emerges as a literal "newly born woman."

Like the ritual, the dream provides a domain unhindered by time and space. Within the context of the dream the limitations of Brewster Place are torn down by the power of the community of women. In the dream space the narrative comes full circle: Ciel returns to Brewster Place, healed and whole, and the women destroy, brick by brick, the wall which closes off the street.

We never know if Mattie's dream is prophetic, for in the narrative time of the story, the women do not tear down the wall that surrounds them. Perhaps like the dream of Brooks's poem it is unable to survive in the Brewster Place tenements. By the end of the text Brewster Place dies, but the women leave "some to the arms of a world that they would have to pry open to take them, most to inherit another aging street and the privilege of clinging to its decay."

Because the resistance of the women of Brewster Place occurs only in the context of these female spaces, they are acts that serve to ensure survival but not to guarantee any ongoing resistance to the social order. A return to the mother is healing and nurturing, but alone it is not enough to dismantle the wall which circumscribes their lives. As Ann Rosalind Jones asserts, "the female body hardly seems the best site to launch an attack on the forces that have alienated us."[33] Michael Awkward extends Jones's critique in his reading of *The Women of Brewster Place:* "However profitable individual acts of sisterly love . . . prove, they do not have the power to alter significantly the deleterious conditions for Brewster Place's females as a group."[34]

The ultimate vision of Brewster Place asserts that the process of change is painful and ever so slow, one nurtured by the existence of safe womanspaces. Naylor also provides an alternative to the fates of Lutie and Lizabeth: the safe space of a women-centered community. However, it seems safe space is available only to the heterosexual women of Brewster Place. The lesbian couple, Theresa and Lorraine, are denied entrée into the sisterhood and Lorraine is forced to suffer a violent death at the hands of young men. Interestingly, her death occurs at the brick wall dead-end which encloses Brewster Place. The wall, domain of the street culture of Brewster Place's Bigger Thomas, C. C. Baker, here signifies the literal end that awaits women denied safe space on Brewster Place. The dream of dismantling the wall is an effort to reclaim a dangerous street space and gain control of it.

The dream imagery, though displacing more material notions of resistance, is nonetheless very important to Naylor's vision. In a wonderful discussion of the dream imagery in the novel, critic Jill L. Matus has argued that "the dreams of Brewster's inhabitants are what keep them alive."[35] Their dreams ensure their survival. The final lines of her text are:

> But the colored daughters of Brewster, spread over the canvas of time, still wake up with their dreams misted on the edge of a yawn. They get up and pin those dreams to wet laundry hung out to dry, they're mixed with a pinch of salt and thrown into pots of soup, and they're diapered around babies. They ebb and flow, ebb and flow, but never disappear. So Brewster Place still waits to die. [p. 192]

Like the dwellers of Brooks's "Kitchenette Building," the women of Brewster Place manage to keep their dreams alive and to pass them on in the healing sustenance they provide for their families. Who knows but that one of those dreams "diapered around babies" will be realized in the future of one of Brewster's many children? After all, Naylor dedicates her novel to people in her own life who helped her realize the dream of writing: "Marcia, who gave me the dream; Lauren, who believed in it; Rich, who nurtured and shaped it, and George, who applauded the loudest in his heart." As with Gwendolyn Brooks, Gloria Naylor's dream is realized in her art: a novel devoted to the dreams of countless black women of Brewster Place(s).

To the extent that safe spaces work in *The Women of Brewster Place* they do so because the women suffer from sexual as well as racial oppression. Because of this, women's spaces serve as healing spaces. Their sex is one cause of their suffering as well as a source of their healing community. Naylor's text revises the tropes of the two earlier texts; her refiguration of the tropes of entrapment—the brick wall, motherhood, and the fictional urban neighborhoods—are directly related to the historical and political moment in which she writes. *Brewster Place* does not simply emerge in response to the changing political and social relationships between black men and black women following the Black Power Movement, it also helps to helps to create that change. Naylor's text emerges as a black feminist attempt to show that black women's intraracial gender-based oppression necessitates the construction of a black women's community and the utilization of safe space. Of the three writers considered here, her narrative technique best exploits the literary potential of the safe space and also follows and contributes to a feminist literary construction.

Naylor's vision is limited by her denial to extend the benefits of women-defined safe space to her lesbian characters. While relationships between women serve as a source of safe space for other female characters, in the context of the lesbian relationship it is the source of oppression not only by whites and men but also by other women.

IV

> We
> Die soon.
>
> Gwendolyn Brooks, "We Real Cool"

Melvin Dixon has argued that "one difference between [black male] and [black female] writers . . . lies in the various ways their protagonists reinvent self through verbal performances in alternative landscapes."[36] While the women of Brewster Place create women-defined safe spaces in order to sustain themselves, male protagonists participate in street space and often enact more violent efforts to counter their oppression. In Richard Wright's *Native Son*, Ralph Ellison's *Invisible Man*, and *The Autobiography of Malcolm X* domestic space is stifling and provincial. The male migrant characters of these texts attempt to develop a street culture and/or attempt to acquire a critical consciousness as a means of resisting the negative impact of the city.[37] Malcolm X and Bigger Thomas actively participate in a street culture that is detrimental to women like Lutie and those of Brewster Place.

The three factors that most concern Bigger Thomas, Invisible Man, and Malcolm X are an escape from the stifling nature of domestic safe space, the acquisition of a critical consciousness, and the attempt to resist the power of the dominant white society to control their acquisition of knowledge and to shape their desire. In each case, the protagonist feels that any retention of the South inhibits his personal growth and development. For Invisible Man this dismissal of his Southern past is further evidence of his arrogance and ignorance. It is a stance of which Ellison is clearly critical.

All three characters seek to gain a higher level of consciousness. Because all other outlets are closed to him, Bigger is able to gain a higher level of consciousness only by committing murders. Invisible Man seeks a critical consciousness in all the wrong places—the black college and then a predominantly white left-wing organization, The Brotherhood. Both prove to be sites that are hostile to critical thinking. Malcolm X revises the tropes of the street culture and prison first established by Wright, to stress their significance and importance in his ability to acquire the consciousness to resist the dominant society.

It is significant that each character links resistance to his possession of white women. As noted in Chapter 1, a black man's desire for a white woman is the taboo which most likely leads to a lynching. In the mind of the male migrant characters, white women are linked with fear. In the North, black men are bombarded with images of white women that construct their desire for them; they also have access to and a physical proximity with white women that was denied in the South. This fear-desire dialectic is dominant in these urban male narratives and each protagonist responds to it differently. At some point in each novel, the protagonist is controlled through the manipulation of his desire. Interestingly, none of the authors presents us with a healthy, loving interracial relationship.[38] Although much of the narrative focuses on the manipulation of the protagonist through his desire, in all three cases he is capable of sustaining a stance of resistance.

Richard Wright establishes the tropes others who follow him must respond to and/or reject. The relationship of Wright's text to that of Ellison has been the subject of many critical and theoretical works.[39] Ellison's Invisible Man is most often viewed as a revision and alternative to Bigger. However, critics have paid little attention to the earlier text's relationship to the *Autobiography of Malcolm X*. Not only did Malcolm X read these narratives in prison, the writer who constructs his autobiography into a migration narrative, Alex Haley, was certainly aware of the defining tropes of Wright and Ellison. An exploration of X's revision of the tropes first presented in Wright and Ellison reveals new insight into notions of urban black male subjectivity and resistance.

In "How Bigger Was Born," Richard Wright asserts that African-Americans have responded in one of six ways to their oppression: the acquisition of religion, efforts at reform, the creation of new art forms, addiction to alcohol, formal education, and aimless rebellion. According to Wright formal education creates bourgeois race leaders; uneducated men like Bigger Thomas (and the personae of Brooks's "We Real Cool") act in aimless rebellion. Bigger revolts because he is estranged from the "safe spaces" of religion and folk culture and because he is "reacting to and answering the call of the dominant civilization" as it is set forth in newspapers, magazines, radios, and movies. In other words, the religion and folk culture prove to be too provincial, and the media create his desire for those things that the dominant society denies him: "Chicago . . . did so much more to dazzle the mind with a taunting sense of possible achievement that the segregation it did impose brought forth . . . a reaction more obstreperous than in the South."[40]

The dominant discourse, represented throughout the novel in advertisements, newspapers, and social service reports, constructs him as a troublesome, unintelligent, inferior being.[41] The movies and advertisements bombard him with images of power, wealth, and white women and in so doing create his desire for all of them. Throughout the text there is evidence of the manner in which the dominant discourse constructs Bigger. The social welfare organization constructs him as a good worker who is always in trouble. The discourse of this bureaucracy seeks to turn him into a good and efficient worker. "Using the analysis contained in the case record the relief sent to us, I think we should invoke an immediate feeling of confidence," says Mrs. Dalton. She and her husband act not on the real young man who stands before them but on the character that emerges from the pages of the relief records. Their efforts will include formal education so that he may enter the place that society holds for him and so that he might consider that place a desirable one. Their efforts differ from those of the Urban League in that the latter also fought for better living conditions, while the Daltons are the slumlords of the kitchenette apartment in which Bigger and his family live.

"The long strange words they used made no sense to him; it was another language. He felt from the tone of their voices. . . . It made him feel uneasy, tense, as though there were influences and presences about him which he could feel but not see" (p. 48). Here Bigger is confronted with a discourse that constructs him, but he also realizes that he has no access to understanding that discourse. At first this inability to understand makes his efforts at resisting it somewhat futile. When finally he does find a means of resisting it, through the construction of an alternative narrative, another more powerful and more destructive discourse emerges to contain him. The newspaper stories that cover his crime, his flight, his incarceration, and his trial establish him as the oversexed black beast.

Bigger's violent rebellion constitutes his efforts to create an alternative construction of himself. These efforts take place on three levels. The first occurs at the naive level of enacting petty crimes and his participation in manhood rituals of signifying and bullying his peers. In this instance signifying and street culture provide a space where he can claim verbal and physical authority denied him in the white world. These are all responses to his frustration at having no influence over a situation that controls him. "Let's play white," he says after watching a plane overhead. The closest he gets to holding the power of the white man is through this game, and yet inherent in the game is a critique of white people. In mimicking white people he parodies them. Here again, parody grants him a degree of verbal authority over whites. Bigger's desire to rob a white-owned store is another example of his aimless rebellion; however, fear paralyzes and prohibits him from following through on the plan. Instead he internalizes the pain and frustration of his desire by striking out at his friend Gus in the pool hall and establishing his power within this arena. He is feared and admired by his peers.

The dominant society denies him opportunity; however, it also creates his desire for access to what it denies him. This is evident in the construction of his desire for white women. Like Petry, Wright uses the cinema to illustrate the way that popular culture creates the desire for a mythological white woman and white society. The same movies that give images of white wealth and power also provide images of black savagery and primitivism:

> Two features were advertised: one, "The Gay Woman," was pictured on the posters in images of white men and women lolling on beaches, swimming and dancing in night clubs; the other, "Trader Horn," was shown on the posters in terms of black men and black women dancing against a wild background of barbaric jungle. [p. 32]

Bigger and his friend Jack, choose *The Gay Woman*. Initially they desire the white movie star sexually, but it soon becomes evident that the desire to possess her is linked with a desire to possess all that she represents for them: "I'd like to be invited to a place like that just to find out what it feels like," Bigger says. To which Jack responds, "Man, if them folks saw you, they'd run. . . . They'd think a gorilla broke loose from the zoo and put on a tuxedo" (p. 33). Here the two images displayed on the movie posters have helped Bigger and Jack construct an image of themselves in relation to the dominant white society. The cinematic representation is one which Bigger desires; as a spectator he attempts to place himself in the picture on the screen. This fantasy moment is ruptured by his own understanding, reinforced by Jack, that there is no place for him in that world, that, like the characters of *Trader Horn*, he is no more than a savage beast. Like the gorilla in the tuxedo, Bigger does not fit; he is awkward and out of place in the world portrayed by *The Gay Woman*. Note how he and Jack accept the racist construction of themselves as "gorillas." Bigger does not challenge or question Jack's use of the term. Instead of challenging the "gorilla" as a racist construct, Bigger fantasizes about the image of the white world presented on the screen. In his imagination he creates a space for himself in the context of the white narrative. In Bigger's imagined narrative possession of the white woman by the black chauffeur leads to the possession of white wealth and therefore a degree of white power.

While the dominant society creates his desire for opportunity and for access to white women, it also fills him with fear of acting on that desire. It is this deadly combination which leads him to murder Mary Dalton. As he attempts to put the drunken Mary to bed, "He leaned over her, excited, looking at her face in the dim light, not wanting to take his hands from her breasts. She tossed and mumbled sleepily. He tightened his fingers on her breasts, kissing her again, feeling her move toward him." When Mrs. Dalton enters the room, this desire manifests itself in fear. The fear and desire culminate in the enactment of a murder described in sexual terms:

> Frantically, he caught a corner of the pillow and brought it to her lips . . . he grew tight and full, as though about to explode. Mary's fingernails tore at his hands and he caught the pillow and covered her entire face with it, firmly. Mary's body surged upward and he pushed downward upon the pillow with all of his weight. . . . Mary's body heaved. . . .
>
> He clenched his teeth and held his breath. . . . His muscles flexed taut as steel and he pressed the pillow, feeling the bed give slowly, evenly, but silently. . . .
>
> *He relaxed and sank to the floor, his breath going in a long gasp. He was weak and wet with sweat. . . . Gradually, the intensity of his sensations subsided.* [pp. 84–86; emphasis added]

For the first time in his life, Bigger acts on his desire for a white woman. Because of the circumstances, it takes the form of murder and not sexual intercourse. The murder is described in very sexual language. He is "tight," "full," "about to explode." Her body "surges upward" to meet his downward pushes. The final sentences might have been used to describe Bigger after he achieved an orgasm. In contrast, Wright's description of Mary's body following the murder is especially significant: "Her mouth was open and her eyes bulged glassily" (p. 87). This sentence uses a very familiar description to describe an unfamiliar subject. The open mouth, the bulging eyes are descriptors used for lynched black bodies, echoing Billie Holiday's "the bulging eyes and the twisted mouth." The description is familiar to Wright's audience (much of which is made up of those same people to whom Holiday sang "Strange Fruit" at Cafe Society). The description is familiar, but the sex and race of the victim is different. In this one sentence, Wright turns centuries of terror experienced by black people on to whites. Here Wright does what Bigger will attempt to do. He claims the power of fear over whites through his manipulation of their language and signs of racial terror. Valerie Smith notes, "Not only do both Bigger and Wright rebel against the strictures of black and white authority, but both also rely on their ability to manipulate language and its assumptions—to tell their own stories—as a means of liberating themselves from the plots others impose on them."[42]

Because of the context in which Mary's murder takes place, this first murder, though not a conscious choice on Bigger's part, initiates the beginning of his own critical awareness of his life. The murder of Mary Dalton makes Bigger acutely aware of the mechanisms of power that dominate him and the means of his access to it.

Crime allows him to snatch a modicum of power from white people. It provides him his only access to this power:

> He felt a certain sense of power, a power born of a latent capacity to live. He was conscious of . . . the wealthy white people living in a smugness, a security, a certainty that he had never known. The knowledge that he had killed a white girl they loved and regarded as their symbol of beauty made him feel the equal of them, like a man who had been somehow cheated, but had now evened the score. [p. 155]

Here we have the true source of Bigger's desire for Mary. It is not for Mary as woman, but for Mary as symbol of that which he is denied. Her body becomes the means of acquiring power over her father. As he initiates each of his crimes, he gains a greater sense of clarity. Action and the ability to construct something heighten his intellectual sense, his own understanding of and disgust with the place society has created for him. Because the dominant society considers him incapable of conceiving of a plot to murder and/or kidnap Mary Dalton, he is able to strike his first significant blow to the power that affects him. Relying on their ignorance, Bigger is able to hide his guilt as well as demand ransom money.

Bigger's attempts to act on his own creativity are his most significant acts of rebellion. The writing of the phony ransom note is another creative effort linked to his crime. However, when he attempts to act upon this creativity, his black girlfriend, Bessie, threatens to thwart it. His second murder, the killing of Bessie, is another attempt to rebel against those things he thinks repress him. In killing Bessie, he strikes out against the stifling nature of black women as they appear in all of Wright's texts. Black women bind Bigger to a provincial racial past. Although he does have intercourse with Bessie prior to murdering her, it is not an act of desire; it is rape—an act of violence. The murder of Bessie is not described in terms of desire:

> Then he took a deep breath and his hand gripped the brick and shot upward and paused a second and then plunged downward through the darkness to the accompaniment of a deep short grunt from his chest and landed with a thud. *Yes!* There was a dull gasp of surprise, then a moan. No, that must not be! He lifted the brick again and again, until in falling it struck a sodden mass that gave softly but stoutly to each landing blow. Soon he seemed to be striking a wet wad of cotton, of some damp substance whose only life was the jarring of the brick's impact. He stopped, hearing his own breath heaving in and out of his chest. He was wet all over, and cold. How many times he had lifted the brick and brought it down, he did not know. All he knew was that the room was quiet and cold and that the job was done. [p. 222]

"Shot," "short grunt," and "thud" are not words of desire but words of violence. In contrast to the passage describing the murder of Mary, here Bessie does not respond to him. She is like a "wet wad of cotton." Intercourse is no longer the appropriate metaphor for murder. There is no desire for the black woman's body. If the language is at all sexual, it is the violent sexuality of a rape. Her murder is not a mistake; it is premeditated, calculated, and precise. Here he is no longer acting out of fear. He kills Bessie out of hate—hate for what she represents to

128

him as a black woman. "He hated his mother for that way of hers which was like Bessie's. What his mother had was Bessie's whiskey, and Bessie's whiskey was his mother's religion." The use of the sexual metaphor in the earlier murder suggested a distorted sense of human connection. With Bessie, this connection is completely dissolved. James A. Miller notes, "when Bigger rapes and murders Bessie, he effectively severs his ties to the black community. From this point in the novel until its conclusion, Bigger functions essentially as a soloist."[43]

As was the case with Mary's death, the murder of Bessie is followed by a greater consciousness, an intellectual and spiritual longing that becomes clearer with each crime Bigger commits:

> He did not want to sit on a bench and sing, or lie in a corner and sleep. It was when he read the newspapers or magazines, went to the movies, or walked along the streets with crowds, that he felt what he wanted: to merge himself with others and be part of this world, to lose himself in it so he could find himself, to be allowed a chance to live like others, even though he was black. [p. 226]

The language of this passage is exactly like that of *12 Million Black Voices*. Bigger aspires to the position of modern man as described in Wright's vision in the documentary text. Up to this point, he has not experienced such a clear understanding of that to which he aspires—the chance to participate in civilization with other modern men; a chance denied him by the dominant society and by what he perceives to be the provinciality of the text's black women. After each criminal act Bigger grows closer to a critical understanding of his actions.

As Bigger becomes a suspect in Mary's murder, a discourse emerges that creates him as an oversexed black beast. He becomes "some half-human black animal . . . climbing through the windows of [white] homes to rape murder, and burn [white] daughters" (p. 373).

It is this Bigger of the media who is pursued, captured, tried, and executed. The overwhelming state apparatus leaps to violence when it can no longer contain him through housing and discourse. Significantly, he is tried in the court and in the press for a crime he did not commit—the rape of Mary Dalton. The media-defined image of him sparks the lynch mob mentality of the Northern judicial system. Like the Daltons, who respond to the discursive Bigger, so too does the judicial system.[44] It is the image of black man as rapist of white women which is on trial, not Bigger Thomas. As was the case in the South, a black man's greatest crime is acting on his desire for white women. He is never tried for the rape and murder of Bessie.

While white society acts on the Bigger of their discourse, Bigger Thomas again attempts to create an alternative Bigger, a young man who, through the acquisition of a critical consciousness, faces and takes responsibility for his actions. However, Bigger realizes that this consciousness only makes him more intently aware of his predicament, without providing him a means to escape it. He comes to possess it too late to restructure the direction of his life:

Having been thrown by an accidental murder into a position where he had sensed a possible order and meaning in his relations with the people about him; having accepted the moral guilt and responsibility for that murder because it had made him feel free for the first time in his life; having felt in his heart some obscure need to be at home with people and having demanded ransom money to enable him to do it—having done all this and failed, he chose not to struggle any more. With a supreme act of will springing from the essence of his being, he turned away from his life and the long train of disastrous consequences that had flowed from it and looked wistfully upon the dark face of ancient waters upon which some spirit had breathed and created him, the dark face of the waters from which he had been first made in the image of a man with a man's obscure need and urge; feeling that he wanted to sink back into those waters and rest eternally. [p. 255]

Like thousands of black men imprisoned in America's jails, Bigger is one who possesses a critical intelligence and the restless energy to act upon it. However, the society in which he lives provides little opportunity for him; in fact, it seeks to crush his spirit and drive. The only realm Wright makes available to him is the criminal realm, which thrusts him further outside society. Here he experiences a sense of resignation that comes about as a result of his recognition of the futility of "hope." Like Ciel, he travels over ancient waters which obliterate the boundaries of race; unlike her, he travels there not to be reborn, but to die.

In Bigger's world "safe" domestic space is female—stifling and provincial—capable only of creating complacent black subjects. Formal education is denied him, and if he had access to it Wright believes it might have produced a petty bourgeois race leader, like those who ultimately fail him. The acquisition of a critical consciousness comes too late to affect his life in any significant way.

Of the male artists considered here, only Ralph Ellison suggests the significance and importance of safe spaces and ancestors to his migrant protagonist.[45] Though Invisible Man tends to ignore them, the reader knows that this naive dismissal is to his detriment. In many ways Invisible Man is the male counterpart to Ann Petry's Lutie. Safe space is available to him throughout the narrative in the form of ancestors and elders: the grandfather and the veteran in the South and Mary, Petie Wheatstraw, and Brother Tarp in the North. He always greets them with "Why?" "What does this mean?" He blindly follows those characters that embody the stranger, especially Bledsoe and Brother Jack, a literal stranger he meets in the crowd.

Invisible Man mistakes distance from ancestors for critical intelligence. He does not realize that his "education" is an empty one if it denies the importance and significance of the wisdom embodied in the text's ancestral figures. Because Bledsoe and Brother Jack speak to his ambition, he mistakenly believes them capable of informing his critical consciousness. He follows their advice while ignoring that of those who possess wisdom.

Shortly after his arrival in New York, the protagonist meets a blues-singing pushcart man, Petie Wheatstraw. Immediately the man's song takes him back home: "It was a blues and I walked along behind him remembering the times that I had heard such singing at home. It seemed that here some memories slipped around my life at the campus and went far back to things I had long ago shut out of my mind. There was no escaping such reminders."[46] Instead of finding comfort in something familiar, Invisible Man hears the blues as the remnant of a past he seeks to escape. Unlike the migrants of the last chapter, who sought solace and comfort in blues performances, he is annoyed by them. By the end of the novel, Invisible Man learns to find safe space in black music.

Wheatstraw tries to engage Invisible Man in a dialogue whose language he cannot understand: "What I want to know is, is you got the dog. . . . Now I know you from down home, how come you trying to ack [*sic*] like you never heard that before! Hell, ain't nobody out here this morning but us colored—Why you trying to deny me?" asks Wheatstraw. The narrator notes, "I wanted to leave him, and yet I found a certain comfort in walking along beside him" (p. 172). The comfort is that of safe space: through his use of a black vernacular Wheatstraw invokes a coded language with which Invisible Man should be familiar. Like Lutie, Invisible Man senses the value the man's presence has for him, but he is unable to rationalize it sufficiently. Instead, he asks, "What does it mean?"

This question, "What does it mean?" is Invisible Man's constant refrain. He is ambitious and somewhat pretentious. He feels that in order to reach his goal of leadership, he must shun those elements that bind him to a racial past. While he seeks to lead black people, it is an empty aspiration that fails to recognize the value of racial wisdom. Nowhere is this contradiction more evident than in his relationship with Mary, the black woman who takes him in when he decides to stay in New York.

Mary's home, especially her cooking, provides him with safe space, a space that he values but finds suffocating. When he is approached by the Brotherhood to join their ranks—requiring that he put his past behind him—he thinks, "What a vast difference between Mary and those for whom I was leaving her. And why should it be this way, that the very job which might make it possible for me to do some of the things which she expected of me required that I leave her?" (p. 315). If he is to represent Mary's interest, it seems he ought to maintain contact with her. However, once again, he fails to recognize the significance of his own question and instead he asserts the stifling nature of people like Mary. "They seldom know where their personalities end and yours begins; they usually think in terms of 'we' while I have always tended to think in terms of 'me'—and that has caused some friction even with my own family." Again Ellison demonstrates Invisible Man's fatal flaw. He possesses the ability to raise crucial questions, but he fails time and again to adequately address them. Instead, he pushes the questions aside with substantive, un-self-reflective assertions that justify his empty ambition. For Invisible Man the stifling provinciality of race is illustrated by Mary's kitchen—an important metaphor for the apronstrings of race.

That Ellison is critical of Invisible Man is evident throughout the text as well as in the story "Out of the Hospital and under the Bar." The story, first published in Herbert Hill's 1963 anthology *Soon One Morning*, was to have been the Mary chapter of Ellison's novel. According to Ellison, the chapter—which illustrates Mary's pivotal role of freeing the protagonist from the surveillance of the hospital—was removed at the suggestion of the publisher. Ellison later wrote, "[Harlem] was Mary's world, the world of the urbanized (or partially urbanized) Negro folk, and I found it quite pleasurable to discover, during those expansive days of composition before the necessities of publication became a reality, that it was Mary, a woman of the folk, who helped to release the hero from the machine."[47]

In the short story Invisible Man demonstrates the same ignorance of Mary's importance that he shows throughout the novel. This ignorance does not inhibit his aspiration to leadership; in fact, it fosters it. His aspiration to black leadership consistently removes him further and further from those he is supposed to represent. He first aspires to a position of racial manager like Bledsoe; later he is selected by and groomed through the Brotherhood. This grooming prepares him to be leader as stranger—a stranger with the appearance of kinship. "You shall be the new Booker T. Washington, but even greater than he" (p. 307), Brother Jack tells him. In order to acquire this status, he is told, "You must put aside your past" (p. 309). The final act in their construction of him is a new name: "Remember your new identity" (p. 310).

The nature of his leadership role and his new name link him to a past and a history from which he hopes to distance himself. On the one hand, the trope of a new white-given name and the loss of his past are used here to signify his slave status. On the other hand, his position of leadership is no different from that created by white people in the post-Reconstruction South and embodied in the figure of Washington. In making this connection, Ellison provides the reader with a sense of historical continuity. However, it is a continuity of which Invisible Man remains ignorant.

When he accepts the name given him by the Brotherhood, the memory of his grandfather emerges to remind him of this history and to warn him: "The thing to do was to be prepared—as my grandfather had been when it was demanded that he quote the entire United States Constitution as a test of his fitness to vote. He had confounded them all by passing the test although they refused him the ballot. . . . Anyway, these were different" (p. 315). Once again, Invisible Man raises and ignores the important question embodied in the memory of his grandfather's experience with those white people who established poll taxes. Like Lutie, he fails to heed his grandfather's advice. In fact, he misinterprets it. His grandfather's example is to not only be prepared for the test that white people place before you, but also (and this is most important) to be prepared when they still deny you even after you have passed it. The "prepared" of his grandfather's advice is not to be prepared to perform—as Invisible Man mistakenly believes—

but to be prepared for white people's continued refusal to allow a black man equal access.

In joining the ranks of the Brotherhood, Invisible Man suppresses all aspects of the ancestor even though he knows that the only real promise of successful resistance lay in the possession of ancestral perspectives. "Perhaps the part of me that observed listlessly but saw all, missing nothing, was still the malicious, arguing part, the dissenting voice, my grandfather part, the cynical, disbelieving part—the traitor self that always threatened internal discord. Whatever it was, I knew that I had to keep it pressed down" (p. 335). Invisible Man denies that which would inform a critical consciousness. His "grandfather part" would help him negotiate all of the situations in which he finds himself. As he gets more deeply entrenched in the Brotherhood, he more readily dismisses his grandfather. "For a moment I thought of my grandfather and quickly dismissed him. What had an old slave to do with humanity?" (p. 354). His grandfather, an old slave like Toomer's Father John, is an ancestor like Lutie's grandmother who survives in his memory and who has everything to do with humanity.

Instead of realizing that the ancestor holds the key to his sustenance, he chooses to exploit white women to gain power and control over white men. He claims to use them as a tool of resistance. In his first encounter with a nameless white woman, Invisible Man is forced to face his own fear and desire. "I was headed for the door, torn between anger and a fierce excitement" (p. 416). Unlike Bigger, his encounter does end in intercourse. The white woman is sexually assertive, using the Brotherhood as a point of entrée for articulating her desire for him. Though Ellison makes explicit her seductive intentions, Invisible Man does not recognize them until she blatantly ushers him into her bedroom and removes her clothing. In this instance, his grandfather's advice would have been useful, if only he had understood it. While he is "prepared" to perform, he is not prepared for the compromising situation in which she places him. As she lies in his arms in a postcoital slumber, her husband returns home. Invisible Man is surprised when he is able to escape without incident. Still, he is unable to answer the crucial question he raises: "Why did they insist upon confusing the class struggle with the ass struggle, debasing both us and them—all human motives?" (p. 418).

By his second encounter, he is better "prepared" to read the signals being thrown him by another white woman, Sybil. This time, he wishes to take advantage of her in order to gain access to information about the Brotherhood, an organization of which he is now skeptical. She requests that he indulge her in a rape fantasy, the very suggestion of which brings fear and images of lynching to his mind. This time, he has no desire for her. Instead, white men have created her desire for him, by creating the stereotype of black male sexuality and then making relations between black men and white women taboo. In this instance, Invisible Man does not indulge the white woman; instead he intoxicates her and leads her to believe that her fantasies have been fulfilled.

Having done this, he begins to pump her for information about her husband. It is not long before he realizes that his grand scheme is a dud. Sybil "had no idea of the schemes that occupied her husband night and day." Although he is "prepared" to manipulate her fantasies, again, he is not prepared for what has always been the case—she provides him no access to the power that controls his destiny.

By the end of the text, Invisible Man has been constructed as a false leader of black people. Though he seeks to resist this construction, he fails to utilize the power of the ancestor and the elders. Reflecting on his failed career from his underground refuge, he finally realizes his grandfather's humanity: "Hell, he never had any doubts about his humanity—that was left to his 'free' offspring. He accepted his humanity" (p. 580). Situated underground, at his greatest physical distance from the ancestor, he finally becomes closest to him. This closeness to his grandfather is embodied in Invisible Man's ability to finally understand the language of another ancestor—the music of Louis Armstrong. In the prologue he says: "I want to feel [the music's] vibration, not only with my ear but with my whole body. I'd like to hear five recordings of Louis Armstrong playing and singing 'What did I do to be so Black and Blue'—all at the same time" (p. 8). Robert Stepto notes that here Invisible Man moves beyond "embracing the music" to hearing and claiming that music.[48] To both feel and hear is a distinct contrast to his hearing the ancestor but not listening to it. By hearing and feeling he can experience the music (and the history and culture it embodies) as safe space, a space like Naylor's ritual space where one has

> a slightly different sense of time, you're never quite on the beat. Sometimes you're ahead and sometimes behind. Instead of the swift and imperceptible flowing of time you are aware of its nodes, those points where time stands still or from which it leaps ahead. And you slip into the breaks and look around. That's what you hear vaguely in Louis' music. [p. 8]

Interestingly, in the epilogue, Invisible Man tells us: "Gin, jazz, and dreams were not enough." As was the case with the women of Brewster Place, "safe space" and "safe time" are necessary components for healing and coming to terms with one's history; however, in and of themselves they are not acts of resistance.

In creating Invisible Man, a Negro leader who distances himself from racial history, Ellison suggest that such leadership is the construction of whites who do not have the best interest of black people at hand. Malcolm X offers an alternative conception of black leadership, one that is constructed in radical resistance to the dominant society.

Alex Haley's Malcolm X is aware of his naïveté and of the control white society has exerted over him. *The Autobiography* is a constant commentary on white dominance as well as a documentation of the various ways Malcolm attempts to resist it. While Richard Wright documents the failure of an attempt to construct an alternative self, Haley uses some of the same cultural tropes to illustrate a successful attempt, one that also leads to a violent death but that ultimately leaves behind a legacy that acts as an alternative space for a younger generation of black people. The image of Malcolm X refuses to die and remains a space where contemporary urban black men can create their own sense of identity in contrast to the construction of them by the dominant society.[49]

For Malcolm X the street provides an alternative for the creation of an urban identity in stark contrast to that of white racists or of black middle-class organizations like the Urban League. Within his narrative, the Northern safe space of home is but an agent for the socializing work done by these organizations. He values the street over the provinciality and stifling atmosphere of the middle-class-defined safe spaces. This is something he seems to share with Wright, who dismisses homespaces as viable alternatives to oppression. He too seems to think that the street life provides a resisting alternative.[50] However, unlike Wright, the preconversion Malcolm sees safe space in the culture of the street, especially in its night life and music.

Finally, for Wright and Ellison lack of access to white women is a fundamental aspect of the limitations placed on their freedom. For Malcolm X desiring and acquiring white women is primarily evidence of the hold white society has on black men. The dominant society produces desire for white women and then punishes those who act on it. For Wright and Ellison to act on that desire is an act of defiance. For Malcolm X it is an act of compliance. In his autobiography, white women become consumable objects.

"I looked like Li'l Abner. Mason, Michigan, was written all over me."[51] So opens the "'Homeboy'" chapter of Malcolm X's autobiography. His body is the text on which his country status is written. The signs of this identity include "kinky, reddish hair . . . cut in hick style" and a green suit that is too small. The chapter "'Homeboy'" painstakingly details his transformation from Midwestern hick to Boston hipster. The name Homeboy is one of the many titles he earns during the course of his life. It is the name given to him by Shorty, a street-smart man he meets in Boston, who befriends and mentors him. Like Malcolm, Shorty also migrates from Lansing, Michigan. In the context of the street life, Homeboy becomes a term of affection, a symbol of friendship, a "safe space" not unlike Mattie's use of Tut to identify her friend Etta in *The Women of Brewster Place*.

The homeboy period serves as his high school education in the street life. It is followed by the "college" of Harlem, where his edges are smoothed and his skills sharpened. Finally, the intense graduate training of the Charlestown State Prison completes his education. His early education allows him to resist the disciplinary efforts of his middle-class sister Ella. Instead, he surrenders to the discipline of the street. The prison stay initiates his critical awareness but leads to his surrender to the discipline of the Nation of Islam.[52]

Ella's disciplinary work begins in her provision of domestic safe space, homespace. Upon arriving in Boston, Malcolm immediately goes to Ella's house and here begins the process of balancing and nurturing in her "Georgia"-style kitchen: "She was truly a Georgia Negro woman when she got into the kitchen with her pots and pans. She was the kind of cook who would heap up your plate with such as ham hock, greens, black-eyed peas, fried fish, cabbage, sweet potatoes, grits and gravy, and cornbread. . . . I worked out at Ella's kitchen table like there was no tomorrow (p. 39). Like Ellison's Mary, Ella uses food to physically nourish the young Malcolm and also provides him with safe space by invoking the South through her culinary skills. While Malcolm eagerly partakes of her food, he finds her other, more disciplinary work less appetizing. Like Christian missions that provide balanced meals and follow them with attempts to convert those in attendance, Ella encourages Malcolm to "mingle with nice young people" in her neighborhood. He responds by progressively seeking company with the poorer blacks down the hill.

For Malcolm, it is immediately clear that the middle-class blacks of "the Hill" are middle class in affected manner only: "Eight out of ten of the Hill Negroes of Roxbury, despite the impressive-sounding job titles they affected [*sic*] actually worked as menials and servants" (p. 41). This class of blacks appears to be the same class that Dorothy West portrays in *The Living Is Easy*. In stark contrast, Malcolm found the poorer blacks were "Negroes who were being their natural selves and not putting on airs" (p. 43).

Although Malcolm X is aware of the control white society has in shaping the desires and aspirations of the black middle class, at first he is not as aware of its control on those with whom he identifies. Like the daughter of Bonner's "The Whipping," he straightens his hair. The tortuous "conk scene" illustrates the length to which he goes in order to imitate his oppressor. After his humorous description of the process where kinky hair is burned into submission with lye, Malcolm notes:

> This was my first really big step toward self-degradation: when I endured all of that pain, literally burning my flesh to have it look like a white man's hair. I had joined that multitude of Negro men and women in America who are brainwashed into believing that the black people are "inferior"—and white people "superior"—that they will even violate and mutilate their God-created bodies to try to look "pretty" by white standards. [p. 54]

The street life embodies a love–hate relationship with the dominant white society. Efforts to resist are thwarted by an unconscious aspiration to "whiteness." The first step toward initiation into the street life is the acquisition of a new language: stud, cat, chick, cool, hip: "Every night as I lay in bed I turned these new words over in my mind. It was shocking to me that in town, especially after dark, you'd occasionally see a white girl and a Negro man strolling arm in arm" (p. 43). In his consciousness, he juxtaposes a new language with the possession of white women. While to walk openly with a white woman is an act of defiance of American racial norms, the obsessive desire for white women documented by X is the direct result of the white society's power in shaping the desires of those it oppresses. Many black women and men desire white women. Some black women desire to look and live like the popular images of white women and some black men desire sexual possession of these same images. The black subject who successfully resists such a desire does so in the face of constant efforts to undermine him or her. At this moment in the text, Malcolm X has not yet reached this latter point of resistance.

Malcolm X illustrates the manner in which black peoples' bodies become inscribed with the power of their oppressors, not in the form of scars and dismemberment, but in the form of a self-inflicted discipline which quite literally "tames all the anger down," as Gwendolyn Brooks so eloquently describes straightening black hair.[53] As long as he is willing to undergo this process, he is not willing to reject the standards of white society. While he may consider himself a resisting subject, in that he participates in illegal activities of the street—he sells marijuana, gambles, and eventually steals in order to support his drug habit—he is controlled by the dominant white society without it ever laying a hand on him.

The great quest for whiteness does not stop here. Its ultimate fulfillment in the streetspace is the acquisition of a white woman. This gains him respect among hicks and hustlers alike. It is also the factor which accounts for the severity of his punishment when he is arrested years later. His union with a white woman, Sophia, causes him to be given five times the standard prison sentence for burglary. The social service system that is supposed to come to his aid, the judicial system, and the prosecuting attorney all seek to punish him for his flagrant association with a white woman. To possess a white woman openly is a blow to the dominant white society, but to desire one in the way that Malcolm's friend Shorty does is to be bound by this very society: "Shorty was so obsessed with the white girl that even if the lights were out, he would pull up the shade to be able to see that white flesh by the street lamp from outside" (p. 145). Shorty's obsession with white skin serves as a mental prison.

Unlike Invisible Man, who sought to use a white woman for access to white men, Malcolm X eventually uses Sophia for financial gain. His desire for her is not for her as a person, but as a symbol and a means to counter his frustrations with white men. By emotionally and physically abusing her, he claims to "possess" her. He believes that his possession of a beautiful white woman is indicative of defiant resistance as well as acceptance of white male definitions of manhood. When his domination over Sophia comes to the attention of white authorities, he is severely punished. Instead of being lynched, as he would be in the South, he is sent to the Charlestown State Prison. There is a particular irony in his prison sentence. While it is the ultimate method, second only to death, of controlling a resisting subject, in this context it helps to create one. In prison Malcolm begins the pursuit of knowledge that will eventually free his psyche from the reins of white power:

> I found books like Will Durant's *Story of Civilization*. I read H. G. Wells'
> *Outline of History*. *Souls Of Black Folk* by W. E. B. Du Bois gave me a glimpse

into the black people's history before they came to this country. Carter G. Woodson's *Negro History* opened my eyes about black empires before the black slave was brought to the United States, and the early Negro struggles for freedom. . . . I will never forget how shocked I was when I began reading about slavery's total horror. It made such an impact upon me that it later became one of my favorite subjects. . . . The world's most monstrous crime, the sin and the blood on the white man's hands, are almost impossible to believe. [p. 175]

During his prison stay, Malcolm X retreats into himself, he studies, he reads, and he begins to prepare for the leadership role that awaits him. This period marks the true beginning of his construction of himself as a resistant agent. Along with this study he starts a correspondence with Elijah Muhammad, who becomes his spiritual and intellectual mentor. While at first he is equally controlled by the power of this black demigod, he eventually escapes this as well and emerges as an individually thinking subject, capable of resistance and leadership.[54] He undergoes the same kind of reflection, study, and meditation on his trip to Mecca, which further leads to his independence from Elijah Muhammad.

Only after this myriad of experiences does Malcolm X become a leader independent of Elijah Muhammad. He is not elected and he is not chosen by whites, but he is accepted by his poor, urban black constituency because he has proven himself on their terms. Unlike Bigger, Malcolm X gains a critical consciousness of America's racism in time to share an analysis of it with other African-Americans. Unlike Invisible Man, he never distances himself from the majority of black people. Instead, like Toomer's Lewis, he is a man with the courage of his convictions; but Malcolm X offers a challenge not only to whites but to the Black Muslims from whom he arises. These challenges lead to his death.

Leadership is here defined quite differently than in Wright or Ellison. Because Malcolm X's road to a critical consciousness includes stopovers in street-space and prison and not formal education, he emerges as an alternative, resisting black male leader. He is not vulnerable to the compromising efforts of the power structure.

Malcolm X closes his text with the prophetic prediction of his own violent death. This prophecy affirms his understanding of the power of the dominant society to stop those who transcend efforts to construct them and create their own resisting subjectivities. Interestingly, Malcolm X is murdered by those people whom he assumed offered him safe space. When he ventures from the confines of that space he suffers their wrath. This is an extreme example of the negative possibilities of safe spaces. In this context, "safe space" is so stifling that one risks death in the attempt to leave it.

Although Malcolm X was murdered by an act of black violence, violence was also done to his legacy by the dominant society in attempting to deny his place in history. In so doing, it sought to ensure that no other would rise to his example.

Interestingly, the link between his assassins and the racial powers that be has not yet been firmly established or denied, so we still cannot determine the extent to which the American government might have been involved in his death. Malcolm X's life and death continue to carry a legacy of radical black male subjectivity. He has become the resisting ancestor to whom younger generations of urban blacks consistently return.

It is quite significant that X's role of ancestor is most evident in black popular culture, because it is this very culture that served as "safe space" for him during his homeboy days. Swing bands, jazz stars, and lindy hopping all serve as moments of cultural pleasure and affirmation of black humanity for Malcolm Little. Though he never implies that these spaces are resistant spaces, he acknowledges the significance of them in sustaining a sense of community and joy. In fact, in his renunciation of dance and night life, he seems to suggest that partaking of it is antithetical to resistance.[55] The Malcolm who denies the resistant capacities of black popular culture is the same Malcolm who is resurrected in the most influential form of that culture, film and rap music. Many of the rap artists who resurrect him would claim that by so doing, they are indeed acting in resistance to black oppression.

V

Don't push me, 'cause I'm close to the edge."

Grandmaster Flash and the Furious Five, *The Message*

Excerpts from Malcolm X's "Ballot or the Bullet" speech frame the opening and closing of the rap song "Self-Destruction," the anthem of the Stop the Violence Movement. The movement is an effort of hip-hop's most progressive artists, in conjunction with the Urban League, to discourage black-on-black violence (particularly at rap concerts) and an attempt to reclaim and redefine streetspace. Like Malcolm X, the rap and the Urban League book that accompanies it[56] attempt to provide young African-Americans with a critical awareness of their history, in their own language, on their own grounds. This is indeed a departure from earlier Urban League efforts outlined at the opening of this chapter. It is not an attempt to create "complacent" black subjects, but to inform young African-Americans. While the lyrics and the text do seek to contain aimless, self-directed rebellion, they also seek to turn that energy into more constructive ways of resisting racial oppression.

Much media attention has been given to those rap lyrics that encourage gang violence and the abuse of black women. Rhymes by the Ghetto Boyz, Dr. Dre, and Snoop Doggy Dog are indeed reflective of the street culture from which rap emerges. However, the rappers of "Stop the Violence" as well as a growing number of other hip-hop artists constitute another strain. Public Enemy, KRS-One, Arrested Development, Salt and Pepa, Queen Latifah, MC Lyte, and Me'Shell NdegéOcello all create raps of resisting discourses: Two examples are black nationalism and black feminism. They espouse doctrines of self-determination, education, and social responsibility not unlike those espoused by Malcolm X. His legacy is central to all of them. His words and image are peppered throughout their rhymes; his image graces their videos.

Just as rap groups "sample" earlier black musical artists as a means of paying homage to them, they also "sample" Malcolm X's speeches.[57] While it often seems that the revival of interest in Malcolm X has only ensured that his image become a consumable object, it has also assured his place in the pantheon of cultural icons revered by young urban blacks.[58]

Few have spoken to the urban context in which these young people find themselves. More than ever they battle with the complexity of urban power, with fewer and fewer spaces available to them to gain a critical consciousness that would help them understand and escape the morass that ensnares their lives. Like those who came before them, they are in search of means to negotiate the urban landscape. For some, rap provides a possible map. In some cases it has become their safe space. The Stop the Violence Movement seeks to reclaim the spaces of rap as safe spaces which nurture and inform rap's primary constituency. As is always the case, the terms of the space are contested and the conflict is yet to be resolved.

Like the efforts of rap artists, the tropes which are used to represent the Southern migrant's attempt to negotiate the urban landscape undergo significant revision throughout the period considered. The earlier narratives of both male and female authors portray this process as one leading directly to the destruction of the protagonist. There is little or no use of safe space as a place of resistance. The middle narratives focus on the possibilities of ancestors and safe space, but they give us protagonists who dismiss their value. The late narratives—one setting the standard for sixties-era urban male narratives, the other responding to these during the feminist-influenced decades following the Black Power and Civil Rights movements—show the possibility of constructing an alternative black self through the use of migrant-defined spaces but warn us against any utopian notions of complete resistance and survival. The manner in which the protagonists negotiate this process is deeply affected by gender.

While the earlier narratives are fully aware of the subtlety and sophistication of modern power, of its ability to construct subjects through the creation of discourse and desire, they do not provide successful models of resistance. *The Autobiography of Malcolm X* and *The Women of Brewster Place* provide us with two very different attempts at resistance. Malcolm X asserts the necessity of a historically grounded critical consciousness for the emergence of a resisting subject. Gloria Naylor asserts the necessity of participation in nurturing female spaces for the emergence of a surviving one. Neither provides us with a realization of their alternative worldviews; instead they stress the necessity of working for it. However, because Malcolm X is assassinated in an urban ballroom (an alternative space) by black assassins, and because the women of Brewster Place leave only for other ghetto streets or to "ascend" into an unwelcoming world that continues to treat them as daughters of a despised race, the vision of the city remains a pessimistic one.

Similarly, the majority of socially conscious rappers join the authors of the migration narratives in creating an image of the urban landscape like that described by Grand Master Flash's classic "The Message":

> Broken glass everywhere—people pissin on the stairs
> You know they just don't care
> I can't take the smell—I can't take the noise
> Got no money to move out—I guess I got no choice
> Rats in the front room—roaches in the back
> Junkies in the alley with a baseball bat
> I tried to get away but I couldn't get far
> Cause a man with a tow truck repossessed my car.[59]

Here, as is the case with Richard Wright and Ann Petry, we have an image of a closed-in world from which there is no escape. As readers of the metanarrative of migration, we are left wondering: "Where do we go from here?"

4

To Where from Here?
The Final Vision of the
Migration Narrative

In 1973 Gladys Knight and the Pips answered the question "To Where from Here?" with the anthem of black countermigration, "Midnight Train to Georgia." The song, written by James Weatherly and released by Motown, was on *Billboard*'s rhythm and blues charts for eighteen weeks. On August 5, 1973, the song peaked at number one, a position it held for four weeks. It also reached number one on the pop charts. Like the trains of earlier spirituals and blues, the midnight train to Georgia is also bound to "a different place in time," but unlike its precursors, this train is headed South. It is not the first to do so; southbound blues songs were recorded in the early twenties. But "Midnight Train to Georgia" is the first post–Civil Rights Movement song to accompany the growing number of blacks and to document possible reasons for their return to the South:

(Parentheses indicate the Pips's background vocals, which alternate from call to response throughout.)

<blockquote>

L.A. proved too much for the man
(Too much for the man. He couldn't make it)
So he's leaving life, he's come to know.
(He said he's going)
He said he's going back to find.
(Going back to find)
What's left of his world,
A world he left behind
Not so long ago.
He's leaving,
(Leaving)
On that Midnight Train to Georgia.
(Leaving on the Midnight train)
Said he's going back to a simpler place in time.
(Guess you're gonna be right by his side)
I'll be with him
(I know you will)

</blockquote>

> On that Midnight Train to Georgia.
> (Midnight Train to Georgia . . . Hoo-Hooo)
> I'd rather live in his world, than live without him in mine.
> (Live in his world. World, World, its his. His and hers.)
> He kept dreaming, that someday he'd be a star.
> (A superstar but he didn't get far)
> But he sure found out the hard way
> That dreams don't always come true
> So he turned all his hopes
> And he even sold his car
> Bought a one way ticket back
> To the life he once knew. . . .
> [*CHORUS*]
> On a board the midnight train
> To Go
> My world, his world, our world
> My man, his girl
> I got to go, I got to go.[1]

Consider three striking aspects of the lyrics of the song. First, the mention of racial or economic oppression is virtually absent. The narrative tells of the failure of the migrant in the city (a Western metropolis). Second, the South is romanticized as "a simpler place in time." And third, the female persona's almost antifeminist assertions appear in a song released at the beginning of the black feminist literary movement. Throughout, the South is a haven where the failed migrant might heal from his failure. The city is a place of failed dreams and lost hope.

Musically, the song follows in the tradition of African-American oral culture. The background vocals of the Pips act to comment upon, add to, support, and suggest the lead vocals of Gladys Knight as well as onomatopoetically suggesting the train. Technically, the song has no claims to musical innovations like Stevie Wonder's "Living for the City." Its significance lies in the story that it tells and the manner in which it tells it. "Midnight Train to Georgia" heralds the return migration of thousands of African-Americans to the South. It also makes claims for a South that was a simpler place without acknowledging the racism and the horror of the Southern past. "Simpler place in time" mimics Toomer's timeless canefield. The song furthers this notion of simplicity by asserting a return to traditional gender roles where the good woman follows her man to "his world" (which becomes her world), where he is her man and she his "girl."

In an attempt to construct the South as the safe space of return for African-Americans "Midnight Train to Georgia" fails to confront the reality of the racist past of the American South; it also suggests that the South is free of the problems that plague Northern, Western, and Midwestern cities.

The tendency to romanticize the South and return migration is evident in mainstream American culture as well. However, American popular culture departs from the tendency of African-American lore in that its romanticization of the South is part of a nostalgic longing for the "good old days" of the American South: The award-winning *Driving Miss Daisy*, the sleeper movie hit *Fried Green Tomatoes*, the fiftieth anniversary of the publication of *Gone with the Wind* and the subsequent enormous commercial popularity of its sequel, *Scarlett*, are all evidence of America's need to escape into a past that never was.

During the 1991–92 television season, the credit sequence of CBS's Monday-night hit *Designing Women* opens with Ray Charles, seated at a black piano, singing one of his signature tunes, "Georgia on My Mind." Charles is surrounded by the four designing women: Annie Potts, Julia Duffy, Dixie Carter, and Jan Hooks. All of them are situated seductively around the piano. Dressed in elegant but sexy gowns, each woman offers an inviting glance and suggestive smile to the camera and thus to millions of American viewers. At the head of the piano sits another black male, the otherwise desexualized leading man, Meshach Taylor, "Anthony."[2] In the opening sequence, Taylor is given his only opportunity for an explicitly sexual persona, as he too peers suggestively into the camera. The visual imagery combined with Charles's soulful rendering of "Georgia" emphatically states, "This is the New South." Four sensual Southern white women, two black men in the same room, joined by their love of Atlanta, Georgia.

This rendering of the song contrasts with an earlier recording. When Charles first recorded Hoagy Carmichael's "Georgia on My Mind" in 1964, it was one song on an album filled with sentimental, nostalgic songs about various Southern states. The Charles of *Designing Women* sings the song in the state of Georgia with four white women. In 1964, the state itself can be only "an old sweet song in [his] mind"—a safe space to which he nostalgically retreats in his imagination, but a physical site to which he cannot return. Billie Holiday and Ethel Waters also recorded "Georgia," and their versions, like Charles's evoke a sad nostalgia about a beautiful place, a homeland of sorts to which they cannot return. One need only listen to Holiday singing while reading the portion of her autobiography that deals with the South to appreciate the irony of her performance.[3]

Designing Women attempts to portray a New South where traditional racial and gender roles have disappeared. The women are independent, feminine, feminist; they consistently challenge the conventional status quo. Nonetheless, with a continued stress on the charm and gracious sensibility of the South, they are not above evoking romanticized visions about the place and its history.[4] In so doing the show participates in a current tendency to romanticize a mythic Southern past.

The trend toward romanticizing the Southern past is in many ways a reflection of some very real social changes that have occurred there over the past twenty years. While the significant changes in the South do warrant a new attitude about race relations, they in no way warrant the uncritical stance currently being taken in American popular culture.

The romanticization of a Southern past combined with the changes in race relations that occurred in the South following the Civil Rights Movement and the violent chaos of Northern cities have contributed to a very real reconsideration of the South on the part of African-Americans. In May 1945, *Negro Digest* published the results of a survey of black and white Americans about the South. A roundtable focusing on attitudes about the South followed the survey results. The question "Are race relations improving in the South?" was answered as follows:

Resepondents	Yes	No	Undecided
Northern whites	54%	21%	25%
Northern blacks	31%	49%	20%
Southern blacks	35%	39%	26%

Clearly in 1945, there was not an overwhelming sense that things were better in the South for black people. In fact, in 1945, African-Americans were still migrating out of the South. The *Negro Digest* survey stated that blacks in the North and West "felt that race relations were getting worse in Dixie. Much of this belief stems from the treatment of Northern Negro soldiers in the South." According to the survey, "Among Southern Negroes, unofficial repressive measures in a number of cities by police in using vagrancy and draft laws against colored citizens were cited . . . as a sign of worsening racial tensions."[5] Perhaps the clearest evidence of black attitudes about the South is reflected in the continuing large numbers of those black Southerners who migrated north.

In his portion of the roundtable discussion, "What the Negro Thinks of the South," noted journalist and satirist George S. Schuyler asserted the ambivalence blacks felt toward the area:

> Their thoughts about Dixie are similar to the opinion of Jews about Germany. They love the South (especially if they are Southern-born) for its beauty, its climate, its fecundity and its better ways of life; but they hate, with a bitter corroding hatred, the color prejudice, the discrimination, the violence, the crudities, the insults and humiliations, and the racial segregation of the South, and they hate all those who keep these evils alive.[6]

According to Schuyler, "A Negro who migrates South is as rare as a Jew seeking transportation to Berlin."

Today, it is not so rare to find a black person who migrates south. Features in the *Philadelphia Inquirer* and the *New York Times*,[7] as well as segments on the "Today Show," have focused on the trend of black middle-class families returning to the South or moving there for the first time. Between 1975 and 1989 the net migration of blacks to the South from the rest of the country totaled 637,000. According to the *Times* article, the "South's new blacks find comfort laced with strain."

The changes that have occurred in the South since the Civil Rights Movement, a sense of the tradition, history, and values embodied there, combined with the rising crime and cost of living in Northern cities, are all offered as reasons for the large return migration to the South over the past fifteen years. African-American literature and music have anticipated and embodied the tendencies evident in the countermigration. Prior to the Civil Rights Movement, the dominant images of a Northern black's return were embodied in the beaten and bruised body of the fourteen-year-old Emmett Till. In the midst of the movement, the murder of civil rights workers James Chaney, Andrew Goodman, and Michael Schwerner was continued proof of the South's reputation.

The decades of the seventies and eighties found black writers and literary critics participating in a reconsideration of the South and of black folk culture. The view of the South as a place of possibility is apparent in the renewed attention given to the works of Zora Neale Hurston and in the most recently published migration narratives. This is indicative not only of a tendency to romanticize the South, but also of an attempt to reconsider its significance to black people, an attempt that in many ways would have proven futile prior to the Civil Rights Movement. Many of the authors of post–Civil Rights Movement migration narratives answer the question of this chapter, "To Where from Here?" with an emphatic, "Back Down South."

The early fiction of Paul Laurence Dunbar and Jean Toomer first establish a return to the South as a possibility for black migrants. However, for the most part, the South remained the site of racial horror and shame for black writers. While they might have shared some fond memories of a Southern home, writers like Richard Wright and Ann Petry did not see return as a viable option for their characters. For Wright migration to Europe is a more viable option than a return to the South. While Ellison seems to suggest the importance of the South, his protagonist retreats to a Dostoevsky-like underground, and Baldwin's second novel goes to Europe. (He does not venture into a fictional South until the late sixties.) Even Toomer's contemporary Nella Larsen provides us with a protagonist, Helga, whose return to the South signals her metaphoric death. In the 1960s Amiri Baraka contributes a questing protagonist who must return to the South for a necessary understanding of African-American culture. Yet in this novel, *The System of Dante's Hell*, the South is an obligatory site of cultural sojourn, but not a destiny. It is not until the seventies and eighties that writers like Toni Morrison, Alice Walker, Maya Angelou, Ernest Gaines, James McPherson, and Albert Murray begin to seriously reconsider the South as a viable option for black people.[8]

These writers differ from Toomer and Dunbar in two important ways. For Toomer, like Du Bois, a journey of immersion to the South is a necessary stop for the African-American intellectual; it is not, however, his ultimate destiny. His work is to be accomplished in the North. For Dunbar, like Washington, the South is a place for African-Americans to cast down their buckets, accept racial inequities, and build around them. With the exception of Baraka, latter-day writers differ from both these views in that they see the South as a place to stay because it has changed. For these writers the South is a site of racial memory and redemption. Unlike Toomer, they portray the South as a final resting place for black people. Unlike Dunbar, they portray it as a place of changed racial mores and in this way a much better place than the North for black people.

I

> Pour O pour that parting soul in song,
> O pour it in the sawdust glow of night,
> Into the velvet pine-smoke air to-night,
>   And let the valley carry it along.
>   And let the valley carry it along.
>
> O land and soil, red soil and sweet-gum tree,
>   So scant of grass, so profligate of pines,
>   Now just before an epoch's sun declines
> Thy son, in time, I have returned to thee,
> Thy son, I have in time returned to thee.
>
>   In time, for though the sun is setting on
>   A song-lit race of slaves, it has not set;
>   Though late, O soil, it is not too late yet
> To catch thy plaintive soul, leaving, soon gone,
> Leaving, to catch thy plaintive soul soon gone.
>
>   O Negro slaves, dark purple ripened plums,
>   Squeezed, and bursting in the pine-wood air,
>   Passing, before they stripped the old tree bare
> One plum was saved for me, one seed becomes
>
>   An everlasting song, a singing tree,
>   Caroling softly souls of slavery,
> What they were, and what they are to me,
>   Caroling softly souls of slavery.
>
>   Jean Toomer, "Song of the Son"

Jean Toomer's "Kabnis" marks *Cane*'s return to the South. It is a return foreshadowed in the first part of the text in the poem "Song of the Son." "Song of the Son" sends out the call; "Kabnis" portrays one response. In content, Kabnis documents the failure of the poet to fulfill the ideal set forth in "Song of the Son"; however, in its form, it represents Toomer's achievement of that ideal.[9] Robert Stepto defines the relationship of call and response within the African-American literary tradition: "A response is fundamentally an artistic act of closure performed upon a formal unit that already possesses substantial coherence. There can be no one response, no one and final closure; there can only be appropriate and inappropriate responses, and what is appropriate is defined by the prefiguring call that has come before."[10]

In light of Stepto's definition, the character Kabnis provides an inappropriate response. The return, "the journey of immersion" traveled by Kabnis, is also traveled by African-American protagonists in the works of Du Bois, James Weldon Johnson, Zora Neale Hurston, Amiri Baraka, Paule Marshall, and Speech of the rap group Arrested Development. Again, according to Stepto, the journey of immersion is

> a ritualized journey into a symbolic South, in which the protagonist seeks those aspects of tribal literacy that ameliorate, if not obliterate, the conditions imposed by solitude. The conventional immersion narrative ends almost paradoxically with the questing figure located in or near the narrative's most oppressive social structure, but free in the sense that he has gained sufficient tribal literacy to assume the mantle of an articulate kinsman.[11]

This is certainly the stance sought in "Song of the Son." The persona in "Song of the Son" aspires to the fulfillment of Stepto's mandate. In many ways Jean Toomer, during his ever so brief sojourn into an African-American identity, does fulfill it. Of his trip South Toomer noted, "Georgia . . . There one finds soil, soil in the sense the Russians know it, the soil every art and literature that is to live, must be embedded in."[12] *Cane* embodies a tale of the Georgia soil. Because of the conditions imposed upon him by a fragmented (post)modern identity, Ralph Kabnis is not capable of the synthesis implied by Stepto's definition.

"Song of the Son" is a tribute, elegy, and plea. The black artist returns to the South, land of the ancestor—just before the epoch of the folk dies; he turns to the folk for sources and inspiration. He seeks to turn folk culture into art. The song of the slaves exists side by side with the terror inflicted upon them. The slaves are dark purple plums. One plum is plucked by the poet to become a seed nourished in him and eventually a poem of the race. When Toomer said of Georgia that its soil held the ingredient for the art and literature of black Americans, he was establishing the South as a symbolic space. In this poem the song that the poet must grasp exists in the soil and in the night. Within the frame of the text, no character is able to accomplish the task set forth in the poem. In "Song of the Son" the poet grasps the song from the slaves; Kabnis cannot hear the music in their religious shouting. Here the poet hears the song in the night winds; they only evoke fear in Kabnis. Here the poet acknowledges his kinship with plum-colored slaves; Kabnis denies and rejects it. "Song of the Son" represents the ideal destiny of the returning artist. The artist cannot be true to his art without confronting and accepting this culture. The impotent, incompetent Kabnis strives for this ideal but fails to reach it. In his autobiographical writings, Toomer suggests that he is closer to the persona of "Song of the Son" than he is to Kabnis. While in Georgia, Toomer noted, "I'd never heard the folk songs and the spirituals. They were very rich and sad and joyous and beautiful. But I learned that the Negroes of the town objected to them. They called them shouting."[13]

Ralph Kabnis seems to join the pantheon of modernist antiheroes that includes J. Alfred Prufrock and Willie Loman. He shares with them weakness of character and a sense of sexual and creative impotence. Yet unlike them, he is in search of the possibility which he believes exists in a Southern racial past. *Cane* represents possibility in a way that the "Love Song of J. Alfred Prufrock" and *Death of a Salesman* do not. It is Kabnis's own fear and weakness, linked with his disdain for the black folk to whom he is connected by an oppressive history, that make it almost impossible for him to grasp that possibility.

In asserting the possibility of the South to which Kabnis returns, Toomer does not deny the real and present horror that the South embodies for a black man. This South is a place where the lynching of black men and women is a reality; however, the repressiveness of the Southern black community constitutes a much more immediate threat for those who are likely to go against the grain. Kabnis experiences this repression at the hands of a figure resembling Booker T. Washington, Hanby, head of the school where Kabnis teaches. Hanby is the literary forefather to Ellison's Bledsoe; the school over which he presides is the precursor to Larsen's Naxos. These schools, produced and maintained by whites, act as a means of self-disciplining within the black community.

Although Hanby and the black institution attempt to circumscribe his freedom, it is the legacy of racial terrorism that most haunts Kabnis. He cannot hear the poetry in the night winds, he cannot translate it, because he is too paralyzed by fear. In the movement of chickens and calves he hears night riders and the ghosts of lynched black people, doomed to walk the red clay earth chained to the trees upon which their bodies were strapped. Like the persona in "Song of the Son," Kabnis declares: "If I . . . could become the face of the South. How my lips would sing for it, my songs being the lips of its soul." But before he is able to fulfill this wish he counters with, "Soul. Soul hell. There ain't no such thing" (p. 81). His impotence comes from a literal fear of castration, which continues to be a possibility, as well as his own weakness of character. Toomer gives us a foil for Kabnis in the character of Lewis. In many ways Lewis is the other side of Kabnis.[14] He is the flawed hero of this text, a man who possesses the courage of his convictions and who suffers the consequence of this by falling victim to the repressive tendencies of the black community when he tries to force them to face their own subjugation. Lewis has the strength and the courage but lacks Kabnis's artistic sensibility. He can recognize the song, he can be sustained by the history and confront it fearlessly, but he cannot translate it into poetry.

The fifth section of the play brings both Kabnis and Lewis into a confrontation with the ancestor—the embodiment of history. The failure of either to enact a fusion with the ancestor, a fusion that will result in the production of the song of the son, is the consequence of their fragmentation: As fragmented sides of one self neither is capable of creating art. Of the two, only Lewis, who has a sense of history, is able to have a meaningful, if not lasting, connection with the ancestor.

Kabnis and the other characters descend into an Inferno-like hole where an old, blind black man sits amid other relics, liquor, and cards. "He is like a bust in black walnut. Gray-bearded. Gray-haired. Prophetic. Immobile" (p. 104). Kabnis calls him Father of Hell, someone who reigns over a past of racial shame and a cellar of debauchery. Lewis calls him Father John—a black John the Baptist who at once represents the past and holds the key to redemption in the future. John the Baptist bore the wisdom of the risen Savior—a wisdom, if accepted by the hearer, that holds the promise of redemption. However, Father John is a "mute John the Baptist." He holds the wisdom of redemption but he cannot communicate that wisdom verbally.

For Lewis the old man is "Slave boy whom some Christian mistress taught to read the Bible. Black man who saw Jesus in the rice fields, and began preaching to his people. Moses- and Christ-words used for songs. Dead blind father of a muted folk who feel their way upward to a life that crushes and absorbs them" (p. 106). Here Lewis reads the old man as a text of African-American history. It is a history linked both to a biblical past and to the story of the African struggle for liberation in the New World. In this description, the old man becomes Frederick Douglass, taught to read by a Christian mistress; Nat Turner and Denmark Vesey, who both saw Jesus and acted to liberate their people; and the embodiment of the spirituals, words of Christ and Moses set to song. Father John is the father of a folk without a poet, a folk whom the future absorbs or kills. This keen and insightful sensitivity allows Lewis to acquire that which Kabnis aspires to but cannot reach—a fusion with the past. Yet because Lewis lacks the artist's sensibility, he cannot turn the horror, terror, and beauty into song; as Melvin Dixon notes, "The ancestral ground becomes obscured and can be approached only through the imagination."[15] Without this ability, when faced with it, he can only flee in fear of the true horror and power of that history:

> Lewis, seated now so that his eyes rest upon the old man, merges with his source and lets the pain and beauty of the South meet him there. White faces, pain pollen, settle downward through a cane-sweet mist and touch the ovaries of yellow flowers. Cotton-bolls bloom, droop. Black roots twist in a parched red soil beneath a blazing sky. Magnolias, fragrant, a trifle futile, lovely, far off. . . . His eyelids close. A force begins to heave and rise. . . .
>
> Lewis' skin is tight and glowing over the fine bones of his face. His lips tremble. His nostrils quiver. [p. 106]

This passage records Lewis's connection not only with the past history of the South, but also with the pain and beauty born out of the interracial union that occurs there. A union grounded in pain and exploitation, a union in which the earth and roots are a black woman, the flower a mulatto daughter, and the pollen a white man. The result is the beauty of the South, a fusion of all the races who have met there. The pain of the history results in possibilities for a beautiful art. As Lewis emerges from the state of ecstasy imposed upon him by the connection with the ancestor, he confronts Kabnis, who responds defensively. Aware of his own failure to acquire such a bond with the black ancestor, Kabnis attempts to overcome his spiritual bankruptcy by establishing his racial bond with white people. In doing so, he hopes to invoke his status in the material world: "He ain't my past. My ancestors were Southern blue-bloods." Lewis challenges the stability of the order upon which Kabnis relies by deconstructing received notions of difference between black and white. His vision, provoked by the ancestor, provides him with the tools to deconstruct the foundation upon which Kabnis grounds his status: "Master; slave. Soil; and the overarching heavens. Dusk; dawn. They fight and bastardize you. The sun tint of your cheeks, flame of the great season's multi-colored leaves, tarnished, burned. Split, shredded: easily burned" (p. 107). Together, each pair fuses to create Kabnis and the present South. Each is dependent on its opposite. There is no master without the slave; no sense of the heavens without a sense of the ground upon which you stand; dusk is meaningless unless compared to dawn.

The first three sentences or phrases set out the apparent oppositions. The following sentence gives the oppositional pairs their verb. One is not the subject and the other an object which is acted upon. Instead, they both fight and create a bastard culture. They both create a new mixed race represented by Stella, Halsey, and Kabnis. The result of this violent fusion is the beauty of sun-tinted cheeks, compared here with the lovely image of multicolored leaves, leaves of gold, red, crimson, peach—the various hues of the New World Africans. This act of deconstruction provides the others with the voice to tell their own personal histories and confrontations with racism. The cellar becomes a site of testimony—a testimony made possible by Lewis's sermon after a visitation with the prophetic Father John. Lewis returns from viewing the face of God, to give voice to the others.

Kabnis confronts the call to testify with a bitter accusation against Lewis: Lewis is but a mere black preacher, who can speak only to the racial past, not to the soul. Kabnis counters Lewis's sermon—a sermon grounded in an understanding of history—with his own empty alternative:

> Lewis don't know it all, an I'm a tellin' y. Ugh. Th form thats burned int my soul is some twisted and awful thing that crept in from a dream, a goddamn nightmare, an wont stay still unless I feed it. An it lives on words. Not beautiful words. God Almighty no. Misshapen, split-gut, tortured, twisted words. . . . White folks feed it cause their looks are words. Niggers, black niggers feed it cause theyre evil an their looks are words. Yallar niggers feed it. . . . I want to feed the soul—I know what that is; the preachers don't—but I've got t feed it. I wish t God some lynchin white man ud stick his knife through it an pin it to a tree. An pin it to a tree. [p. 110]

According to John Callahan, Kabnis "acts out the distinction between a closed version of oratory and the open participatory sermons of the black church. For in an uncreative, dead-end way he is an orator."[16] He is an orator, not a poet, for there is no possibility for poetry in the world painted by Kabnis—who likens his poetry to the child ripped and torn from its dying mother's belly only to be pinned to a tree by a white mob. Poetry, like the black baby, has no opportunity in the South. Kabnis seems to paraphrase Theodor Adorno: How can there be poetry after slavery, or after the Nadir of black history? There can only be ugly, unpoetic words. There can be no heroes, there can only be the likes of Ralph Kabnis. For Kabnis there is no possible fusion with history, only an incomplete sexual one with the whore Cora.

Lewis, who has no sexual partner in the resulting orgy, is "completely cut out. The glowing within him subsides. It is followed by a dead chill" (p. 110). The intimacy achieved by the fusion with history cannot sustain him in the denial of poetry. History, the souls of black folk, can be immortalized only in art. "Kabnis, Carrie, Stella, Halsey, Cora, the old man, the cellar and the work-shop, the southern town descend upon him. Their pain is too intense. He cannot stand it. He bolts from the table. Leaps up the stairs. Plunges through the work-shop and out into the night" (p. 110–11). In Toomer's vision, the past, when not sifted through poetry, is too ugly and painful to confront.

Michael Cooke provides great insight into Lewis's inability to sustain the connection with the ancestor and the other inhabitants of the cellar:

> Lewis is the only character in *Cane* who can boast, on both personal and professional levels, the capacity for expanded consciousness that Toomer regarded as indispensable for human fulfillment. And Lewis "cannot stand it." He illustrates an underlying problem for *Cane* as a whole, the absence of a suitable medium for substantiating Toomer's vision. . . . Lewis plunges out of the story because of a fear of staying in it.[17]

If Lewis is not to be the son of "Song of the Son," then in the fifth act of "Kabnis," Kabnis is an impostor to this throne also. Only Toomer emerges as the poet who will turn the Georgia night and red clay earth into a morning song.

The sixth and final act of "Kabnis" portrays the real redemptive possibilities inhabited in the ancestor; however, Kabnis, the fragmented antihero of the text, cannot gain access to this possibility because he is unable to attain the value of the history embedded in the ancestral figure. Act 6 marks the only dawn of the play, thus foreshadowing the possibility for hope and renewal; in this act, we hear the ancestor speak and in his voice lies the truth that might nurture black redemption. The opening scene is described like the pregnant womb just before the birth of the child. This is fitting in that the Southern night has been likened to a pregnant black woman throughout the drama: "The cellar swims in a pale phosphorescence. The table, the chairs, the figure of the old man are amoeba-like shadows which move about and float in it. In the corner under the steps, close to the floor, a solid blackness. A sound comes from it. A forcible yawn. Part of the blackness detaches itself so that it may be seen against the grayness of the wall. It moves forward and then seems to be clothing itself in odd dangling bits of shadow" (p. 111).

The womblike description sets the stage for the birth that is to follow. Kabnis accuses Father John of "feeding that angry thing thats livin on my insides." He has made the distinction between that angry thing and his soul earlier, yet in his early state of fragmentation he does not realize that they are, in fact, one in the same thing. His soul is the place of beauty and ugliness, pleasure and pain. He, like Muriel of "Box Seat," is incapable of recognizing their unity:

> T hell with you too. What do I care whether you can see or hear? You know what hell is cause youve been there. Its a feelin an its ragin in my soul in a way that'll pop out of me an run you through, an scorch y, and burn an rip your soul. Your soul. Ha. Nigger soul. A gin soul that gets drunk on a preacher's words. An screams. An shouts. God almighty, how I hate that shoutin. Where's th beauty in that? Give a buzzard a windpipe an I'll bet a dollar to a dime th buzzard ud beat y to it. Aint surprisin th white folks hate y so. [p. 113]

For Kabnis, the history embodied in the ancestor is an ugly history filled with shame and horror. He cannot imagine it as a source that nourishes his artistic imagination. He thinks that if he grounds himself in it, he is going to be capable of producing only ugly, empty words, words that do not nourish the soul as poetry must, but words that scorch and burn and rip it, as that history has done to black bodies. These are words that lynch in the manner of the lynching of "Blood-Burning Moon." Furthermore, Kabnis is so far alienated from the black side of his personal history that he is incapable of hearing the poetry in black oral culture. He hates the shouting; he does not understand the poetics of black preaching. He sees himself as an orator and is unable to see that the tradition of oration in which he situates himself is only made richer with the inclusion of black homiletics. John Callahan notes that in rejecting the shouts and the sermons of the black descendants of slaves, "Kabnis turns away from the mission of voice—'Caroling softly souls of slavery'—that Toomer embrace[s] in 'Song of the Son.'"[18] He identifies himself with white people in their lack of appreciation and thus inability to comprehend the coded beauty of black oral culture.

Carrie Kate, the only woman of the play to resemble the women of the Southern section and Avey in Washington, D.C., attempts to usher Kabnis into racial awareness. She seeks to facilitate his fusion with the ancestor and in so doing to lead him to a spiritual ecstasy not unlike the sexual ecstasy he achieved earlier with Cora. In her presence, the old man gives Kabnis the song of the real atrocity of slavery: "O th sin th white folks 'mitted when they made the Bible lie" (p. 115). The sin of slavery is the justification that white masters claimed to have found in the Bible. The sin of slavery is the sin against black humanity: White people committed this sin by claiming that the Bible justified the enslavement of Africans. Here lies the source of the song Kabnis is to sing. This is the charge of the ancestor. The legacy of the poet is to correct this wrong to redeem this sin. Yet Kabnis is not inspired. While Carrie Kate cries at the truth of this revelation, Kabnis is "contemptuous." He, like Lutie in relation to her grandmother, does not want the simple truth provided by Father John's revelation. He is looking for something more earth-shattering. He does not recognize the earth-shattering potential of this revelation. The white folks made the Bible lie—a simple falsehood that pardoned the enslavement of generations of New World Africans.

Carrie Kate attempts to facilitate Kabnis's redemption. In an image like a black pietà—with Carrie as the Virgin Mary and Kabnis as a recently crucified Christ who has just doubted the Father—Toomer provides us with the final attempt to resurrect Kabnis: "She turns him to her and takes his hot cheeks in her firm cool hands. Her palms draw the fever out. With its passing, Kabnis crumples. He sinks to his knees before her, ashamed, exhausted. His eyes squeeze tight. Carrie presses his face tenderly against her. The suffocation of her fresh starched dress feels good to him. Carrie is about to lift her hands in prayer" (p. 116). Kabnis is the crucified savior as well as penitent sinner at the feet of the virgin. She lays hands on him. After this pietà moment, he "rises and is going doggedly towards the steps. Carrie notices his robe. She catches up to him, points to it and helps him take it off. . . . Carrie's gaze follows him till he is gone. Then she goes to the old man and slips to her knees before him. Her lips murmur, 'Jesus come'" (p. 116).

Kabnis, like a reluctant risen savior, enacts an awkward resurrection. But it is an empty resurrection in that it does not leave a song. Like Jesus ascending from the three days in hell before going toward heaven, he leaves behind his robe for the two Marys and Martha, here embodied in Carrie Kate. Carrie Kate as Mary Magdalene then kneels at the feet of the father. Carrie Kate as Martha is the first to preach of the risen savior. The final image embodies both Mary Magdalene at the feet of Jesus and Mary the Mother of Christ: "Light streaks through the iron-barred cellar window. Within its soft circle, the figures of Carrie and Father John."

The final vision of the text is a vision of dawn, birth, and beauty told in the song of the true son of the text, Jean Toomer: "Outside, the sun arises from its cradle in the tree-tops of the forest. Shadows of pines are dreams the sun shakes from its eyes. The sun arises. Gold-glowing child, it steps into the sky and sends a birth-song slanting down gray dust streets and sleepy windows of the Southern town" (p. 116). Here the blood-burning moon of the first section delivers its promise. That moon warned of crucifixion and in so doing promised resurrection as well. Here, the blood-burning moon gives way to the gold-glowing sun—the Southern dawn. In the Southern dawn lies the possibility of racial redemption embodied in the creation of an art that is grounded in the history of a dying black folk. The gold-glowing child is the mulatto artist born of black mother and white father who is not only a son of the South, but also a son of God. In his song lies redemption.

II

> The South. Naxos. Negro education. Suddenly she hated them all.
>
> Nella Larsen, *Quicksand*

In striking contrast to Toomer's view of a Southern sojourn as necessary for black redemption, Nella Larsen, Toomer's contemporary, paints a picture of the South as a stifling hell which provokes her understanding of the truly doomed fate of black people. In *Quicksand* (1928) we see two alternative responses to "To Where from Here?" Helga Crane, the alienated and fragmented biracial protagonist of Larsen's text, attempts to escape the confinement of American cities and the racial provincialism of the Harlem black bourgeoisie by escaping first to Europe and finally to the American South. These are two alternatives that are more fully developed in the later migration narratives, but Larsen lays out the problems with either of these attempts.

In Europe, Helga thinks she finds an appreciation of black beauty and a rejection of the aesthetic norms of American society. However, she soon realizes that Europeans objectify her as a colorful exotic and as a somewhat grotesque other. Her body becomes the text on which the narrative of a sexualized other is written. Nowhere is this more evident than in the sequences that portray her adorning and that culminate in the portrait of her painted by her Danish intended, Axel Olson.

While the Europeans reduce her to a dark and mysterious sexuality embodied in primitive performance, black Southerners reduce her to a reproductive sexuality enacted in the constant birthing of children. For Helga, the South is not only a place of sexual oppression, it is also the place where her unflinching disdain for poor, illiterate, dark-skinned Southern blacks leads her to conclude the black race is doomed to the role of history's despised burden. She is most convinced by the people themselves and not the racial oppression from which they suffer. In contrast to the elegant cream, banana, and beige women who populate the city sections of the text, here the women are strong, sturdy, matronly, and black. Larsen paints a picture of them that is in many ways as grotesque as the portrait of Helga painted by Olson. If the muck is a place where Hurston's Janie comes into an affirming personal, spiritual, cultural, and sexual self-realization, the South for Helga is the site of confrontation with racial shame. There are no wisdom-bearing sages in Larsen's South—only ignorant, superstitious black folk.

A close reading of these two destinations, an expatriate's escape to Europe and a journey of immersion to the South, reveals neither to be a viable alternative for this questing heroine. In many ways the difference between Larsen's final vision and that of Toomer is a difference of sex, but just as important, it is a difference of the value that each author places on a sense of racial connectedness and a difference in the degree of disdain and contempt held for the black "folk."

Helga Crane goes to Denmark to visit her Danish ancestors in an attempt to escape the racial provincialism and class pretensions of her black middle-class Harlem. She also seeks refuge from the American system of racial classification which does not recognize her biracial identity. In Denmark she is overwhelmed by her family's enthusiastic welcoming of her. However, it is not long before she realizes that for them she is nothing more than the exotic currency with which they hope to purchase social status. Larsen tells us that Helga's aunt "had determined the role that Helga was to play in advancing the social fortunes of the

Dahls of Copenhagen."[19] Consequently, like Sarah Bartman, the Hottentot Venus, she is dressed up and shown off like an exciting souvenir brought back from a foreign land.

Although Helga experiences some resentment of the effort to portray her as an exotic object, she nonetheless begins to grow comfortable in her role:

> Certainly she loved color with a passion that perhaps only Negroes and Gypsies know. But she had a deep faith in the perfection of her own taste, and no mind to be bedecked in flaunting flashy things. Still—she had to admit that Fru Dahl was right about the dressing-gown. It did suit her. Perhaps an evening dress. And she knew that she had lovely shoulders, and her feet *were* nice. [p. 69]

Helga rationalizes her own objectification, because here in Denmark, at least her difference is considered attractive, desirable. In the United States, where all that is related to black is defined as ugly, she is "a despised mulatto." Helga has made comments on the pain of seeing black Americans agonizingly trying to cover their blackness, to alter it, through a rejection of bright colors that enhance their hue, and by turning "nice live crinkly hair, perfectly suited to [their] smooth dark skin and agreeable round features, into a dead straight, greasy, ugly mass" (p. 14). However, while she agrees to her display at a round of teas, cocktail parties, openings, lunches, dinners, and parties, she is always uncomfortable with the spectacle of herself. After she is adorned with "long enameled" earrings, "glittering shoe-buckles," and bracelets, "Helga felt like a veritable savage."

Eventually, Helga, like Josephine Baker, participates in her own objectification in exchange for material comfort and attention.[20] She does not manipulate or control this image of herself:

> She began to feel a little excited, incited.
>
> Incited. That was it, the guiding principle of her life in Copenhagen. She was incited to make an impression, a voluptuous impression. She was incited to inflame attention and admiration. She was dressed for it, subtly schooled for it. And after a little while she gave herself up wholly to the fascinating business of being seen, gaped at, desired. Against the solid background of Herr Dahl's wealth and generosity she submitted to her aunt's arrangement of her life to one end, the amusing one of being noticed and flattered. Intentionally she kept to the slow, faltering Danish. It was, she decided, more attractive than a nearer perfection. She grew used to the extravagant things with which Aunt Katrina chose to dress her. [p. 74]

The verb "incited" sets the tone for this passage and describes not only Helga's state of being in Denmark but also the consequences of her acceptance of her objectification as quintessential other. To incite according to *Webster's*, is "to put in motion; to move to action; stir up; spur on." It does not imply "initiating." With this verb, Helga is the object that is acted upon. She does not instigate, she does not abet, she is incited. That Larsen places such stress on this verb indicates her intention to portray Helga as lacking in agency, as accepting her status as object.

She is schooled, gaped at, seen, desired. There is only one suggestion that she has control over the choices available to her: She can choose to master the language. However, even where she is able to enact her own agency, she undermines it by choosing not to do so. It is a choice that does not resist but supports her objectification, which might be read as an act of subversion. Her willingness to use the Danes' image of her is a means of maintaining financial stability and a modicum of power, yet, as Larsen asserts, Helga, thus undermines her agency. In accepting Danish images of her, she is caught in a representational bind from which she cannot escape.

In Denmark, Helga becomes more exotic, more "black," in order to escape the prison of race. She does not immediately see the inherent contradiction and flaw in this reasoning. Instead, Helga believes that she has found a way out:

> She had resolved never to return to the existence of ignominy which the New World of opportunity and promise forced upon Negroes. How stupid she had been ever to have thought that she could marry and perhaps have children in a land where every dark child was handicapped at the start by the shroud of color! She saw, suddenly, the giving birth to little, helpless, unprotesting Negro children as a sin, an unforgivable outrage. More black folk to suffer Negro indignities. More dark bodies for mobs to lynch. No, Helga Crane didn't think often of America. It was too humiliating, too disturbing. And she wanted to be left to the peace which had come to her. [p. 75]

Helga Crane's understanding of racism is circumscribed by her experience of American race relations. For her racism equals the lynching of black bodies and the denial of opportunity to African-Americans and their children. In fact, she even seems to deny the significance of African-American humanity in her critical stance toward reproducing the race. She is unable to recognize the racism enveloping her in Denmark. It is not until she is confronted with it blatantly in the words of Axel Olson, the man she hopes to marry, that she begins to recognize the contours of Europe's romantic racism. Olson tells her, "You have the warm impulsive nature of the women of Africa, but my lovely, you have, I fear, the soul of a prostitute. You sell yourself to the highest buyer. I should of course be happy that it is I" (p. 87). Olson's portrayal of Helga is reiterated in the portrait he paints of her. "It wasn't, she contended, herself at all, but some disgusting sensual creature with her features" (p. 89). Helga has occupied the space of the grotesque, sensual exotic throughout her stay in Denmark. It is only when confronted with blatant racism in the form of the portrait and Olson's words that she stops denying its existence. In America, a white man would think the same thing of her, without the proposal of marriage. In Denmark, she gets the offer, but her status nonetheless remains that of whore.

Her newfound understanding of Danish racism makes her distinguish between the racism of white Americans' and black Americans' existence. Two theatrical moments usher in Helga's own moment of self-recognition.[21] The first, a vaudeville act by traveling black Americans, makes her reflect upon her

157

own grotesque comedy in the eyes of the Danish: "Helga Crane was not amused. Instead she was filled with a fierce hatred for the cavorting Negroes on the stage. She felt ashamed, betrayed, as if these pale pink and white people had been invited to look upon something in her which she had hidden away and wanted to forget" (p. 83). This is a moment of self-hatred. She internalizes the pain of racism, which makes her white friends so enjoy the spectacle before them. Later, Helga returns time and again to the circus in an attempt to answer the question that the performance raises for her.

It is not until the second theatrical moment that she comes upon her answer. Upon hearing a rendition of "Swing Low Sweet Chariot" she is reminded of her affinity with the race and she decides to return home—not home to America, but home to African-Americans.[22] She says, "I'm homesick, not for America, but for Negroes" (p. 92).

Shortly after her return to the United States, however, Helga realizes that "Negroes" as she knows them are still not able to fulfill her longings. If in Denmark she is defined in terms of her sexuality, among her bourgeois black peers she is defined devoid of it. Robert Anderson, husband of her best friend, and the man whom she most desires, categorizes her as "a lady" and therefore too good and pure to meet his own sexual desires.

In an effort to gain some degree of sexual satisfaction without being classified as whore, Helga marries an unsophisticated Southern black minister and returns South with him. She covers her need for sexual satisfaction in the cloak of religion and within the confines of a stifling marriage. The consequences are a series of difficult and unwanted births.

When Helga left the South in the first part of the novel, she did so to escape the narrow-minded provincialism of a black college—the Tuskegee-like Naxos. There, because of her lack of family, she was a nobody; here, "as the wife of the preacher, she was a person of relative importance. Only relative" (p. 118). Once again her personhood is defined by something outside of herself.

Sexuality, then, is a villain because the consequence of acting on it is the horror of childbirth, an act, Helga is convinced, that only contributes to the demise of black people. In giving birth to brown children, Helga becomes guilty of an act that, while in Denmark, she had determined never to commit: "giving birth to little, helpless, unprotesting . . . Negro indignities. More dark bodies for mobs to lynch." For Helga, giving birth is her contribution to "a despised race" (p. 127).[23]

If the North of Helga's days as a single woman was populated with "slim cream" and "ivory hands," "biscuit-colored feet," and "yellow satin" and "pale amber skin," the South of her married life is bursting with strapping black beauties, dirty brown children, and little bronze figures. The only amber in this section of Alabama are Helga's own "little dab[s] of amber humanity which [she] had contributed to a despised race" (p. 127). Unlike Toomer's, Larsen's South is not a place reeking with the fear of institutionalized racial terrorism or of cultural and historical redemption. Instead it is a provincial, black living hell. Whereas Toomer's Southern section ends with the affirmation of a resurrection, Larsen's closes with Helga's rejection of God and the likening of yet another birth to Helga's own death. Instead of resurrection, for Helga there is crucifixion. She experiences "asphyxiation."

During her immersion in black folk life, Helga comes to have an even greater disdain for black people, and she is even more convinced of the curse that has visited them. Religion and sexuality become the villains here. For Helga, the two are inseparable: "And she had her religion . . . she believed in it. Because in its coming it had brought this other thing, this anesthetic satisfaction for her senses" (p. 118). Sexuality is linked to religion, because the latter allows her to act upon her sexual desires within the confines of marriage. Sexual ecstasy becomes conflated with Helga's own sense of religious ecstasy. When her sexual activity leads to the misery of childbirth, she immediately begins to reject religion.

Religion is the other villain for Helga because of its delusional quality. Black people suffer constant strikes against their dignity and their humanity when they accept its promise of justice in another world:

> The cruel, unrelieved suffering [of childbirth] had beaten down her protective wall of artificial faith in the infinite wisdom, in the mercy, of God. For had she not called in her agony on Him? And He had not heard. Why? Because, she knew now, He wasn't there. Didn't exist. Into that yawning gap of unspeakable brutality had gone, too her belief in the miracle and wonder of life. . . . Life wasn't a miracle, a wonder. It was, for Negroes at least, only a great disappointment. Something to be gotten through with as best one could. No one was interested in them or helped them. God! Bah! And they were only a nuisance to other people. [p. 130]

In *Cane*, Father John tells Kabnis that the greatest sin committed by white people was their having made the Bible lie. Like the grandfather's principle in *Invisible Man*, this assertion implies that the Bible does hold possibilities for black people once its interpretation is purged of white lies. In *Quicksand*, religion itself is guilty of oppressing black people:

> Religion had, after all, its uses. It blunted the perceptions. Robbed life of its crudest truth. Especially it had its uses for the poor—and the blacks. . . .
>
> And this, Helga decided, was what ailed the whole Negro race in America, this fatuous belief in the white man's God. . . . How the white man's God must laugh at the great joke he had played on them! Bound them to slavery, then to poverty and insult, and made them bear it unresistingly, uncomplainingly almost, by sweet promises of mansions in the sky by and by. [pp. 133–34]

By defining black people as cursed and despised, Helga can see nothing worth salvaging. There are no redemptive possibilities. Larsen's South is not one haunted by the stirring, haunting beauty of the spirituals. For readers awaiting a Toomeresque South, there are two striking absences here: There is no evidence of white oppression, no mention of lynchings and the other horrors of the post-

Reconstruction South, and there is no mention of a folk culture. By seeing only a cursed and despised people, Helga seems to feel that their condition is one they bring upon themselves in their insistence on furthering the race through childbirth and their blind faith in a white man's god.

Unlike the persona in Toomer's "Song of the Son," Helga Crane only despises the descendants of slaves; for her they serve simply as a link to a shameful past and an oppressive present. "She hated their raucous laughter, their stupid acceptance of all things and their unfailing trust in 'de Lawd'" (p. 134). While *Cane* ends with Kabnis's emergence from the hole, having been given a piece of racial wisdom, while the final scene is one of a new day, *Quicksand* ends with Helga taking yet one step closer to what in her sight and Larsen's is surely an eternal damnation: "she began to have her fifth child."

For Helga Crane, a return to the South initiates her demise. Interestingly, though Kabnis holds a similar disdain for poor black Southerners, his greatest fear is of the inhumanity of white acts toward blacks. Also, Kabnis has a sense that there is something to nourish his art in the South. We never know if he attains the plum for which he is looking; we do know that Toomer does and that the result is *Cane*. In striking contrast, Helga Crane provides no explicit example of white oppression in the closing section of *Quicksand*. For her the South is a black woman's hell. There are no redemptive possibilities; there is only a confrontation with the curse of the race. There are no ancestors in *Quicksand*. Richard Wright seems to agree with Larsen in that he does not see a return south as necessary or possible. Like Toomer, however, Wright sees the greatest obstacle to Southern blacks as racial and class oppression. He grounds the curse of black people in a very real and present white terror. Interestingly, Zora Neale Hurston, like Larsen, portrays a South without a white presence. However, for her heroine, Janie, the outcome of her journey of immersion is a moment of self-discovery and growth accomplished through a confrontation and melding with the folk. Considered together, the two women appear to occupy two opposing positions on the same spectrum. Both create a South devoid of a threatening white presence. This is certainly not the case in the fiction of Richard Wright.

III

> "Boy, the South's good. . . ."
> ". . . and bad!"
> "It's Heaven. . . ."
> ". . . and Hell. . . ."
> ". . . all rolled into one!"
>
> Richard Wright, *Lawd Today*

None of Richard Wright's migrant characters return to the South. The closing pages of *Native Son* portray the final moments of Bigger's life prior to his execution. Cross Damon of *The Outsider* goes to Europe to lead an existential existence. The black migrants of *12 Million Black Voices* look forward to the dawn of a new day where they along with their poor white comrades forge a different world. Jake of *Lawd Today* falls down drunken and brutalized, sure to return to another day like the one described throughout the course of the novel.

Interestingly, Wright, himself a migrant, does return South. He goes back to do the research for *12 Million Black Voices*, encounters the continuing hostility of Southern racism, and never commits the experience to the fictional page. The only indication of his return is the brief but powerful passage of *Black Boy*, where he renders his final encounter with his father.

Upon studying this nonfiction version of his return South, we can perhaps better understand why Wright chooses alternatives other than a return with which to end his migration narratives.

> A quarter of a century was to elapse between the time when I saw my father sitting with the strange woman and the time when I was to see him again, standing alone upon the red clay of a Mississippi plantation, a sharecropper, clad in ragged overalls, holding a muddy hoe in his gnarled, veined hands—a quarter of a century during which my mind and consciousness had become so greatly and violently altered that when I tried to talk to him I realized that, though ties of blood made us kin, though I could see a shadow of my face in his face, though there was an echo of my voice in his voice, we were forever strangers, speaking a different language, living on vastly distant planes of reality. That day a quarter of a century later when I visited him on the plantation—he was standing against the sky, smiling toothlessly, his hair whitened, his body bent, his eyes glazed with dim recollection, his fearsome aspect of twenty-five years ago gone forever from him—I was overwhelmed to realize that he could never understand me or the scalding experiences that had swept me beyond his life and into an area of living that he could never know. I stood before him poised, my mind aching as it embraced the simple nakedness of his life, feeling how completely his soul was imprisoned by the slow flow of the seasons, by wind and rain and sun, how fastened were his memories to a crude and raw past, how chained were his actions and emotions to the direct, animalistic, impulses of his withering body. From the white landowners above him there had not been handed to him a chance to learn the meaning of loyalty, of sentiment of tradition. Joy was as unknown to him as was despair. As a creature of the earth, he endured, hearty, whole, seemingly indestructible, with no regrets and no hope. . . . From far beyond the horizons that bound this bleak plantation there had come to me through my living the knowledge that my father was a black peasant who had gone to the city seeking life, but who had failed in the city; a black peasant whose life had been hopelessly snarled in the city, and who had at last fled the city—that same city which had lifted me in its burning arms and borne me toward alien and undreamed-of shores of knowing.[24]

Here we observe two returned migrants—one who returned to stay because of his failure in the city; the other who will never stay in the South, who will eventually leave the American city to seek refuge from America's racism in the expatriate experience of Paris. This is the closest we will get to a meeting with the ancestor in Wright; it is a meeting in which the persona defines himself in contrast to the past as it stands before him. There are no nurturing, redemptive, or wisdom-bearing experiences in this meeting. Robert Stepto cites this passage as evidence of a "strident attempt by Wright's persona to condemn and obliterate the haunting image of his father. Every failing with which Negro America is charged is, at base, a failure he has witnessed within his family circle."[25] In releasing himself of the past represented by his father, he is releasing himself from the oppressive burden of history. The only ties that bind him are ties of blood and flesh. In Wright's view these are bonds of an essential blackness, not bonds upon which he can enter into the future. The rhetorical use of a quarter of a century instead of twenty-five years stresses the historical difference between him and his father. When talking about the passage of time in his father's life, he uses "twenty-five years"; when talking about the passage of time between him and his father, he uses "a quarter of a century."

During this quarter of a century Wright has become separated from his father by his acquisition of a critical consciousness. He exists on another plane and in another historical epoch—that of modernity. He speaks a different language than his father. These words could be taken directly from *American Hunger*, where Wright the migrant illustrates the difference between his Southern self and the white city dwellers. It is also similar to the language used to describe the difference between the migrants of *12 Million Black Voices* and the urbanized whites. In both instances, the differences in the experience of time and of language are differences of race. Here they are differences of class, with Wright taking on the white position. His father, like the black peasants of *12 Million Black Voices*, is a premodern man whose experience of time is cyclical. He remains bound to the past with no hope of entering the future.

The white landowners of this passage are the lords of the land in the Southern section of *12 Million Black Voices*. With their introduction into the passage, Wright begins an unrelenting and unfair critique of black Southerners. White landowners exercised enormous control over Southern blacks but they were not successful in stopping them from forging a tradition. Also, it is presumptuous to state that white landowners control the degree of loyalty any black Southerner is able to experience or understand. In *12 Million Black Voices*, Wright eloquently cites the forging of a black tradition in the spirituals—one instance where black slaves and peasants "stole the language" and forged a new one of their own. However, there are no such possibilities in the passage cited above.

Interestingly, it was on a trip south to conduct research for *12 Million Black Voices* that Wright had the encounter documented in the preceding passage. According to Robert Stepto, Wright distances his "persona, in time and achievement, from the black 'specimen' he . . . dissect[s]."[26] As illustrated earlier, this distanced persona also relates the migration narrative of *12 Million Black Voices*.

The fourth and final section of *12 Million Black Voices*, "Men in the Making," furthers the vision of the Wright persona in the passage cited above. The occupants of this section are not migrants but the children of migrants: "We are the children of the black sharecroppers, the first-born of the city tenements."[27] They do not return to the South after having been defeated by the city. Nor do they return for a necessary spiritual and cultural pilgrimage. Instead, they find themselves confronted with a variety of options: some choose racial nationalism, others aspire toward Africa, and still others admire and seek to emulate "the harsh and imperialistic policies of Japan and ardently hope that the Japanese will assume the leadership of the darker races." Both the early Bigger and Jake fall into this category. Those who have gained a critical awareness and analysis of historical forces emerge as modern black *men* who, along with other modern men, forge a more just future. These are the black men upon whom Wright sets his final vision.

This final vision is one that seems to emerge in both the written and photographic texts, although they are again divergent. Three photographs accompany this section. The first is a frontal portrait of a young, handsome worker. The second depicts well-dressed black women forming a picket line around the White House. Their placards call for the end of lynching and other racial injustices. They also identify the women as delegates of different states representing a national movement. Amiri Baraka notes that upon migration, black people become aware of themselves as a national presence.[28] In this photograph, the women are citizens, exercising their constitutional rights, calling for the restoration of democracy. Of the three, this is the only non-FSA photograph. While it does suggest a dissatisfaction with America, it also portrays peaceful, nonviolent protest. The final photograph is a full-length frontal shot of a black man (Figure 4.1). Though he is standing at the back door of what appears to be a Southern shack, surrounded by the debris of poverty, he nonetheless optimistically looks up at the sun.

Although Wright's narrative, like the photographs, ends with an optimistic glance toward tomorrow, the written text sets its sight on a different dawn. The photographic narrative urges a tomorrow with the restoration of capitalistic order; the written narrative ever so subtly wishes for a politically different vision:

> When the depression was at its severest, the courts of many cities, at the instigation of the Bosses of the Buildings, sent armed marshals to evict our jobless black families for their inability to pay rent for the rotting kitchenettes. Organized into groups, we black folk smashed the marshals' locks, picked up the paltry sticks of furniture, and replaced the evicted families. Having hurdled fear's first barrier, we found that many white workers were eager to have us in their organizations, and we were proud to feel that at last our strength was sufficient to awaken in others a desire to work with us. . . . We invited them into our homes and broke our scanty bread with them, and this was our supreme gesture of trust. In this way we encountered for the first time in our lives the full effect of those forces that tended to reshape our folk consciousness, and a few of us stepped forth and accepted within the confines of our

Figure 4.1 Carl Mydans, *Back Yard of Alley Dwelling.* Washington, D.C., Farm Securities Administration. (Reproduced from the Collections of the Library of Congress)

> personalities the death of our old folk lives, an acceptance of a death that enabled us to cross class and racial lines, a death that made us free. [p. 144]

This extremely important paragraph requires close reading, for it reveals several significant insights into Wright's narrative. The organization of the paragraph itself places the independent agency of the urban blacks before their attempts to organize with white workers. The historical value of this cannot be overestimated. According to Wright, poor urban blacks responded to their economic oppression by first organizing and acting in their own behalf, and then later, upon finding themselves welcomed by white organizations, by joining with them. Note that the white organizations were eager to invite black membership because black "strength was sufficient to awaken in others a desire to work" with them. This narrative move places the agency and the value with the urban black community. This is a significant departure from William Stott's extensive misreading of the text: "Wright's Negroes are both piteously weak and improbably heroic." According to Stott *12 Million Black Voices* is full of exaggerated emotion and sentimentalism.[29] I would argue instead that all the photo documentaries are emotional and, in fact, Stott argues elsewhere that this was their strength. However, Wright's text is not without its critical stance.

Upon a closer reading of the silences of this paragraph, it becomes evident that the "white workers" organizational efforts were orchestrated by the Communist party. The scientific and theoretical vision offered by the party helps Wright's blacks to "encounter for the first time . . . the full effect of those forces that tended to reshape our folk consciousness" and allowed "a few of us" to step "forth and accept within the confines of our personalities the death of our old folk lives, an acceptance of a death that enabled us to cross class and racial lines, a death that made us free" (p. 144).

While Wright is careful to note that this acquisition of a necessary critical consciousness was not the fate of all urban blacks, he nonetheless does suggest this possibility as the final vision of his narrative. In fact, a more likely response to the depression was the 1935 Harlem riot, which Wright sees as the expression of "inarticulate black men and women, filled with a naive, peasant anger." These are the blacks whose consciousness has yet to develop the critical sophistication necessary for the making of a future.

Although Wright's fictional narratives suggest that the inarticulate, naive blacks outnumber those who acquire the status of modern men, he nonetheless makes the latter the stars of this narrative. For the men of *12 Million Black Voices*, "The seasons of the plantation no longer dictate the lives of many of us; hundreds of thousands of us are moving into the sphere of conscious history. We are with the new tide. We stand at the crossroads. We watch each new procession. . . . Men are moving! And we shall be with them . . ." (p. 147).

For Richard Wright, a return to the South is a retreat into a dark and ugly history. The only positive movement is a progressive, linear one forward into the future, abroad to Europe, or to a final death on the city pavement. Even this latter option is preferred to a return south. During the time that Wright is writing, the South is not much different from the South from which he fled. It is still a place where the races are segregated and where black men are lynched. Unlike Toomer, who recognized these realities but who nonetheless considered the South a necessary and important spiritual and artistic archive, for Wright it is a place of stagnation and cultural deprivation. From his perspective, the only thing that awaits the returning hero is a lynch mob.

The brutal beating, mutilation, and murder of Emmett Till in 1955 was proof positive that the South was no place for a young Northern black man. Till, a fourteen-year-old Chicagoan visiting relatives in Mississippi, was lynched for whistling at a white woman. His murderers were known, and after a circus of a trial, complete with vendors hawking Cokes, they walked away free men.

In the September 15, 1955, issue of *Jet Magazine*, African-American readers were confronted with the graphic photographs of Till's brutally battered corpse. Till's mother, Mamie Till Mobley, requested that her son's body lie in state for three days "so all the world can see what they did to my boy." Photographs of Till ran in most major black papers throughout the nation as well as in the mainstream press. The photographs of Till and the subsequent acquittal of the white men sent a loud and clear message to all African-Americans: The specter of lynching in Mississippi was not only a threat but a real possibility for young black Northerners.

Less than ten years later, in the midst of a Civil Rights Movement galvanized in part by the response to the Till photographs, writers could begin reclaiming Toomer, and they could firmly assert the South as site of racial memory. After significant social and political changes in the South, brought about by the Civil Rights Movement, such a return was not only a possibility but a prerequisite to gaining and maintaining a sense of ethnic identity and wholeness. For these writers, a journey of immersion seemed necessary to combating the psychic violence inflicted on black people in the urban North.

IV

> It is heresy, against one's own sources, running in terror, from one's deepest responses and insights . . . the denial of feeling . . . that I see as basest evil.
>
> Amiri Baraka (Leroi Jones), *The System of Dante's Hell*

Amiri Baraka's autobiographical novel *The System of Dante's Hell* (1965) portrays the journey of immersion of the young protagonist, Leroi, an aspiring poet. Baraka likens Leroi's journey to that of Dante: a journey south is a journey into hell. But as the persona tells us at the novel's opening, "Dante's hell is heaven." So too, it seems, is Leroi's; however, as Kimberly Benston notes in *Baraka: The Renegade and the Mask*, Leroi's South is actually more like a paradise lost.[30]

The young Leroi, highly literate yet confused, lives a life filled with literature and disconnected, dark, and ugly bisexual encounters. Throughout the text he is caught in a hopeless web of awe and admiration for white Western culture. "The dead are what move me," he says, only to chastise himself with "YOU LOVE THESE DEMONS AND WILL NOT LEAVE THEM."[31] Implicit in this remark is the ambiguous manner in which he both loves and despises the tradition to which he aspires as a poet, the tradition which has the most influence on him. He is aware of the deadness, the lack of fertility in this tradition, yet he cannot overcome his disdain for all that is "black." The last section of the novel finds him in the circle of the heretics, "the deepest part of hell."[32]

On a weekend leave from an Air Force base in Louisiana, he descends into "The Bottom," the segregated section of Shreveport. Unlike Kabnis, he does not go in search of some spiritual sustenance for his work; he goes in search of sex and alcohol. If the South is the place where Helga Crane is used up by the serial births of her children, for Leroi, "the place use(s) him." Here, "books fall by," but his senses awaken. When he opens his "eyes [and] nose," he becomes aware of the sensuality of the Southern night. If Toomer's night is fertile in its likeness to a pregnant and/or nursing black woman, Baraka's Southern night is virile in its likeness to a man: "The Bottom lay like a man under a huge mountain . . . the night had it. Air like mild seasons and come. That simple elegance of semen on the single buds of air" (p. 122). Images of virility are used throughout the novel to signal the life-giving forces of African-American culture.

Like the South of Baldwin and Toomer, Baraka's South is both life-threatening and life-giving. The Bottom is "a culture of violence and food-smells." The blood imagery of the two earlier texts reappears here, again to suggest this dialectic. "The bus, moon and trees floated heavily in blood. It washed down the side of the hill and negroes ran from it" (p. 123). The blood is of black victims of Southern violence, as well as the blood of redemption. For Baldwin, Toomer, and Baraka black people are blood flowing out and pumping in.

In Leroi's inferno white culture is a literate culture; black culture, throbbing, thriving, and emotional. Up to this point, he has been a somewhat passive sexual object of men and an active sexual subject in emotionally disconnected encounters with women—even a rape. Throughout the course of the night he will experience a new type of sexual encounter, one that brings him closer to the sensual wealth of black culture. Under the guidance of Don, a fellow Air Force pilot and Virgil to his Dante, Leroi encounters black Southern night life. Like Kabnis, he is distanced from and somewhat disdainful of black Southerners and they are mocking of him and his "shy clipped speech." In the bar, "The Joint," he meets not the ancestor but Peaches, a seventeen-year-old whore who is the embodiment of all that he hates and fears: "Fat with short baked hair split at the ends. Pregnant empty stomach. Thin shrieky voice like knives against a black-board. Speeded up records. Big feet in white, shiny polished shoes. Fat tiny hands full of rings. A purple dress with wrinkles across the stomach. And perspiring flesh that made my khakis wet" (p. 127). Peaches *is* body. She has a belly just waiting for his seed. She possesses none of the soft Southern beauty or hardened wisdom of Kabnis's whores. Instead she is Mammy, Jezebel, and Sapphire all rolled into one.

Peaches takes him out on the dance floor, where she initiates his spiritual and sexual revival:

> On the dance floor people hung on each other. Clutched their separate flesh and thought, my god, their separate thots. They stunk. They screamed. They moved hard against each other. They pushed. And wiggled to keep the music

on. . . . All that screaming came together with the smells and the music, the people bumped their asses and squeezed their eyes shut. [p. 129]

At this moment, the dance floor is like the very center of hell for Leroi. The smell and the screams resemble the descriptions of hell passed down in a Western literary tradition beginning with the Bible. But he soon learns that the dance floor is what Kimberly Benston calls "the threshing floor":

> The dancing like a rite no one knew, or had use for outside their secret lives. The flesh they felt when they moved, or I felt all their flesh and was happy and drunk and looked at the black faces knowing all the world thot they were my own, and lusted at that anonymous America I broke out of, and long for it now, where I am.
>
> We danced, this face and I, close so I had her sweat in my mouth, her flesh the only sound my brain could use. Stinking, and the music over us like a sky, choked any other movement off. I danced. And my history was there, had passed no further. Where it ended, here, the light white talking jig, died in the arms of some sentry of Africa. Some short-haired witch out of my mother's most hideous dreams. I was nobody now, mama. Nobody. Another secret nigger. No one the white world wanted or would look at. [pp. 129–30]

Through the communal ritual of the dance floor he meets the ancestor,[33] melds his spirit and body with the movement of other black people, and is both elated and afraid. He lives a nightmare and yet he is drawn to its possibilities—drawn and repulsed at the same time.

Leroi is a reluctant questing protagonist. He attempts to escape the Bottom three times, only to unwillingly return. He is a self-described "imitation white boy" who says of himself: "I've been fucked in the ass. I love books and smells and my own voice" (p. 131). Peaches takes him further down the Bottom where his outsider status is even more evident: "Rich nigger. Porch sitter. . . . So cute. . . . Yellow thing. . . . Sissy motherfucker" (pp. 134–35).

When Peaches takes him down for the third time it is "down some steps and thru A dark low hall to where she lived." Once there, like Prufrock, he wants to talk with her "about my life. my thots. What I'd found out and tried to use. Who I was." Peaches does not want talk, she wants sex. He vividly remembers his first sexual encounter with a man, but with her he is impotent. He says, "I'm beautiful. Stephen Dedalus. A mind. . . . My eyes. My soul is white, pure white, and soars. Is the God himself" (p. 140). During his homosexual encounters, the men listen to his identification with the princes of high modernism or exchange their knowledge of Western culture for sex with him. For Peaches he is "Faggot. Faggot. Sissy," impotent, and incapable of a sexual act that would lead to reproduction.

When finally he is able to copulate, he rushes immediately from her, only to encounter another resident of the hellish Bottom, the Belacqua-like "sweet-peter-eater," a man with "sand-colored Jew hair . . . yellow soggy skin full of red freckles" who propositions him. Unlike earlier encounters, this time he does not indulge the man's request to "Lemme suck yo dick, honey." After his confrontation with the ancestor on the dance floor, his sexual connection with Peaches, he now runs from the possibility of homosexual sex. The culturally immersed hero of this text rejects homosexual encounters. The black manhood to emerge from this journey of immersion is the macho, heterosexual black male of the Black Power Movement.

Still ready to leave his brief but eventful sojourn, he attempts again to escape the Bottom. He wants to be " the anonymous seer again." He seeks to occupy the space of the stranger, familiar with but not bound by a black culture. However, upon seeing a near-dead black soldier, he knows that despite his innocence, he will be accused by the white authorities of murder. This possible injustice makes him return unwillingly to the Bottom. Chased by two white police officers, he runs in search of Peaches and the cover of night. This time with Peaches, "we talked about our lives: then she pushed back the sheets, helped me undress again, got me hard and pulled me into her" (p. 146). She promises to teach him about sex.

When he awakes, it is to a sun that warms him and to a smell that he no longer finds distasteful. He has been completely immersed and emerges as a member of the tribe. He is not only literate but sensual. "And I heard daytime voices thru the window up and fat with optimism" (p. 147). The sun has arisen as has his soul, for now. The room is full of light and music, "heavy blues and twangy guitar." He and the greasy-haired Peaches eat a breakfast of watermelon and he is not ashamed of the ethnic implications of the music or the food. The novel's only tender moment, an eloquent and beautiful statement of the consequences of his immersion, occurs at this point:

> And I felt myself smiling, and it seemed that things had come to an order. Peaches sitting on the edge of the bed, just beginning to perspire around her forehead, eating the melon in both hands. . . . It seemed settled. That she was to talk softly in her vague american, and I was to listen and nod, or remark on the heat or the sweetness of the melon. And that the sun was to be hot on our faces and the day smell come in with dry smells of knuckles or greens or peas cooking somewhere. Things moving naturally for us. At what bliss we took. At our words. . . . And slumped together in anonymous houses. I thought of black men sitting on their beds this saturday of my life listening quietly to their wives' soft talk. And felt the world grow together as I hadn't known it. All lies before, I thought. All fraud and sickness. This was the world of flesh, of smells, of soft black harmonies and color. The dead maelstrom of my head, a sickness. The sun so warm and lovely on my face. . . . Peaches' music and her radio's I cursed chicago, and softed at the world. "You look so sweet," she was saying. "Like you're real rested." [pp. 147–48]

While the passage appears to settle his conflicting yearnings, in fact it embodies the very source of his discontent. On the one hand, he is now immersed in black culture, a warm, sensual culture of sounds, smells, and touches. He has come to love not only the sound of his own voice but also the sound of another's—to be the ear to her stories. In this simple act of listening he communes with other black men, who also listen to their wives' soft voices. These voices, the voices of the women and the men, are communal—another characteristic of this new culture, they are spoken, experienced in unison, not individually on the written page. Here, in her bed, he likens his obsession with white culture to sickness. He is made warm and welcome by the safe spaces of black food and music. However, because he creates this binary opposition between black and white culture—one living, the other dead; one oral, the other written; one communal, the other individual; one sensual, the other intellectual—he is still dividing and fragmenting his needs and himself. Under this set of oppositions he cannot possibly be whole. For now he momentarily belongs to this paradise: "People walked by me smiling. And waved 'Hey' (a greeting) and they all knew I was Peaches' man" (p. 149).[34]

However, it is not long before he realizes that the black South of Peaches is not a destination; it is but a stop on his journey of artistic development. There is no eternal redemption—there are only redemptive moments. He cannot abandon the white demons that drive him. Leaving Peaches to purchase fresh tomatoes for their dinner, he walks into a storm. Although Peaches represents a sense of home, his relationship with her is nonetheless "a heavy iron to this tomb." This sense of connectedness, while appreciated and necessary, is not ultimately fulfilling. The heaven of the Bottom is a paradise lost. Leroi, like Adam, must fall from Grace. "To come to see the world, and yet lose it." He goes once again "Up the road, to go out of the Bottom," only to eventually find himself in a cave "with white men, screaming for God to help me." He cannot live by black bread alone. It is not enough to have his soul fed and not his intellect. He embodies the dilemma of the black artist, drawn to the accomplishment of the Western tradition, addicted to it even, yet needing the source and the sustenance of the black tradition as well. Like Kabnis before him, he goes to have his soul nourished so that he can become an artist.

The South to which he returns is not romanticized or sentimentalized. It is dark, dank, and ugly. Like Dan's vision in "Box Seat," it is both beautiful and ugly; painful and wonderful. The questing protagonist of Baraka's journey of immersion must shed himself of a past of white Western poets and homosexual encounters. The two are not separate; his love affair with the white poets is likened to a homosexual encounter. The point of the immersion journey is to gain critical insight into the nature of this relationship. The black culture that Baraka envisions is a "dynamic," heterosexist culture where "men are men" and "women are women." At this early point of transition between the personae of Leroi Jones and Amiri Baraka, we can see an emerging sensibility about black manhood, one that certainly informs his formation of the Black Arts Movement, a sensibility that has no place for "sissy" men or, eventually, women as aggressive as Peaches.

In many ways it is in response to the foundations laid by Baraka, Ron Karenga, and Haki Madhubuti that the black women writers of the decades following the sixties rewrite the migration narrative. Two of the most successful writers of this period, Alice Walker and Toni Morrison, helped to reshape the journey of immersion as a final vision of the migration narrative and to rewrite the character of the questing black male of these narratives. Both women wrote novels whose central figures were black males who, upon returning to the South, discover the nurturing side of themselves and in so doing contribute to the well-being of other, female characters. Walker's *The Third Life of Grange Copeland* (1970) and Morrison's *Song of Solomon* (1977) portray the South as a place of racial history and the site of the ancestor. It is a place where their male protagonists find the female in themselves and begin a process of redemption. Of the two, Toni Morrison's *Song of Solomon* is most fitting for the concerns of this project.

V

> He wondered why black people had ever left the South.
>
> Toni Morrison, *Song of Solomon*

Milkman, the protagonist of *Song of Solomon* (1977), is one of those first-generation city-born African-Americans about whom Wright speaks in the final pages of *12 Million Black Voices*. However, Milkman is neither nationalist nor militant. (His best friend, Guitar, is both.) Nor does he seek to gain a critical awareness of the forces that shape history, as do the ideal young men of the Wright text. He is comfortably middle class, spoiled, and rather self-indulgent.

Morrison's *Song of Solomon* can be positioned in the tradition of urban male narratives discussed in the previous chapter. Both Emmett Till and Malcolm X have cameo appearances in her novel. The first is used to initiate a dialogue about the precarious condition of black manhood. Upon hearing news of Till's murder, the men in the barbershop

> began to trade tales of atrocities, first stories they had heard, then those they'd witnessed, and finally the things that had happened to themselves. A litany of personal humiliation, outrage, and anger turned sicklelike back to themselves as humor. They laughed then, uproariously, about the speed with which they had run, the pose they had assumed, the ruse they had invented to escape or decrease some threat to their manliness, their humanness.[35]

This is a conversation in which Milkman remains silent. His comfortable life has protected him from the experiences they share; however, the conversation reveals to him and to the reader the impossibility of a black man returning south without risking his life.

Malcolm X is used to suggest an alternative to returning, the alternative of a militant black nationalism which seeks vengeance on white people for their inhumane acts. When Guitar tells Milkman of his membership in a secret vigilante society, the Seven Days, Milkman tells him, "You sound like that red-headed Negro named X. Why don't you join him and call yourself Guitar X?" (p. 161). Morrison uses Till and X to situate the novel historically. The reference to Till tells us that at that point in the novel, we are in the year 1955. The reference to Malcolm X tells us that the novel is now in the early 1960s. We can measure Milkman's growth and development with these historical signposts. More significantly, however, these two historical figures serve as symbols of black manhood in America.

Morrison's novel is about the quest for black manhood following the Black Power Movement. She reconsiders many of the concerns set forth in the narratives of Wright, Ellison, and Malcolm X. In so doing she redefines masculinity, making the connectedness that would have seemed stifling to the former absolutely necessary for the achievement of manhood. Milkman does not suffer the fate of Emmett Till when he returns to the South. He does, like Malcolm X, make a spiritual journey and become the prey of another black man. However, the consequence of Milkman's journey is a redefinition of manhood that includes a less selfish, more nurturing component. He does not leave the United States for his pilgrimage. His Mecca is the American South, where the earth "is soggy with black people's blood" (p. 159).

In this novel, we have the synthesis of two perspectives, one emphasizing the importance of safe spaces in the achievement of wholeness and the other documenting the difficulty of accomplishing this for a black man in American society. Central to the achievement of a healthy manhood is the journey back and a sustained relationship with the ancestor. Finally, Morrison rewrites the narrative of immersion first written by Jean Toomer in *Cane*. Unlike the antihero Kabnis, Milkman emerges heroic, because he can sing and reinvent the song of the ancestor. He is able to adapt the ancestor's song to meet present-day needs. While Kabnis never occupies the space of the son in "Song of the Son," Milkman does indeed "sing caroling forth the songs of slavery" in a soothsaying melody to comfort the dying Pilate.

Milkman embarks on a Southern journey in search of gold. His trip is a journey of immersion par excellence. He emerges as a true "articulate kinsman," who though he does not feel "close" to the people he meets on his journey, feels "connected" to them[36] and finally, after linking his history with theirs, is able to attain the status of storyteller. The journey is divided into three segments and culminates in his having learned his family's history and his acquiring the ability to memorize, sing, and adopt the family song to meet present needs. During the course of the journey, he finally traces the history of the ancestor—not just his immediate grandfather, but the African who is the subject of the Song of Solomon. Learning the meaning of the song introduces him to his own lack of responsibility.

Early in the novel, Morrison situates Danville, Pennsylvania, as the site of one ancestor, Macon Dead I, by telling of his brutal death at the hands of white people. Milkman is familiar with this story as he arrives in Danville on the first leg of his journey. Through the safe space of song and storytelling, he becomes acquainted with the ancestor. A series of elders grant him a better understanding of the circumstances surrounding the death of his most immediate ancestor, Macon Dead I, and an introduction to those ancestors who preceded Macon Dead I. The first elders are Pilate and Macon Dead II, both of whom first relay to him the story of their father. In Danville, he is introduced to several more elders, the male contemporaries of his father, most notably Reverend Cooper and surreal Circe, the midwife who birthed Pilate and hid her and Macon following the lynching of their father. By example, Reverend Cooper teaches Milkman the art of framing and telling a story. "Milkman felt a glow listening to a story come from this man that he'd heard many times before but only half listened to" (p. 233). History comes to life for him. He can identify the sites of the story—it no longer has a distanced exoticism.

During his stay in Danville, he meets other elders, boyhood companions of his father, who flesh out his family's history, make a living, breathing, folk hero of his grandfather, and listen attentively to his own rendering of a tale. He is empowered by them to construct his own narrative, the sequel to theirs—The Dead Clan in the City. This story is told not only to entertain but also to uplift the spirits of the listeners, to help them share in the success of the characters, to give them a sense of pride. During the period of listening to and relaying his story, Milkman is forced to reconceptualize his notion of time. The urgency with which he wants to move on in his journey, in his search for the lost gold, is checked when he must wait days before someone is able to give him a ride to the home where Pilate and Macon hid.

Although the slowness with which Reverend Cooper responds to his request to be driven to the house appears to Milkman as evidence of country incompetence, in fact, it prepares him for the meeting with the most important elder of this section, Circe. He must experience a different notion of temporality before meeting Circe: Circe who was one hundred years old when she helped to bring Pilate into the world; Circe who, like the biblical figures of the Old Testament, lives close to two centuries. In his meeting with Circe he is snatched literally from reality: "She grabbed him, grabbed his shoulders and pulled him right up against her and tightened her arms around him" (p. 241–242).

From Circe he learns more of his family's history. He learns the real name of Macon Dead I, Jake. He learns of his Indian grandmother, Sing. He learns that while his father left Danville and headed north for the city, Pilate traveled further south. He learns that Macon Dead I never received a proper burial. But, most important, he learns of the necessity of being patient with time, which will redeem all injustice. Angry with Circe for staying on in the Butler's home, he accuses her: "You loved those white folks that much?" Circe explains to him that she stays because in time she emerges as triumphant: "Everything in this world they lived for will crumble and rot. . . . And I want to see it all go, make sure it does go, and that nobody fixes it up" (p. 248–50). Circe's method of vengeance is strikingly different from that of Guitar and the Seven Days, who seek to even the score at every moment between blacks and whites. Circe's method is grounded in an understanding of history. It is an understanding best explained by Reverend Cooper when he tells Milkman, "Things work out, son. The ways of God are mysterious, but if you live it out, just live it out, you see that it always works out. Nothing they stole or killed for did 'em a bit a good. Not one bit" (p. 234). This is also a warning to Milkman, that his quest for gold is ultimately a futile one.

In Danville, Milkman begins for the first time in his life to listen. Still he is not cognizant of the true mission of his journey. He still is in search of the gold, although the driving force behind the second leg of his journey is the need to trace the history of his family. He has heard part of the story; he must hear the rest and he must experience a part of it before he realizes his own destiny as articulate kinsman. In exchange for the tools provided him by the elders, Milkman must give up the luxury of trains and planes and begin to lose some of his material trappings. In giving up the man-made flight of planes, he embarks on a surrealistic journey into history.

The second leg of his journey takes him to Shalimar, Virginia, home of the original ancestor. Here he begins a rite of passage that will allow him to find the true gold (goal) of his journey—his history. In Shalimar, he undergoes a process of initiation that starts with his insulting local men first by asking about their women and then by making a pretentious but sincere statement about buying a new car if his old one cannot be fixed:

> They looked with hatred at the city Negro who could buy a car as if it were a bottle of whiskey because the one he had was broken. And what's more, who had said so in front of them. He hadn't bothered to say his name, nor ask theirs, had called them "them," and would certainly despise their days, which should have been spent harvesting their own crops, instead of waiting around the general store hoping a truck would come looking for mill hands or tobacco pickers in the flatlands that belonged to somebody else. His manner, his clothes were reminders that they had no crops of their own and no land to speak of either. . . . He was telling them that they weren't men, that they relied on women and children for their food. . . . That thin shoes and suits with vests and smooth smooth hands were the measure. That eyes that had seen big cities and the inside of airplanes were the measure. They had seen him watching their women and rubbing his fly as he stood on the steps. . . . He hadn't found them fit enough or good enough to want to know their names, and believed himself too good to tell them his. They looked at his skin and saw it was as black as theirs, but they knew he had the heart of the white men who came to pick them up in the trucks when they needed anonymous, faceless laborers. [p. 269]

Here, again, in this novel about black manhood, there emerges yet another set of criteria for measuring it—a set based on certain class assumptions of which these men fall short. They opt to test Milkman's manhood from their own criteria,

criteria which include oral virtuosity, fighting, and finally a familiarity with and relationship to nature.

The younger men engage him in the rhetorical game of signifying that challenges his sexuality. The signifying session ends in a duel where Milkman faces his knife-bearing opponent with a broken bottle. After his peer group initiates his rite of passage, "the older men . . . take over. Their style, of course, would be different. No name-calling toilet contest for them. No knives either, or hot breath and knotted neck muscles. They would test him, match and beat him, probably on some other ground" (p. 272).

The ground is quite literal. These Shalimar elders take Milkman on a midnight hunting trip where he confronts his own incompetence and where he is forced into a process of self-evaluation:

> When he was breathing almost normally, he began to wonder what he was doing sitting in the middle of a woods in Blue Ridge country. He had come here to find traces of Pilate's journey, to find relatives she might have visited, to find anything he could that would either lead him to the gold or convince him that it no longer existed. How had he got himself involved in a hunt, involved in a knife-and-broken-bottle fight in the first place? . . . He had done nothing to deserve their contempt. Nothing to deserve the explosive hostility that engulfed him when he said he might have to buy a car. . . . It sounded old. *Deserve.* Old and tired and beaten to death. Deserve. Now it seemed to him that he was always saying or thinking that he didn't deserve some bad luck, or some bad treatment from others. . . .
>
> Apparently he thought he deserved only to be loved—from a distance, though—and given what he wanted. And in return he would be . . . what? Pleasant? Generous? Maybe all he was really saying was: I am not responsible for your pain; share your happiness with me but not your unhappiness. [pp. 279–80]

The first half of this quotation maps out the contours of Milkman as we have come to know him. He is greedy—in search of gold; self-centered—he sees negative responses to him as the consequence of the character of others and not a response to his own flawed character. Still the fact that the first sentences are questions suggests Milkman's first self-reflective moment. Questions are openended; there is always room for exploration on the other side of them.

"Deserve" is the word that the first and second paragraphs share. Deserve is stated at first as something taken for granted, then questioned and finally implicitly compared to the word "earn." When Milkman examines his relationships to the word deserve he comes to a moment of recognition and engages in a self-critique necessary for personal growth. Milkman sees himself, for the first time, as Guitar, Magdalene, and the reader have come to know him. This seeing marks a turning point in Milkman's life and in the narrative of immersion.[37]

He emerges from the forest as a member of the tribe, having been initiated by this rite of passage—the midnight hunting trip—where he had to confront all his fears about himself. The men, who at first were insulted at his expressed desire for the women of the group, now point him in the direction of one of them, Sweet.

Milkman has now been prepared to receive the full family history. From this moment on, he is in a constant state of self-reflection, and following each moment of self-discovery he is rewarded with information. After realizing that he had used Hagar, betrayed Pilate, and taken his immediate family for granted, he again listens to the game song of the Shalimar children. However, this time he is able to crack the code embedded in the lyrics:

> Jake the only son of Solomon
> Come booba yalle, come booba tambee
> Whirled about and touched the sun
> Come konka yalle, come konka tambee
>
> Left that baby in a white man's house
> Come booba yalle, come booba tambee
> Heddy took him to a red man's house
> Come konka yalle, come konka tambee
>
> Black lady fell down on the ground
> Come booba yalle, come booba tambee
> Threw her body all around
> Come konka yalle, come konka tambee
>
> Solomon and Ryna Belali Shalut
> Yaruba Medina Muhammet too.
> Nestor Kalina Saraka cake.
> Twenty-one children, the last one Jake!
>
> O Solomon don't leave me here
> Cotton balls to choke me
> O Solomon don't leave me here
> Buckra's arms to yoke me
>
> Solomon done fly, Solomon done gone
> Solomon cut across the sky, Solomon gone home. [p. 307]

This is the "Song of Solomon"—song of the son—the "one plum saved" for Milkman. The song not only tells Milkman his family history, but it also embodies a history of the African in the New World. The mythologies informing the song are the Greek tale of Icarus and Daedelus and the African-American folk tale of the Flying African. Embodied within the lyrics are a documentation of the diversity of African ethnicities and religions that converge on the American continent, the horror of fragmentation and destruction of black families and black bodies, and their economic exploitation—all in a plea to the ancestor, Solomon, who flew off and left these bodies on these hostile shores. Caroling softly souls of slavery.

Milkman is the son, returned to take the wisdom, beauty, and pathos of this song into the future. He is nourished by this journey of immersion and prepared to provide this spiritual sustenance to Pilate by informing her of the family history. However, the true sustenance he provides to Pilate is in singing the song, transformed now, into her dying ear: "Sugargirl don't leave me here / Cotton balls to choke me / Sugargirl don't leave me here / Buckra's arms to yoke me" (p. 342).

For Milkman, a return to the Southern home of his ancestors is absolutely necessary for finding himself, for the acquisition of a historical consciousness, for his standing on a higher spiritual and intellectual plane. The South to which he goes is not a place of racial horror and shame, it is a site of history and redemption for him—a place where he can begin to piece together the fragments and where he can grasp and sing that which Kabnis sought, the Song of the Son.

In singing the Song of the Son, Milkman becomes the literate tribesman and the nurturer of Pilate. In writing *Song of Solomon*, Morrison seeks to accomplish the same tasks. This text is the novel as ancestor. In "Rootednesss: The Ancestor as Foundation," Morrsion asserts:

> The novel is needed by African-Americans now in ways that it was not needed before-and it is following along the lines of the function of novels everywhere. We don't live in places where we can hear those stories anymore; parents don't sit around and tell their children those classical, mythological archetypal stories that we heard years ago. But new information has got to get out, and there are several ways to do it. One is the novel.[38]

By retelling the folk story of the Flying African, by embodying the history of the Dead Clan and a history of Africans in the New World, Morrison's novel is itself a site of the ancestor. However, as Michael Awkward has shown us, the function of the novel as ancestor is twofold:

> 1) to preserve the traditional Afro-American folktales, folk wisdom, and general cultural beliefs, and 2) to adapt to contemporary times and needs such traditional beliefs by infusing them with "new information," and to transmit the resultant amalgam of traditional and "new" to succeeding generations.[39]

One of the things that Morrison clearly wants to revise, to infuse with new information, and to transmit to new generations is the notion of black manhood which she inherits from writers like Wright, Ellison, and Baraka. It is quite significant that her revision of manhood goes hand in hand with her revision of the tropes of the migration narrative. Both insist on an understanding of the necessity of confronting, knowing, and transcending the past, and they insist on a notion of manhood that is balanced in its so-called feminine and masculine qualities. However, although Morrison offers revised notions of manhood, it is quite notable that it remains a manhood that is achieved by sacrificing women. Just as Bigger had to kill Bessie, so too must Hagar die before Milkman is able to learn and grow from her death. In Morrison's world, even Pilate must suffer so that she can be the recipient of Milkman's nurturance.

Oddly, it is within the migration narrative of hip-hop, a genre that has been overdetermined by its misogynist masculinity, that the voices of male and female finally lie side by side in their attempts to claim the South as a black homeland and, in so doing, to embody the ancestor.

VI

Tennessee . . . Home

Arrested Development, "Tennessee"

In its opening, the rap song "Tennessee" relays a vision of the South that is very similar to that of *Cane*, *System of Dante's Hell*, and *Song of Solomon*. Looking at the same closed-in world of Richard Wright, Ann Petry, Marita Bonner, and Grandmaster Flash, the protagonist of Arrested Development's "Tennessee" prays:

> Lord i've really been real stressed
> down and out, losin
> ground.
> Although i am black and
> proud
> problems got me
> pessimistic.
> Brothers and sisters
> keep messin up.
> Why does it have to be
> so dam tuff?
> I don't know where I
> could go
> to let these ghost out
> of my skull . . .
> He guided me to
> Tennessee . . . home.

In Tennessee, the protagonist embraces and is enlightened by both the beauty and the terror of the Southern past:

> Walk the roads my forefathers walked
> Climb the trees my forefathers hung from.
> Ask those trees for all their wisdom,
> They tell me my ears are
> So young . . . home.
> Go Back to from
> Whence you
> Came. . . . Home.
> My family tree-My
> Family name . . . Home.
> For some strange
> Reason it had to
> Be . . . Home
> He guided me to
> Tennessee . . . Home.[40]

178

Billie Holiday, Jacob Lawrence, Jean Toomer, and James Baldwin all established the connection between the Southern landscape and the terrorization of black people. In so doing they also suggested that landscape held not only black blood, but also possibilities for black redemption. In this song, the very trees from which black bodies were lynched now provide the descendants of those bodies with ancestral wisdom. Again the black body is an indelible part of the Southern landscape. But now the site of that terror is a source of wisdom, spirituality, and redemption. Billie Holiday's trees of strange fruit, Toomer's trees that drag the chains of the lynched through the night, have here become Morrison's tree that embraces the questing son, Milkman: "Down either side of [Milkman's] thighs he felt the sweet gum's surface roots cradling him like the rough but maternal hands of a grandfather" (p. 282). Note that in the song, lynching is a phenomenon of the past. There is no sense that the South to which the questing narrator returns continues to be a place where black men might be burned by a gang of white teenagers, or even lynched by the Klan.

The persona of this rap may very well have been like the migrant of Stevie Wonder's "Living for the City." This time his prayers are answered. In fact, many connections can be made between the earlier migration narrative and this one. While in Wonder's song those aspects of black culture signified by black women's voices remain as background vocals, reminders of the values and community of a Southern black church, those voices emerge as soloists in the Arrested Development song. The insertion of women's spoken and singing voices directly in the context of the song suggests that the stories and experiences of men and women, though different, are nonetheless both integral to the telling of the tale. The first woman's voice is the spoken free verse conversation of Aerle Taree. Her words are one side of a dialogue. This dialogue contrasts with the individual rap of the male protagonist. She speaks of games like horseshoes and she names the various Southern towns where the new migrants from the North (members of the Arrested Development family) have gone: "Ehse? She went down to Holland Springs. Rasa Don and Baba? They went down to Peachtree." While Taree lists literal geographic sites, the beautiful singing voice of Dionne Farris takes the listener to a symbolic site—Home. At first Farris sings the word "Home" as a background to Speech's rap. Then her voice emerges front and center: "Take me home. Take me home. Home. Take me to another place / take me Hooome. I know I need to go hooommme." With the word home, Farris's voice rises several octaves, making that portion of the song a space of transcendence. The singing woman's voice is a safe space within the context of the song, the context of the spoken (not sung) words of Speech, the narrator. The woman's voice carries us "home"—a place that is more symbolic than literal.

It is this symbolic, almost mythical sense of the South as home, as the site of ancestral wisdom and spirituality, that is also the subject of Julie Dash's *Daughters of the Dust* (1992). In Dash's film, black women's voices and visions relay the narrative. *Daughters*, the story of a Gullah family on the eve of their migration north, is one example of the migration theme in recent black film. Dash's film is unique because it is the first feature by an African-American woman; moreover, it is the only one of the recent black films that is set in a rural context.

The film contemplates the consequences of migration by returning to the eve of the migration of the Peazant family from the Georgia Sea Islands. In many ways Dash's film is an overly romanticized vision of a mythical premigration moment.[41] However, Dash does not deny the legacy of racial terrorism—there are references to an antilynching movement and one of the central figures, Eula Peazant (Alva Rogers), has been raped by a white man. In this way, Dash's choice to return to a mythological premigration moment in this time of heightened urban crisis shares much with Hurston's choice to represent the folk in the South at the very moment of their migration to the North.[42] Dash also utilizes and at times revises many of the central tropes of the migration narrative: Nana Peazant, the wise elder of the Peazant clan, speaks with and imparts wisdom from the ancestors. Dash portrays the influence of the stranger as well in her juxtaposition of the Western Christianity of Viola Peazant (Cheryl Lynn Bruce), one of Nana's daughters who lives on the mainland and who returns to organize and to oversee the migration of the rest of the family, against Nana's traditional Yoruba-based folk practices. By giving Nana Peazant the authoritative voiceover, Dash privileges her view of migration as a mistake for black Southerners.

This view is emphasized in more subtle ways with Dash's use of optical devices like the kaleidoscope and stereoscope—nineteenth-century inventions associated with the modernity of urban life—which she juxtaposes with images of black women's artistry in the form of quilts, culinary skills, basket weaving, and braiding. The colorful star design of the kaleidoscope is situated against the same starlike pattern of the quilt. One is an optical illusion, the other a usable piece of art that is both aesthetically pleasing and practical, as well as a source of family history in that it is made of scraps from generations of family garments. The other optical device in the film, the stereoscopic lens, is used to juxtapose black and white images of Northern cities crowded with immigrants (the newsreel-style photographs appear in the stereoscope) with the beautiful, open color landscape of the Sea Islands. Throughout the film these romanticized efforts to privilege a view of the South as African-American homeland, and of Northern migration as a mistake, are underscored by the simple fact that Dash's audience watches it from a present awareness of the chaos of urban America and the tragedy of black life in the city. This tragedy is nowhere more apparent than in the documentation of violence and despair in the more dominant forms of black popular music and film.

VII

I feel really at home.

Barbara Logan

The recent return migration of African-Americans to the South is anticipated by their literature, and in many ways the narrative of return has helped to shape the discourse around this countermigration. However, there are significant differences between the literary narratives and interviews with return migrants. While the former tend to stress history and ancestors as the reason for "journeys of immersion," return migrants include other factors as well.

As was the case with Northern migration, return migrants are often in search of better economic opportunities, yet economic factors do not account for several other significant reasons for returning to the South. Anthropologist Carol B. Stack has conducted extensive research around return migration to the South and notes:

> Important for most individuals is the homeplace, often a place of birth, usually the place where childhood was spent, but not necessarily either. Homeplaces are identified as the center of family history, a characteristic shared with no other place. More than other places for which a person develops ties, such as the location of college or vacations, the homeplace persists as a migration destination.[43]

Stack goes on to note that the homeplace offers migrants a "haven of safety." In short, migrants who return do so in search of a safe space from the violence and domination of Northern cities. For Phoebe Benson, a return migrant to South Carolina, the South provides a sense of safety and contributes "to a sense of being plugged into African-American roots." Ms. Benson notes: "There are patterns that are very comforting here; it's like the smell of fresh washed sheets and bacon frying in the morning. These are verities and they are reassuring for me." Other migrants cite the increased violence of Northern gangs and the decay of the urban infrastructure as a reason for returning.[44]

While return migrants note that the racism of the South is more blatant than that of the North, it seems to be less effective in denying them access to opportunities. They cite it as an inconvenience they are willing to bear in exchange for "improved economic opportunities, easier life styles and vastly improved race relations." According to Isaac Robinson, a North Carolina Central University sociologist cited in a *New York Times* article on black return migration, new black migrants are returning to a significantly different South: "There is a whole generation out there whose idea of the South has very little to do with lynchings of blacks, segregation or the Ku Klux Klan. They know that there is some racism, but it is not the predominant thing in their minds."[45] The small day-to-day incidents of racism can be attributed to ignorance and rudeness, according to many return migrants.

As has been the case throughout, the words of the migrants themselves offer a more well-rounded perspective than that of artistic narratives of return. They are influenced but not bound by the dominant migration narrative. It is quite significant that most of the artistic narratives fail to focus on the continued racism of the South. In the later narratives, the South to which the protagonist migrates is most often racially monolithic. Return migrants do not paint such a picture.

Perhaps return migrants Barbara and Marshall Logan best articulate the strengths and weaknesses of return without romanticizing it:

> With [my children's] educational background, their exposure, this is not the place for them. There still aren't great opportunities for young black people in small Southern cities. . . . They would be better off in Atlanta or even a Columbia, S.C. . . . Now, I feel that I have returned to my roots. I go to the church that I grew up in and I have restored an old home next door to my 93-year-old uncle. I feel really at home.[46]

The South of this portrait continues to be a place that suffers from a racist legacy. Nonetheless, it is also a haven of African-American history and community, a site of the ancestor, and for some African-Americans, it is still home.

This sense of the South as "home" is certainly a dominant sentiment in the most recent literary treatments of migration as well. However, while Southern sojourns have come to dominate literary migration narratives, there is a significant departure from this tendency in the cultural production of most African-American filmmakers and rap musicians. This departure might be attributed to the difference of generation. The black male bildungsroman that culminated in the sixties is now finding expression in these newer art forms. Both film and rap are currently dominated by young black men. However, as I have documented even within the context of film and rap music, there is evidence of the narrative of return. Though by no means dominant, the works of artists like filmmaker Julie Dash and rap group Arrested Development nonetheless provide an alternative narrative to those offered by the so-called gangsta rappers and the boyz of black film. Their alternative is not just a geographical one asserting the significance of the South; it also provides a vision that values black history, culture, and women.

It is not insignificant that both Dash and Arrested Development are based in Atlanta, Georgia, the contested site with which this chapter opened. Atlanta has garnered an image as the new mecca of black culture, politics, and achievement. While the city suffers from all the problems that plague Northern urban centers, it also houses a significant black middle class, has been able to sustain a black political presence, and is home to a new black cultural renaissance. It is therefore not surprising that the city has replaced Detroit as a capital of black popular music: The producers and performers L. A. Reid and Bell Biv, Devoe, the performers Pebbles, Another Bad Creation, Tupac Shakur, TLC, Toni Braxton, the playwright and essayist Pearl Cleage, and filmmaker Julie Dash all live and create in Atlanta. The city also has a thriving black literary scene with publications like the literary journals *8Rock* and *Catalyst* and the scholarly journal *SAGE: A Journal of Black Women's History*. In the 1980s and 1990s, Atlanta's black institutions of higher education, Spelman, Morehouse, and Clark Atlanta University, experienced a rise in popularity among the children of the black middle class.

Surely, the South's new popularity among certain African-Americans will lead to more developments within the migration narrative; however, because of the dominance of black film and rap music as forms of African-American cultural production in the late twentieth century, it is to these arenas that we must keep our eyes and ears attuned for the next developments in the African-American migration narrative—developments that will be as shaped by their historical and political moment of production, their mode of production, and their intended audience as were their predecessors.

5

New Directions for the Migration Narrative: Thoughts on *Jazz*

Instead of pretending to sum up everything in a neat and tidy manner, I want to initiate a more sustained reading of one migration narrative—Toni Morrison's *Jazz*. Because Morrison's novel challenges the framework presented within these pages, it serves to open rather than close any further discussion of the migration narrative.

Toni Morrison's oeuvre attests to the dispossession, displacement, and mobility that characterize black life in the Americas. *The Bluest Eye* (1970) and *Sula* (1974) are both situated around the migration of significant characters. *Tar Baby* (1981) explores the lives of "cultural exiles"[1] who live on a Caribbean island. *Beloved* (1987) documents the life of a runaway slave, Sethe, as well as the forced and volunteer wanderings of African-Americans following the Civil War and during the Nadir. As I have demonstrated, *Song of Solomon* (1977) is an especially important migration narrative, but *Jazz* (1992) is Morrison's most explicit migration narrative to date. It revisits the theme of black mobility and modernity. In so doing, it explicitly revises some of the most important tropes of the migration narrative—tropes that Morrison helped to define through her creative and critical writings.

In *Jazz*, Morrison still considers the major moments of the migration narrative: the catalyst to migration, the initial confrontation with the urban landscape, the navigation of that landscape, and the construction of the urban subject. Nevertheless, she challenges her own notions of the possibility of the city for the migrant and she introduces a new notion of the ancestor.

Jazz was published in 1992. It spent eleven weeks on the *New York Times* bestsellers list and even longer on the Blackboard African-American bestsellers list.

Jazz is the story of Joe and Violet Trace and Joe's dead teenage lover, Dorcas. All three are migrants to the city. At the novel's opening, Joe has murdered Dorcas and Violet attends Dorcas's funeral in order to stab the corpse. The novel's primary narrator is a quirky, often unreliable, omniscient presence. As with a jazz performance, the characters are given their solos, moments to flourish—but they

184

always return to the arrangement of the omniscient narrator. She tries to control the tale, but sometimes individual soloists break free of the arrangement that she tries to impose on them. Dorcas, the murdered black woman, is given but one solo at the end of the novel. Throughout the text the dead teenager is a presence (but not a ghost) who helps the other characters come to terms with themselves.

Joe and Violet Trace, the central migrants of the text, migrate from Virginia to New York in 1906. Their Virginia is a place of towns with Old Testament names,[2] dispossession, violence, and orphaned children. After arriving in the North, their experiences in the South still shape their decisions. For instance, because both Violet and Joe were abandoned by their mothers, they associate freedom with a childless urban life.

Whereas in the earlier migration narratives the South is often the site of family, here it is filled with motherless children. Violet describes the events that directly precede the suicide of her own mother, Rose:

> [White men] came, talking low as though nobody was there but themselves, and picked around in our things, lifting out what they wanted—what was theirs, they said, although we cooked in it, washed sheets in it, sat on it, ate off of it. That was after they had hauled away the plow, the scythe, the mule, the sow, the churn and the butter press. Then they came inside the house. . . . When they got to the chair where our mother sat nursing an empty cup, they took the table out from under her and then while she sat there alone, and all by herself like, cup in hand, they came back and tipped the chair she sat in. She didn't jump up right away, so they shook it a bit and since she still stayed seated—looking ahead at nobody—they just tipped her out of it like the way you get the cat off the seat if you don't want to touch it or pick it up in your arms. You tip it forward and it lands on the floor. No harm done if it's a cat because it has four legs. But a person, a woman, might fall forward and just stay there a minute looking at the cup, stronger than she is, unbroken at least and lying a bit beyond her hand. Just out of reach.[3]

Instead of nursing her children, Violet's mother nurses an empty cup, a cup that is stronger than she. Rose's descent into madness begins even before this final act of dispossession. In fact, she has endured so much, her daughter wonders:

> What was the thing, I wonder, the one and final thing she had not been able to endure or repeat? Had the last washing split the shirtwaist so bad it could not take another mend and changed its name to rag? Perhaps word had reached her about the four-day hangings in Rocky Mount: the men on Tuesday, the women two days later. Or had it been the news of the young tenor in the choir mutilated and tied to a log, his grandmother refusing to give up his waste-filled trousers, washing them over and over although the stain had disappeared at the third rinse. They buried him in his brother's pants and the old woman pumped another bucket of clear water. Might it have been the morning after the night when craving (which used to be hope) got out of hand? When longing squeezed, then tossed her before running off promising to return and bounce her again like an India-rubber ball? Or was it that chair they tipped her out of? Did she fall on the floor and lie there deciding right then that she would do it. Someday. . . . What could it have been, I wonder? [p. 101]

The litany of reasons that may have led to her suicide seems endless. They range from the small domestic tearing of an old dress, one she mends and irons for lack of a new one, to the large political terrorization of black people (the lynchings here are similar to the one described by Baldwin in *Go Tell It on the Mountain*); from her longing for a husband forced to leave because of his political activity, to her own dispossession as a result of these activities. Morrison outlines both the political and interior pains of being a black woman during the Nadir of black history.

Rose appears to suffer from depression. Her depression is a long time coming. It is a madness not brought on by her genetic makeup but created by her social circumstances. She is the rounded mourning figure of Jacob Lawrence's panel 15. Black women experience white terror as victims of violence and as mothers and wives. The consequences of their torture lead to motherless children—in this case, Violet and her four siblings.

Joe is also a motherless child: He is abandoned by a mother who appears mad. Rose's madness is quiet and unobtrusive, brought on by years of racial oppression. We never know if Joe's mother is really insane or simply "Wild." We never know the cause of her insanity. If Rose is the mourning figure of Lawrence's painting, then Wild is one of Toomer's Southern women taken to the extreme. She is a madwoman who lives in the cane field, the one who has become an indelible part of the Virginia landscape. As with the reapers of Toomer's *Cane*,[4] here, the men who cut the cane fear cutting her: "Cutting cane could get frenzied sometimes when young men got the feeling she was just yonder, hiding, and probably looking at them. One swing of the cutting blade could lop off her head" (p. 166). Though she gives birth to Joe, Wild is incapable of mothering him.[5] As was the case with Rose, who nursed the teacup instead of her children, Wild refuses to nurse Joe when he is born.

Joe and Violet, two motherless children, find each other under a tree in Virginia. Together, they decide to leave the South and to migrate to the city. Like the "motherless child" of the African-American spiritual, they, too, "spread their wings and fly." The South they leave behind is one where the possible ancestors are driven mad. The only source of ancestral wisdom comes from an elder who mentors Joe, the Hunter's Hunter—Henry Lestory. The wisdom he shares with Joe would help him to navigate the urban landscape, but Joe forgets the advice given to him: "Never kill the tender and nothing female if you can help it." Joe notes that Lestory "taught me two lessons I lived by all my life. One was the secret kindness of white people—they had to pity a thing before they could like it. The other—well I forgot it" (p. 125).

In general, the South that Joe and Violet leave is a place characterized by what Morrison names the Dispossession:

> One week of rumors, two days of packing, and nine hundred Negroes, encouraged by guns and hemp, left Vienna, rode out of town on wagons or walked on their feet to who knew (or cared) where. With two days' notice? How can you

> plan where to go, and if you do know of a place you think will welcome you, where is the money to arrive? [pp. 173–74]

The movement of this paragraph is filled with an overwhelming sense of uncertainty and absurdity. In naming it "The Dispossession," Morrison gives it grand historical proportions; it becomes an era, a signpost of the black experience like the Middle Passage, Slavery, the Civil War, Reconstruction, the Nadir, *the Dispossession*, the Great Migration.

Joe and Violet's migration to the city is situated in the context of this grand historical narrative. First the author gives us the historical and then, within the context of the historical, she situates the individual. Joe and Violet are two individuals in the thousands contained in the word "They":

> They came on a whim because there it was and why not? They came after much planning, many letters written to and from, to make sure and know how much and where. . . .
>
> However they came, when or why, the minute the leather of their soles hit the pavement—there was no turning around. Even if the room they rented was smaller than the heifer's stall and darker than a morning privy, they stayed to look at their number. . . . Part of why they loved it was the specter they left behind. The slumped spines of the veterans of the 27th Battalion betrayed by the commander for whom they had fought like lunatics. The eyes of thousands, stupefied with disgust at having been imported by Mr. Armour, Mr. Swift, Mr. Montgomery Ward to break strikes then dismissed for having done so. The broken shoes of two thousand Galveston longshoremen that Mr. Mallory would never pay fifty cents an hour like the white ones. The praying palms, the raspy breathing, the quiet children of the ones who had escaped from Springfield Ohio, Springfield Indiana, Greensburg Indiana, Wilmington Delaware, New Orleans Louisiana, after raving whites had foamed all over the lanes and yards of home.
>
> The wave of black people running from want and violence crested in the 1870s; the 80s; and the '90s but was a steady stream in 1906 when Joe and Violet joined it. [pp. 32–33]

Note the sites of persecution are not strictly Southern. "Southern" is a metaphor for all sites where black people are dispossessed, disenfranchised, and brutalized. This includes Midwestern and Northern cities like East St. Louis. The race riots of East St. Louis are the catalyst of the migration of the text's third significant migrant, Joe's teenage lover, Dorcas. Dorcas is yet another orphan, having lost both her parents to the racial violence of those riots. She loses her life, however, to the jealous rage of her lover.

Without familial ties, Joe, Violet, and Dorcas are migrants who seek to create themselves anew in the city. Without the maps provided by Southern ancestors, they are ill-equipped to navigate the urban landscape. They, along with all the migrants of *Jazz*, are like the music for which the book is named. These migrants explode onto the cityscape, capturing its character, its rhythm, forever changing it, and it forever changing them. They go to Harlem in search of safe space only to find that the safety of that space is very tenuous.

At first glance, Morrison's descriptions of the migrant's initial confrontation with the urban landscape seem optimistic, filled with vibrancy and color, not unlike Toomer's "Seventh Street." Joe and Violet enter "the lip of the City dancing all the way." Like millions of others they enjoyed "look[ing] at their number, hear[ing] themselves in an audience, feel[ing] themselves moving down the street among hundreds of others who moved the way they did, and who when they spoke, regardless of the accent, treated language like the same intricate, malleable toy designed for their own play." They are part of a thriving, throbbing black crowd. In the city, there are no lone black figures—there is a black throng, who, unlike Wright's migrants, possess and reshape language. Although there is racial violence in the city, "up here if you bust out a hundred'll bust right along with you" (p. 128).

For Violet and Joe, and even for Alice Manfred, aunt of Dorcas and resident prude, Harlem appears to be a "safe space." Alice Manfred notes "she had begun to feel safe nowhere south of 110th Street" (p. 54). White New Yorkers may greet migrants with violence, but Harlem seemed to offer them a safe homespace. Nevertheless, very early in the text, even before the story unfolds, the narrator begins to undercut the sense of Harlem as a free and safe space:

> Breathing hurts in weather that cold, but whatever the problems of being winterbound in the City they put up with them because it is worth anything to be on Lenox Avenue safe from fays and the things they think up; where the sidewalks, snow-covered or not, are wider than the main roads of the towns where they are born and perfectly ordinary people can stand at the stop, get on the streetcar, give the man the nickel, and ride anywhere you please, although you don't please to go many places because everything you want is right where you are: the church, the store, the party, the women, the men, the postbox (but no high schools), the furniture store, street newspaper vendors, the bootleg houses (but no banks), the beauty parlors, the barbershops, the juke joints, the ice wagons, the rag collectors, the pool halls, the open food markets, the number runner, and every club, organization, group order, union, society, brotherhood, sisterhood or association imaginable. The service trails, of course, are worn, and there are paths slick from the forays of members of one group into the territory of another where it is believed something curious or thrilling lies. Some gleaming, cracking, scary stuff. [p. 10–11]

The cityscape painted by this paragraph portrays a place of seemingly endless possibility. It is a place that appears to be free of white people, yet they are that nameless presence, those "members of one group" who "foray" into Harlem, in search of the "curious or thrilling." Even when not visible, a white presence controls and restrains the possibility of Harlem. The limitations are parenthetical, contained by parenthesis much in the way that they contain the aspirations of black Harlemites. At first, whites control black people without violence. They place limits on education and true economic opportunity. This "free, safe" space is neither free nor safe. The white presence will come in search of entertainment and it will also come wielding pipes like the one "those whitemen" took to Joe's head in the summer of 1917.

Harlem is not as safe a space as the migrants anticipated. Even those spaces considered most safe, those sites of the "South in the city," are possible sites of victimization. This is especially true for women. Like Lacy's tenement, Brooks's kitchenette, and Naylor's neighborhood, the apartment buildings of *Jazz* seem to constitute community, hospitality, and home:

> Up those five story apartment buildings and the narrow wooden houses in between people knock on each others doors to see if anything is needed or can be had. A piece of soap? A little kerosene? Some fat, chicken or pork, to brace the soup one more time? Whose husband is getting ready to see if he can find a shop open? Is there time to add turpentine to the list drawn up and handed to him by the wives? [p. 10]

However, for a writer who has stressed the significance of neighborhood and community, it is significant that this attempt to describe community lacks the specificity of a name. Neither the neighborhood nor the city is named, and those five-story apartment buildings do not even have an address.[6] This is our first clue that the building does not really constitute community. Joe Trace is one of those neighborly husbands who help to make the building a community. He is the man the women welcome in their midst, the one with whom they feel safe. His very voice is a site of the "South in the city":

> Besides, [the women] liked his voice. It had a pitch, a note they heard only when they visited stubborn old folks who would not budge from their front yards and overworked fields to come to the city. It reminded them of men who wore hats to plow and to eat supper in; who blew into saucers of coffee, and held knives in their fists when they ate. [p. 71]

His voice is "home." In light of this, it would appear that his voice is the repository of the ancestor. However, it might sound like the ancestor but not embody the substance of the ancestor. After all, Joe Trace has forgotten the most significant advice given to him by a Southern elder. In "City Limits, Village Values: Concepts of the Neighborhood in Black Fiction, " Morrison notes that it is the presence of the ancestor in the city that constitutes the neighborhood, or home. In the city, the ancestor as we have come to know her is absent.

Joe Trace's voice may remind the black women of "home," yet he proves to be fatal to at least one black woman. Alice Manfred thinks,

> The brutalizing men and their women were not just out there, they were in her block, her house. A man had come in her living room and destroyed her niece. His wife had come right in the funeral to nasty and dishonor her. She would have called the police after both of them if everything she knew about Negro life had made it possible to consider. [p. 74]

Neither the church nor the home is a safe space, especially for black women. Morrison challenges the notion that any of the preceding spaces are safe. Sites like the home, the house party, the church, sites where there is no white intrusion, do not constitute safe space. In Harlem, "citylife is streetlife" (p. 119). The street comes into the church and the home. What is worse is that these spaces are violent spaces, not only because of the intrusion of whites, but also because of the violence of other blacks. Dorcas is murdered in an apartment at a house party. In other migration narratives, house parties and rent parties were safe spaces for migrants. Worse still is the lack of anger, indignation, and horror following her murder. Her aunt doesn't call the police because she knows they do not value black lives. Her best friend is angry at her for leaving. Her lover is never punished; he simply wallows in self-pity. And his crazy wife tries to deface her corpse.

The lack of public outcry following Dorcas's death is evidence the lack of value placed on black people. The urban blacks of *Jazz* love desire but not other human beings. The city makes them this way. All of the efforts to combat the dehumanizing effects of the city appear inappropriate.

Alice Manfred tries to contain Dorcas in juvenile clothing, thick hose, and restrained hair. "However tight and tucked in her braids, however clunky her high-topped shoes that covered ankles . . . however black and thick her stockings, nothing hid the boldness swaying under her cast iron skirt." Encouraged by the music that embodies her migrant energy, sensuality, and anger, Dorcas resists her aunt's attempts to contain her. Alice's map for navigating the urban landscape, a map that calls for "deafness and blindness" and restraint, is useless.

Alice Manfred's map calls for deafness and blindness; Violet Trace's attempts to navigate that landscape result in her bouts with insanity. As with her mother, Violet also appears to suffer from mental illness. However, her illness is not depression, but split personality. Depression has depth and substance. It has its own narrative. Violet's split personality is a fragmented self, an especially fitting disorder for the city. The narrator describes Violet's bouts with insanity as cracks. "I call them cracks because that's what they are. Not openings or breaks, but dark fissures in the globe light of the day." These dark fissures make the narrative of her days less coherent. Violet describes her illness in terms of "that other Violet," who "walked about the City in her skin; peeped through her eyes and saw things" (p. 89). That other Violet is Violent:

> Where [Violet] saw a lonesome chair left like an orphan in a park strip facing the river, that other Violet saw how the ice skim gave the railing's black poles a weapony glint. Where she, last in line at the car stop, noticed a child's cold wrist jutting out of a too-short, hand-me-down coat, that Violet slammed past a white woman into the seat of a trolley four minutes late. [p. 90]

Although Violet's musings about "that other Violet" seem to confirm her insanity, it soon becomes apparent that the development of "that other Violet" helps Violet to navigate the city. Where Violet sees images of passive victims, lone orphans, or children who have not been cared for, "that other Violet" seizes the opportunity for action, for self-defense. Perhaps Violet's illness is a mechanism that sustains her. She realizes that what appears to be a literal fragmentation of her psyche is in fact a means of survival. "That Violet" is the decisive, tough, strong Violet who used to live in the South: "*That* Violet is not somebody walking around town, up and down the streets wearing my skin and using my eyes shit no *that* Violet is me! The me that hauled hay in Virginia and handled a four-mule team in the brace" (pp. 95–96).[7]

Violet navigates the city by splitting her personality; Alice Manfred tries to navigate it by becoming deaf and blind to it. Joe Trace tries to buy "safe space" by buying Dorcas's affections and renting a neighbor's apartment for their weekly trysts. In bed, he and Dorcas share the emptiness they feel over the loss of their mothers. He tells her about the South. This rented bed becomes the site of illicit sex, a site of "safe time" and intimacy. It is a tentative safety, though, dependent not on love but on desire, which is fleeting.

In *Jazz*, migrants fall in love with the city and not with each other. They desire the image of themselves against its skyline:

> [They] forget what loving other people was like—if they ever knew, that is. I don't mean they hate them, no, it's just that what they start to love is the way a person is in the City; the way a schoolgirl never pauses at a stoplight but looks up and down the street before stepping off the curb; how men accommodate themselves to tall buildings and wee porches, what a woman looks like moving in a crowd, or how shocking her profile against the backdrop of the East River. [p. 34]

They love an image, a painting, a photograph—where individuals are but backdrops or adornment to the true object of their affection—the city and how it makes them feel: "Their stronger, riskier selves."

The music of the city, the black jazz that comes to define the city and the era, serves as a source for constructing a black urban subject. It helps to create a subject in opposition to the one that the City attempts to create: in opposition and yet somehow still defined by it. Power constructs the resisting subject. Jazz music embodies *and* gives voice to their experience.

Alice Manfred's response to jazz music is one side of the tremendous debate that surrounded the music in the 1920s. At first her view reflects the exhortations of the reactionaries and the fundamentalists: "She knew from sermons and editorials that it wasn't real music—just colored folks' stuff: harmful, certainly; embarrassing, of course; but not real, not serious" (p. 59).[8] Nevertheless, Manfred is very, very perceptive in that she hears anger of antilynching protests in the music. In Alice Manfred, Morrison begins to launch her project of redefining, reclaiming the jazz in the term Jazz Age. The happy-go-lucky, welcome fun sought by white interlopers to Harlem is a mask for the complex of emotions and experiences voiced in the music.

While Alice Manfred hears its anger, her young charge Dorcas hears its sensual seductiveness:

> Dorcas lay on a chenille bedspread, tickled and happy knowing that there was no place to be where somewhere, close by, somebody was not licking his licorice stick, tickling the ivories, beating his skins, blowing his horn while a knowing woman sang ain't nobody going to keep me down you got the right key baby but the wrong keyhole you got to get it bring it and put it right here or else. [p. 61]

The music calls Dorcas; it is "a City seeping music that begged and challenged each and every day. 'Come' it said. 'Come and do wrong.'" Throughout the text, jazz is like an addictive drug. It entices, it seduces, it makes the takers think they can do the impossible, and it makes addicts of them. Like the first-generation urban-born, or those who migrated as children, like "citymen . . . closed off to themselves, wise young roosters," like the "schoolgirl [who] never pauses at the stoplight," the jazz of this novel is urban, urbane, and capable not only of defining a black urban reality but also of shaping American modernity. Jazz is both a character of this book as well as the form it takes.

In content, jazz becomes a metaphor for the migrants. The final vision of this narrative is a vision where migrants and their music are influenced by but also profoundly influence and redefine the city to which they migrate.

In a very important paragraph Morrison details her understanding of the impact the migrants have on American cities and American culture:

> When I see them now they are not sepia, still, losing their edges to the light of a future afternoon. . . . For me they are real. Sharply in focus and clicking. I wonder, do they know they are the sound of snapping fingers under the sycamores lining the streets? When the loud trains pull into their stops and engines pause, attentive listeners can hear it. Even when they are not there, when whole city blocks downtown and acres of lawned neighborhoods in Sag Harbor cannot see them, the clicking is there. In the T-strap shoes of Long Island debutantes, the sparkling fringes of daring short skirts that swish and glide to music that intoxicates them more than the champagne. It is in the eyes of the old men who watch these girls, and the young ones who hold them up. It is in the graceful slouch of the men slopping their hands into the pockets of their tuxedo trousers. Their teeth are bright; their hair is smooth and parted in the middle. And when they take the arms of the T-strap girls and guide them away from the crowd and the too-bright lights, it is the clicking that makes them sway on unlit porches while the Victrola plays in the parlor. The click of dark and snapping fingers drives them to Roseland, to Bunny's; boardwalks by the sea. Into places their fathers have warned them about and their mothers shudder to think of. Both the warning and shudder come from the snapping fingers, the clicking. And the shade. Pushed away into certain streets, restricted from others, making it possible for the inhabitants to sigh and sleep in relief, the shade stretches—just there—at the edge of the dream, or slips into the crevices of a chuckle. It is out there in the privet hedge that lines the avenue. Gliding through rooms as though it is tidying this, straightening that. It

bunches on the curbstone, wrists crossed, and hides its smile under a wide-brim hat. Shade. Protective, available. Or sometimes not; sometimes it seems to lurk rather than hover kindly, and its stretch is not a yawn but an increase to be beaten back with a stick. Before it clicks, or taps or snaps its fingers. [pp. 226–27]

In this paragraph, Morrison begins to redifine the Jazz Age. There are many predominant literary allusions in this passage. The most obvious are the allusions to the writing of F. Scott Fitzgerald, the writer who coined the term "Jazz Age" and who attempts to chronicle it. However, in his documentation, black people and their music provide the colorful backdrop for the center-stage activities of his Long Island debutantes, flappers, and graceful tuxedoed young men. Black migrants and their music are the servants who tidy up Sag Harbor mansions and the musicians who play the music to which daring short skirts swish and glide. In his reflections on the era he helped to document, "Echoes of the Jazz Age" (1931), Fitzgerald barely mentions the music or its creators. For him, the period between May 1919 and October 1929 was a time when "a whole race [went] hedonistic, deciding on pleasure."[9] According to Kathy Ogren,

> F. Scott Fitzgerald's fiction about the exploits of young and perhaps "lost" white American youth usually garnered [the] honor [of being most associated with the Jazz Age.] . . . In fact, there is very little accurate depiction of jazz performance in Fitzgerald's fiction. . . . Fitzgerald's strength as a jazz age scribe rested more in his ability to capture the affection of young white college students for jazz than in his accuracy about musical performance.[10]

However, the presence of jazz music sparks something in Fitzgerald and his characters. It is more than background music at the lavish parties; it initiates a mood and sense of desire and longing. In *The Great Gatsby*, "When the 'Jazz History of the World' was over girls were putting their heads on men's shoulder in a puppyish, convivial way, girls were swooning backward playfully into men's arms, even into groups knowing that someone would arrest their falls" (pp. 54–55).

Fitzgerald's "Echoes of the Jazz Age" is filled with nostalgia:

> Sometimes, though, there is a ghostly rumble among the drums, an asthmatic whisper in the trombones that swings me back into the early twenties when we drank wood alcohol and everyday in every way grew better and better, and there was a shortening of skirts, and girls all looked alike in sweater dresses . . . and it seemed only a question of a few years before the older people would step aside and let the world be run by those who saw things as they were—and it all seems rosy and romantic to us who were young then, because we will never feel quite so intensely about our surroundings any more. [p. 22]

This is one of those moments that Morrison has defined as a narrative space where "black people ignite critical moments of discovery or change or emphasis in literature not written by them."[11] Here as elsewhere in Fitzgerald's work, black people are hidden beneath references to their music or in almost surreal momentary images as they glide by in limousines or appear out of nowhere in the ash heap of *The Great Gatsby*. In contrast, Morrison captures the Jazz Age as a moment of African-American modernity.

Jazz, like Morrison's important critical essay, *Playing in the Dark: Whiteness and the Literary Imagination*, attempts to reveal the black presence lurking in the shadows of the American literary imagination. According to Morrison, "American writers were able to employ an imagined Africanist persona to articulate and imaginatively act out the forbidden in American culture." Morrison defines Africanism as "a term for the denotative and connotative blackness that African peoples have come to signify, as well as the entire range of views, assumptions, readings and misreadings that accompany Eurocentric learning about these people."[12]

During the Jazz Age black migrants and jazz music became that "imagined Africanist persona" that allowed white writers, musicians, and consumers of black culture to "articulate and imaginatively act out the forbidden in American culture." Morrison's novel is an attempt to reclaim the Jazz Age, to place the creators of jazz at its very center and to shed light on the shadows.

In addition to revising the Jazz Age to expose the black presence, Morrison also challenges those portrayals of the Harlem Renaissance that have focused primarily on the literary and visual arts as well as the efforts of Harlem Renaissance "architects" W. E. B. Du Bois and Alain Locke. Again, she does this by constructing her narrative around working class black migrants and the music that defines and sustains their lives.

The second set of allusions to the paragraph cited earlier once again refer to *Cane*, another text that portrays the black migrant experience. Muriel and Mrs. Pribby of "Box Seat" click into their chairs. Dan Moore is the South in the city of that story, the migrant doomed to failure on the urban landscape. Muriel is a migrant who loses much of her Southern past, acquiring in exchange for it a mechanical "click." The click of that story represented a negative of modernization. It is the harsh metallic and mechanic sound that stands in contrast to the soft, sensual lyricism of Toomer's Southern women. In the preceding excerpt, it is transformed to a sound that embodies the migrant. First, she tells us the migrants are no longer "sepia colored . . . losing their edge to light." They are not photographs, but the clicking of the camera. They have become that instrument of modernity. As the paragraph unfolds, the clicking becomes the sharp, quick rhythmic snap of a finger, tap of a foot, click of a high heel. The migrants of her passage share much with the migrants of Toomer's "Seventh Street." Like those migrants of Seventh Street, these migrants are also "pushed into certain streets, restricted from others." Nonetheless, their music infiltrates suburban homes and communities, influencing daughters to defy their fathers. The migrants and their music sometimes appear to be "protective" servant types, who hum a tune as they clean. At other times they are migrants of Seventh Street, aggressive, strong, and threatening. At times like these, the migrants are beaten back with sticks, their music beaten back in the antijazz discourse that fueled public debate. Still, "Everywhere they go they are like a magician-made clock with hands the same size so you can't figure out what time it is, but you can hear the ticking, tap, snap." While Richard Wright's migrants were oppressed by the clock, Morrison's become a new clock, with a new measure of time.

The final vision of the narrative is one where the migrants have been transformed and have transformed American culture and society. There is no looking back, no return to a mythical South. Instead they continue to exist on the urban landscape and they even manage to survive it in order to live and love. In this novel, the text embodies a new figure, not the Southern ancestor or the Stranger, but an odd combination of both—the migrant. The voice of the omniscient narrator is the voice of the book itself. The narrator, like the ancestor, is "indeterminate: it is neither male nor female; neither young nor old; neither rich nor poor. It is both and neither."[13] It is a voice that is playful, unreliable, appearing to be all-knowing yet constantly undermining itself. It is a voice that embodies oral culture, instrumental jazz arrangements, paintings, photographs, and history.

From its very beginning, the "Sth" with which it opens, the narrative suggests the indignant teeth sucking of a black woman. Later the book-narrator becomes a blueswoman. Listen:

> He became a Thursday man and Thursday men are satisfied.

> I can tell from their look some outlaw love is about to be, or already has been, satisfied.

> Weekends and other days of the week are possibilities, but Thursday is a day to be counted on. . . .

> So why is it on Thursday that the men look satisfied? . . .

> For satisfaction pure and *deep*,
> For balance in pleasure and comfort, Thursday can't be *beat*—
> As is clear from the capable expression on the faces of the men and their conquering stride in the *street*.

> They seem to achieve some sort of completion on that day that makes them steady enough on their *feet*
> to appear graceful even if they are not.

> They command the center of the sidewalk;
> whistle softly in unlit doors. [pp. 49–50; emphasis added]

Just as the reader gets used to the oral quality of the narrative, it shifts gears and becomes visual:

> The woman who churned a man's blood as she leaned all alone on a fence by a country road might not expect even to catch his eye in the City. But if she is clipping quickly down the big-city street in heels, swinging her purse, or sitting on a stoop with a cool beer in her hand, dangling her shoe from the toes of her foot, the man, reacting to her posture, to soft skin on stone, the weight of the building stressing the delicate, dangling shoe, is captured. And he'd think it was the woman he wanted and not some combination of curved stone, and a swinging, highheeled shoe moving in and out of sunlight. He would know right away the deception, the trick of shapes and light and movement, but it wouldn't matter at all because the deception was part of it too. [p. 34]

Opening with another reference to *Cane*, here, the text takes on the quality of what Deborah McDowell calls photocollage, incorporating "descriptions of many of [James Van der Zee's] photographs."[14]

In becoming both oral and photographic, the text does not choose between ancestor and stranger for its form. It embodies both the ancestor's orality and the modernity of photography. In this way it is like the migrant, a new subject, and like jazz. In fact, in its entirety, the text is like an arrangement for a jazz orchestra.

The gift of the ancestor that this text gives us is not the ancestor of the South, but an ancestor who is herself a migrant. Like Malcolm X for the hip-hop generation this text offers us an alternative figure, one who carries the wisdom of those first migrants, their music, their history, their vision, and even the literature that defined their moment. It also carries a warning against doing what the narrator admits to:

> It was loving the City that distracted me and gave me ideas. Made me think I could speak its loud voice and make that sound human. . . . I missed the people altogether. I was watching the streets, thrilled by the buildings pressing and pressed by stone; so glad to be looking out and in on things I dismissed what went on in heart-pockets closed to me. [pp. 220–21]

Loving the City, loving the desire it creates, "distracts" from the humans who inhabit it. Seeing images, illusions, plays of light, and shadow "distract" from seeing women, full-bodied flesh and heart. Under these conditions, black women may die at the hands of their lovers without a cry of remorse from the "community" they inhabit. There is no anger, indignation, and horror following Dorcas's murder. Her aunt does not call the police because she knows they do not value black lives. Her lover is never punished, he simply wallows in self-pity. And his crazy wife tries to deface her corpse. Throughout she is painted as a character who does not deserve our sympathy, as a selfish, uncaring young woman. The lack of public outcry following Dorcas's death is evidence the lack of value placed on black women's lives by her very own communities. As readers we must ask Morrison, "Is this the price of black modernity?"

Morrison's narrative not only seeks to redefine notions of the Jazz Age and

196

the Harlem Renaissance, but also comments on the negative and positive consequences of migration. These consequences are evident in the crisis and the creativity that emerge from contemporary black urban communities. *Jazz* is a portrait of a people in the midst of self-creation, a document of what they created and what they lost along the way.

Notes

Introduction

1. While the experience of migration is different and varied, the many portrayals of this moment have enough in common to constitute them as a new form of cultural production.

2. Susan Willis, *Specifying: Black Women Writing the American Experience* (Madison: University of Wisconsin Press, 1987). Willis argues that "no other body of writing . . . so intimately partakes of the transformation from rural to urban society or so cogently articulates the change in its content as well as its form" (p. 4); Hazel Carby, *Reconstructing Womanhood: The Emergence of the Black Woman Novelist* (New York: Oxford University Press, 1987) ; " 'It Jus Be's Dat Way Sometime': The Sexual Politics of Women's Blues," in *Unequal Sisters: A Multicultural Reader in U.S. Women's History* ed. Ellen Carol DuBois and Vicki L. Ruiz (New York: Routledge, 1990), pp. 238–49 (first published in *Radical America* 20 [1986]: 9–24); "Policing the Black Woman's Body in an Urban Context," *Critical Inquiry* 18 (Summer 1992): 738–55; Lawrence R. Rodgers, "Dorothy West's *The Living Is Easy* and the Ideal of Southern Folk Community," *African American Review* 26 (Spring 1992): 167–68; "Paul Laurence Dunbar's *The Sport of the Gods*: The Doubly Conscious World of Plantation Fiction, Migration, and Ascent," *American Literary Realism* 24 (Spring 1992): 42–57 (Rodgers is also the author of a very important dissertation from which these two articles are drawn: "The Afro-American Great Migration Novel," Ph.D. dissertation, University of Wisconsin-Madison, 1989); Charles Scruggs, *Sweet Home: Invisible Cities in the Afro-American Novel* (Baltimore: Johns Hopkins University Press, 1993).

3. Carby, "Policing the Black Woman's Body," p. 754.

4. Trudier Harris has detailed the portrayal of lynchings in African-American fiction in *Exorcising Blackness: Historical and Literary Lynching and Burning Rituals* (Bloomington: Indiana University Press, 1984).

5. Michel Foucault, *Discipline and Punish: The Birth of the Prison* (New York: Pantheon Books, 1977), pp. 8–16. While Foucault notes that "by the end of the 18th century and the beginning of the 19th century the gloomy festival of punishment was dying out, though here and there it flickered momentarily into life," in the American South these "festivals" occurred well into the twentieth century. Foucault continues, "Most changes [in punishment are] achieved by 1840 but the hold on the body did not entirely disappear in the mid-19th century." Beneath the qualifying phrases of these two statements lies the continuous history of the torture and punishment of black people in the New World. Foucault is talking about violence imposed by the state; the acts committed against black people in the American South were usually acts of vigilantism, although they were sanctioned by the state.

6. Toni Morrison, "Rootedness: The Ancestor in Afro-American Fiction," in *Black Women Writers at Work: A Critical Evaluation*, ed. Mari Evans (Garden City, N.Y.: Anchor Press, 1984), p. 343.

7. See Theodore O. Mason, "The Novelist as Conservator: Stories and Comprehension in Toni Morrison's *Song of Solomon*," *Contemporary Literature* 29 (1988): 565–81. Mason notes: "Morrison is an example of the novelist as conservator. She is a writer particularly interested in depicting, and thereby preserving and perpetuating, the cultural practices of black communities" (p. 565).

8. Morrison, "Rootedness," p. 345.

9. Thomas Leclair, "'The Language Must Not Sweat': A Conversation with Toni Morrison," in *Toni Morrison: Critical Perspectives Past and Present*, ed. Henry Louis Gates, Jr., and K. A. Appiah (New York: Amistad Press, 1993).

10. Georg Simmel, "The Stranger," in *On Individuality and Social Forms*, ed. Donald Levine (Chicago: University of Chicago Press, 1971), p. 143; "The Metropolis and the Mental Life," in *Classic Essays on the Culture of Cities*, ed. Richard Sennett (New York: Appleton-Century-Crofts, 1969).

11. Jerry G. Watts has noted very important differences between Simmel's Stranger and Park's Marginal Man. "Park's marginal man was a racial or cultural hybrid. He lived as an 'outsider' inside two worlds. He is a person who 'aspires to be but is denied full membership in the new group.' Simmel's stranger by contrast has no assimilationist desires. He remains a potential wanderer who stays. Whereas Park's marginal man was a tormented man suffering from 'spiritual instability, intensified self-consciousness, restlessness and malaise,' the stranger endured no such anxieties. Instead, he was described as a judge and trusted confidant." Jerry Watts, "Victim's Revolt," unpublished manuscript, pp. 4–5. See also E. Franklin Frazier, *The Negro Family in Chicago* (Chicago: University of Chicago Press, 1932).

12. Robert Park, "The Marginal Man," in *Race and Culture* (London: Free Press of Glencoe, 1950), p. 351.

13. Julia Kristeva, *Strangers to Ourselves* (New York: Columbia University Press, 1991). See also Abdul R. JanMohamed, "Negating the Negation as a Form of Affirmation in Minority Discourse: The Construction of Richard Wright as Subject," *Cultural Critique* 7 (Fall 1987): 245–66.

14. Richard Wright, "Blueprint for Negro Writing," *New Challenge*, Fall 1937, pp. 53–65.

15. Carla Cappetti explores Wright's relationship to sociology in detail in *Writing Chicago: Modernism, Ethnography, and the Novel* (New York: Columbia University Press, 1993).

16. Patricia Hill Collins, *Black Feminist Thought* (Boston: Unwin Hyman, 1990), p. 97.

17. bell hooks identifies a similar concept in her essay "Homeplace: A Site of Resistance," in *Yearning: Race, Gender, and Cultural Politics* (Boston: South End Press, 1990), pp. 41–51. According to hooks, these spaces are the domain of black women. They differ from the Marxist conception of the worker's home as a site where the oppressed are sustained in order to maintain their place in the social order. In contrast, Hooks's homeplaces lay the foundation for radical resistance.

18. Leroi Jones, *Blues People: The Negro Experience in White America and the Music That Developed From It* (New York: William Morrow, 1968), p. 107.

19. Because of racial segregation in the South, even the library is not always a safe space for Richard Wright. See *Black Boy* (New York: Harper and Row, 1945).

20. Interpretations that are dominant in mainstream culture are not always dominant in African-American culture. Where possible, I have selected texts that fall into both categories. This is easier to do with musical works than with books. Until recently there were no mechanisms that charted the popularity of books by black authors with black audiences. In light of this, I measure a book's dominance in African-American culture by

its influence on other African-American writers, and by reviews in African-American publications.

21. Alice Walker, *The Third Life of Grange Copeland* (New York: Harcourt Brace Jovanovich, 1970); Albert Murray, *South to a Very Old Place* (New York: McGraw-Hill, 1971).

22. The migration of African-Americans from the South to the North during the early years of the century is representative of the larger movements of formerly enslaved and colonized peoples into Western metropolises following World War II. This movement is perhaps one of the most significant moments in the modern history of the West. The historical significance of these migrations is not limited to the people who participated in them. The mass movement of peoples of color to major urban centers of the West changed the faces of these cities and profoundly influenced Western culture as well. Certainly there are texts from throughout the black diaspora that may also be considered a variation on the migration narrative.

23. Chester Himes, *If He Hollers Let Him Go* (Garden City, N.Y.: Doubleday, Doran, 1946); Charles Burnett *Killer of Sheep* (Independent, 1977); *To Sleep With Anger* (Samuel Goldwyn, 1990); Carrie Mae Weems, *Family Pictures and Stories, 1978–84.* Exhibition Catalogue (Washington, D.C.: National Museum of Women in the Arts, 1993).

Chapter 1

1. Regenia Perry, *Free Within Ourselves: African-American Artists in the Collection of the National Museum of American Art* (Washington, D.C.: National Museum of American Art, Smithsonian Institution, 1992), p. 129. Lawrence was twenty-four years old when these paintings were exhibited. This painting is only one of several that describe the various reasons migrants left the South. Other panels portray floods and boll weevils, which ruined crops, injustice in Southern courts, lack of educational and economic opportunity, and racial discrimination.

2. The Museum of Modern Art sponsored a national tour of the Migration Series. The paintings were shown in Poughkeepsie, New York; Kalamazoo, Michigan; Norton, Massachusetts; Portland, Oregon; Sacramento, California; and other cities. They were also on exhibit at Harvard University.

For an extensive discussion of the creation and exhibition of the Migration Series, see Elizabeth Hutton Turner, ed., *Jacob Lawrence: The Migration Series* (Washington, D.C.: Rappahannock Press, 1993).

3. Robert O'Meally, *Lady Day: The Many Faces of Billie Holiday* (New York: Little, Brown, 1991), p. 33.

4. Ibid. In his biography of Billie Holiday, O'Meally notes Holiday "learned the song's melody and then radically altered it, compressing it into her best range and concentrating its power. In this sense, Holiday the recomposer did write the song herself. . . . Whatever the name on the sheet music, 'Strange Fruit' became an unmistakable part of Billie Holiday's artistic territory" (p. 136).

5. Ibid.

6. Michel Foucault, *Power/Knowledge: Selected Interviews and Other Writings 1972–77*, ed. Colin Gordon (New York: Pantheon Books, 1980), pp. 57–58.

7. Stewart E. Tolnay and E. M. Beck have begun the very important work of revising traditional thinking on the role of violence in the Great Migration. See their "Rethinking the Role of Racial Violence in the Great Migration," in *Black Exodus: The Great Migration from the American South*, ed. Alferdteen Harrison (Jackson: University Press of Mississippi, 1991), pp. 20–35.

8. James Grossman, *Land of Hope* (Chicago: University of Chicago Press, 1989); Florette Henri, *Black Migration: Movement North 1900–1920: The Road from Myth to Man.* (Garden City, N.Y.: Anchor Press, 1976); Carole Marks, *Farewell, We're Good and Gone* (Bloomington: Indiana University Press, 1989).

9. Lawrence Levine, *Black Culture, Black Consciousness: Afro-American Folk Thought,* (New York: Oxford University Press, 1981), pp. 264–66.

10. Leroi Jones, *Blues People: The Negro Experience in White America and the Music That Developed from It.* (1963; reprint, New York: William Morrow, 1968), p. 96.

11. William Barlow, *"Looking Up at Down": The Emergence of Blues Culture* (Philadelphia: Temple University Press,1989); Michael Taft, *Blues Lyric Poetry: A Concordance,* 3 vols. (New York: Garland, 1984); *Sorry but I Can't Take You: Women's Railroad Blues* (Rosetta Records, 1301, 1985); Hazel Carby, "'It Jus Be's Dat Way Sometimes': The Sexual Politics of Women's Blues," in *Unequal Sisters,* ed. Ellen Carol DuBois and Vicki L. Ruiz (New York: Routledge, 1990); Sandra Lieb, *Mother of the Blues: A Study of Ma Rainey* (Amherst: University of Massachusetts Press, 1981).

12. Although violence does occur in the blues lyrics, a thorough review of several blues lyric anthologies and Michael Taft's *Blues Lyric Poetry: A Concordance* reveals no blues lyrics mentioning lynching or the threat of violence as the cause of migration. In blues lyrics lynching is usually the punishment bestowed on a man or woman for killing his or her beloved.

13. William Barlow and Hazel Carby both explore the lyrics of the northbound train blues by men and women in detail.

14. Bessie Smith, "Homeless Blues," *Bessie Smith the Empress* (Columbia Records, CG30818, 1972).

15. C. Vann Woodward, *The Strange Career of Jim Crow* (New York: Oxford University Press, 1974), p. 7.

16. Anonymous, "Sometimes I Feel Like a Motherless Child," traditional African-American spiritual.

17. Quoted in Chris Albertson, *Bessie* (New York: Stein and Day, 1985), p. 127.

18. Levine, *Black Culture,* p. 267.

19. Ibid., pp. 267–68.

20. Emit Scott, ed., "Letters of Negro Migrants of 1916–1918," *Journal of Negro History* 4 (July–October 1919): 290–340.

21. Jacob Lawrence's *Migration of the Negro* series, panel 43, portrays the use of Southern violence to keep blacks from migrating. In general, violence was a very real threat to black Southerners. Between 1882 and 1927, there were 4,951 lynchings in the United States. Of that number 3,513 victims were black, and of those 76 were black women. Approximately 85 percent of these occurred in the South. The Chicago Urban League noted, "after a lynching, colored people from that community will arrive in Chicago inside of two weeks."

22. Scott, "Letters of Negro Migrants," p. 456.

23. In the popular press of the day, especially the *Chicago Defender* and the NAACP's *Crisis,* lynching is cited to encourage Southern blacks to migrate. The sensational journalism of the *Defender* carried headlines and editorials which not only documented in detail each lynching that occurred but chided the South and encouraged black Southerners to escape the constant threat of murder by migrating north.

24. Paul Lawrence Dunbar's *Sport of the Gods,* Nella Larsen's *Quicksand,* and Ralph Ellison's *Invisible Man* all depart from this tendency. Dunbar's novel cites the duplicity of one white man, Francis Oakely, as the reason for his character's migration. In contrast, both Larsen and Ellison cite the repressive nature and disciplinary work of white-

controlled black colleges as the causes for their protagonists' migration. This difference is a consequence of their migrants' class status. However, both writers make use of the lynching motif, which enters their texts in mediated ways. For Ellison, the Battle Royale is representative of the violence of the South and in Larsen's second novel, *Passing*, the newspaper story about the lynching, which her characters discuss at the breakfast table, asserts the racial terrorism of the South. I am grateful to Michael Denning for drawing this to my attention.

25. The one exception to this is Paul Lawrence Dunbar's founding text, *Sport of the Gods* (1902).

26. Jones, *Blues People*, p. 95.

27. I chose men here instead of people because more often than not it was men who were the victims of lynching.

28. Jacquelyn Dowd Hall, "'The Mind That Burns in Each Body': Women, Rape, and Racial Violence," in *Powers of Desire: The Politics of Sexuality*, ed. Ann Snitow, Christine Stansell, and Sharon Thompson (New York: Monthly Review Press, 1983), pp. 328–50; *Revolt against Chivalry: Jessie Daniel Ames and the Women's Campaign against Lynching* (New York: Columbia University Press, 1979).

29. For an extensive reading of Dunbar's *Sport of the Gods* as a novel of migration, see Lawrence R. Rodgers, "Paul Laurence Dunbar's *The Sport of the Gods*: The Doubly Conscious World of Plantation Fiction, Migration, and Ascent," *American Literary Realism* 24 (Spring 1992): 42–57.

30. Trudier Harris documents this tendency in a large number of novels, stories, and poems by black male writers in *Exorcising Blackness: Historical and Literary Lynching and Burning Rituals* (Bloomington: Indiana University Press, 1984).

31. Eve Sedgwick, *Between Men: English Literature and Male Homosexual Desire* (New York: Columbia University Press, 1985).

32. Jean Toomer, *Cane* (1923; reprint, New York: Liveright, 1975), p. 28; page numbers cited in the text refer to this edition.

33. Here, my reading of Tom Burwell as folk poet differs significantly from that of Alain Sollard, who claims that

> Toomer's treatment of the psychology of the male protagonist is somewhat stereotyped. Tom Burwell is a "natural" man. He is a fair representative of a countryman—a sturdy, simple type of person. . . . He is not articulate. But when he declares his love, he strikes a true note. . . . The way he puts his feeling is authentic: his words are simple, his message is sensitive. A true black man is speaking here. Consider his syntax: quoting one or two examples will suffice to show that Toomer renders the black form of speech accurately. . . . In the rest of the passage the confusion of tenses and persons—-Ise . . . —is also typical of a black American. Even the tone and content of Tom's message faithfully record the black man's earnestness and enthusiasm. Here we recognize Toomer's expert knowledge of black people.

"Myth and Narrative Fiction in *Cane*: 'Blood-Burning Moon'," *Callaloo* 8 (Fall 1985): 556. It would appear that Sollard is more guilty of stereotyping than Toomer.

34. Nellie McKay notes: "Black women, as symbols of the culture, are identified with nature. In varying degrees, they are beautiful, innocent, sensuous, and strong, yet they are also vulnerable, misunderstood, and unpossessable. Nature is rich, beautiful, lush, benevolent, and always helpless against the onslaughts of industrialization and the ravages of the modern age. The industrial age destroys the pastoral environment, just as racial and sexual oppression are responsible for the alienation, madness, and death of the women in this part of the book." *Jean Toomer, Artist: A Study of His Literary Life and Work, 1894–1936* (Chapel Hill: University of North Carolina Press, 1984), pp. 90–91.

35. Lucinda H. MacKethan notes that in *Cane* "the South, land not only of red soil, canefield and folk song, but also land of lynching and prejudice, primitive violence as well as pastoral peace. . . . Thus irony informs every aspect of Toomer's version of the pastoral." "Jean Toomer's *Cane*: A Pastoral Problem," in *Norton Critical Edition*, ed. Darwin Turner (New York: W. W. Norton, 1988), p. 230.

36. Cowley might better be described as an established independent left critic at the time of his review of *Uncle Tom's Children*. I am grateful to James Miller for bringing this to my attention.

37. See Michel Fabre, *The Unfinished Quest of Richard Wright* (New York: William Morrow, 1973).

38. In his nonfiction autobiography, *Black Boy*, Wright does return to the South to confront his father.

39. Richard Wright, *Lawd Today* (Boston: Northeastern University Press, 1969), p. 97.

40. Harris, *Exorcising Blackness*, p. 95.

41. Robert B. Stepto, *From Behind the Veil: A Study of Afro-American Narrative*. (Urbana: University of Illinois Press,1979).

42. Richard Wright, *Uncle Tom's Children* (1938; reprint, New York: Harper and Row, 1940), p. 27; page numbers cited in the text refer to this edition.

43. John Tagg, *The Burden of Representation: Essays on Photographies and Histories* (Amherst: University of Massachusetts Press, 1988), p. 93; William Stott, *Documentary Expression and Thirties America* (New York: Oxford University Press, 1973), p. 136.

44. For an extensive discussion of the relationship between Wright and Rosskam during the book's publication and an exploration of the politics of the FSA photographs of African-Americans, see Nicholas Natason, *The Black Image in the New Deal: The Politics of FSA Photography*, (Knoxville: University of Tennessee Press, 1992).

45. Richard Wright, *12 Million Black Voices* (1941; reprint, New York: Thunder's Mouth Press, 1988), p. 35; page numbers cited in the text refer to this edition.

46. Richard Wright, *Black Boy: A Record of Childhood and Youth* (1945; reprint, New York: Harper and Row, 1966), p. 45.

47. Author's conversation with James A. Miller, November 13, 1991.

48. Natanson, *The Black Image in the New Deal*, p. 254.

49. Of course, Harriet Jacob's Linda Brent is a precursor to Florence in that she runs away from the slave states because of the sexual harassment she experiences from her master. Jacobs, *Incidents in the Life of a Slave Girl* (New York: Harcourt Brace Jovanovich, 1973).

50. James Baldwin, *Go Tell It on the Mountain* (1952; reprint, New York: Dell, 1985), p. 72; page numbers cited in the text refer to this edition.

51. In asserting Florence's significance as a black woman character, I offer a perspective quite different from that of Trudier Harris in *Black Women in the Fiction of James Baldwin* (Knoxville: University of Tennessee Press, 1985). For Harris, Baldwin fails to create "complex development" of his female characters. She sees all the women of *Go Tell It on the Mountain* as limited by their relationships to men and the church. While Harris acknowledges Florence's independence, she also says that the price of Florence's independence is her guilt. "Florence is torn between duty and self-determination" (p. 34). It seems that Baldwin is perfectly aware of the tensions that circumscribe Florence's life and that by portraying them, he is offering a critique of those values that would seek to limit her determination. These include the patriarchy of the black family and the black church as well as Florence's own status-grasping upward mobility.

52. Darlene Clark Hine, "Black Migration to the Urban Midwest: The Gender Dimension, 1915–1945," in *The Great Migration in Historical Perspective: New Dimensions of*

Race, Class and Gender, ed. Joe William Trotter, Jr. (Bloomington: Indiana University Press, 1991), pp. 127–46.

53. While Baldwin does not explore the redemptive possibilities of the South in *Go Tell It on the Mountain*, his essay "Nobody Knows My Name: A Letter from the South" does consider the relationship of the South to the urban black. "Negroes in the North are right when they refer to the South as the Old Country. A Negro born in the North . . . sees, in effect, his ancestors, who, in everything they do and are, proclaim his inescapable identity." *Nobody Knows My Name: More Notes of a Native Son* (New York: Dial Press, 1961), p. 87.

54. In her first novel, *The Bluest Eye*, Morrison does explore the Southern assault on black manhood and its consequences in the North in the character of Cholly Breedlove.

55. Henry Louis Gates, Jr., "Preface" to *Toni Morrison: Critical Perspectives Past and Present*, ed. Gates and K. A. Appiah (New York: Amistad Press, 1993).

56. Toni Morrison, *Song of Solomon* (New York: New American Library, 1978), pp. 237–38.

57. Melvin Dixon, *Ride Out the Wilderness: Geography and Identity in Afro-American Literature* (Urbana: University of Illinois Press, 1987), p. 163.

58. Ida B.Wells, *Crusade for Justice* (Chicago: University of Chicago Press, 1970), p. 64.

59. According to Michael Awkward, who, along with Susan Willis, is one of the few critics to explore Morrison's choice of a black male protagonist in *Song of Solomon*, "clearly, for Morrison, black female psychic health cannot be achieved without the cooperative participation of both females and males in its creation and nurturance." "Unruly and Let Loose: Myth, Ideology, and Gender in *Song of Solomon*," *Callaloo* 13 (Spring 1990): 489.

60. Dixon, *Ride Out the Wilderness*, p. 164.

61. Toni Morrison, "Life in His Language," in *James Baldwin: The Legacy*, ed. Quincy Troupe (New York: Simon and Schuster, 1970), p. 76.

62. It is significant that Walker's novel, like Morrison's, focuses on the development of a black male protagonist. In so doing, she provides an alternative notion of black manhood to that defined by the Black Power Movement.

63. Gloria Naylor, *The Women of Brewster Place* (New York: Viking Press, 1982), pp. 22–23; page numbers cited in the text refer to this edition.

64. Hine, "Black Migration," p. 138.

Chapter 2

1. Jacob Lawrence has noted that the Southern paintings take their shape from organic forms, whereas the Northern paintings are geometrical. The choice of organic forms for the Southern paintings places an emphasis on nature and the land; in the North, the geometrical imagery is less connected to nature, more abstract and architectural. Jacob Lawrence lecture, February 1990, Wadsworth Athenaeum, Hartford, Conn.

2. As quoted in St. Clair Drake and Horace Cayton, *Black Metropolis* (New York: Harcourt, Brace, 1945), p. 61.

3. Richard Wright uses a similar map in *Native Son*. In Wright's map, the shaded areas represent those parts of the South Side that have been searched for the fugitive, Bigger Thomas. The darkening horde represents the power of the police apparatus. The white portion of the map indicates the spaces that remain "unsafe" for white women because Bigger is still at large.

4. Herbert Shapiro, *White Violence and Black Response: From Reconstruction to Mont-*

gomery (Amherst: University of Massachusetts Press, 1988). This brilliant study documents the history of white violence against blacks in both the North and the South.

5. F. Scott Fitzgerald, *The Great Gatsby* (1925; reprint, New York: Collier Books, 1980), p. 69.

6. Richard Wright, *American Hunger* (New York: Harper and Row, 1977), p. 1; page numbers cited in the text refer to this edition.

7. Rudolph Fisher, *City of Refuge: The Collected Stories of Rudolph Fisher*, ed. John McCluskey (Columbia: University of Missouri Press, 1987).

8. My use of "stranger" is detailed in the introductory essay. The term was initially used by Georg Simmel in his analysis of Jewish migrants to the city.

9. Stephen Kern, *The Culture of Time and Space 1880–1918* (Cambridge, Mass: Harvard University Press, 1983), Introduction.

10. I borrow this title from Brett Williams's article "The South in the City" in *Journal of Popular Culture*. According to Williams, "Migrants bring to cities an expressive culture deeply rooted in another place. Because expressive culture is crucial in defining place, they must revise the often-inappropriate aesthetics of home and join them to more embracing commercial and popular media" (p. 30). Williams's article has greatly influenced my own thinking on black migrant culture as it is discussed in this chapter. Brett Williams, "The South in the City," *Journal of Popular Culture* 16 (1982): 30–41.

11. Leroi Jones, *Blues People: The Negro Experience in White America and the Music That Developed from It* (New York: William Morrow, 1968), p. x.

12. See Jones, *Blues People*; Paul Oliver, *Blues Fell This Morning: The Meaning of the Blues* (London: Cassell, 1960), and *Screening the Blues: Aspects of the Blues Tradition*, (London: Cassell, 1968).

13. Quoted in Jones, *Blues People*, p. 106.

14. In questioning "here," this song resembles the Afro-American spiritual "Lord, How Come Me Here?"

> Lord, how come me here?
> I wish I never was born.
> There ain't no freedom here, Lord.
> I wish I never was born.
> They treat me so mean here, Lord.
> I wish I never was born.
> They sold my chillen away, Lord.
> I wish I never was born.
> Lord, how come me here?
> I wish I never was born.

15. Panel 53 of Lawrence's Migration series provides a similar portrait of the black middle class. The caption beneath the painting reads, "The Negroes who had been North for sometime met their fellow men with disgust and aloofness."

16. Billie Holiday and William Duffy, *Lady Sings the Blues* (Garden City, N.Y.: Doubleday, 1965), p. 33.

17. Charles Keil, *Urban Blues* (Chicago: University of Chicago Press, 1966).

18. Ibid., p. 55.

19. Ibid., p. 76.

20. Linda Dahl, *Stormy Weather: The Music and Lives of a Century of Jazz Women* (New York: Pantheon Books, 1984), p. 120.

21. Chris Albertson, *Bessie* (New York: Stein and Day, 1972), p. 131.

22. Some may argue that the blues performance replaces the church in the lives of the migrants. According to Lawrence Levine, "During the years of transitions from slavery to

freedom, from rural to urban, from South to North, from self-containment to greater exposure to the larger society, black secular music became an increasingly dominant expressive mode reflecting inevitably the decay of the sacred universe." *Black Culture, Black Consciousness: Afro-American Folk Thought* (New York: Oxford University Press, 1977), p. 238. Because the church is in such a state of transformation at this time, the blues performance may, in fact, provide the only source of stability and comfort in this new environment.

23. Albertson, *Bessie*, p. 52.

24. Jones, *Blues People*, p. 103.

25. William Barlow, *"Looking Up at Down": The Emergence of Blues Culture* (Philadelphia: Temple University Press, 1989), p. 169.

26. Jones says that both ragtime and boogie-woogie were "appropriations of white pianistic techniques by black musicians. " However, whereas ragtime aspired to more European "melodic and harmonic variations," boogie-woogie was more percussive and blueslike. *Blues People*, pp. 113–15. Ragtime leaned toward the Stranger, informed by a black past, whereas the uncommercialized form of boogie-woogie invoked and maintained the ancestor while addressing the fragmentation and temporality of the North.

27. Barlow, *"Looking Up at Down,"* p. 4.

28. Jones, *Blues People*, p. 94.

29. Keil, *Urban Blues*, p. 55. Keil's most problematic remarks occur in the introduction to his book, where he describes "the most striking feature of Negro social structure: the battle of the sexes." He asserts, "Men are 'by nature' primarily interested in sexual satisfaction and independence (money will get you both); they are 'strong' sexually, and will take favors from anyone who will grant them. Women are said to be primarily interested in emotional support and their families . . . they are 'weak' sexually, and tend to become attached to one or two men at a time. . . . Relationships between the sexes are usually governed by variations of the 'finance-romance' equation that appears in so many blues lyrics" (p. 9). Keil's gross generalizations are illustrative of the pitfalls that await the critic should he or she read song lyrics as the wholesale literal "truth" of a group of people.

30. Barlow, *"Looking Up at Down,"* p. 181.

31. Ibid., pp. 173–74.

32. Hazel Carby uses the Gramscian category of organic intellectual to describe the blueswomen. As such, she claims, their "music and song embodied the social relations and contradictions of black displacement: of rural migration and the urban flux. In this sense, as singers these women were organic intellectuals; not only were they a part of the community that was the subject of their song but they were also a product of the rural-to-urban migration." "'It Jus Be's Dat Way Sometime': The Sexual Politics of Women's Blues," in *Unequal Sisters: A Multicultural Reader in U.S. Women's History*, ed. Ellen Carol DuBois and Vicki L. Ruiz (New York: Routledge, 1990), p. 242. See also Hazel Carby, "Policing the Black Woman's Body in an Urban Context," *Critical Inquiry* 18 (Summer 1992): 738–55.

33. Keil, *Urban Blues*, p. 218.

34. Jones, *Blues People*, p. 114.

35. Both Richard Wright in *12 Million Black Voices* and Malcolm X in his autobiography provide detailed descriptions of the lindy hop.

36. Richard Wright, *12 Million Black Voices* (New York: Tunder's Mouth Press, 1988), p. 128; page numbers cited in the text refer to this edition.

37. Levine, *Black Culture*, pp. 176–77.

38. Michael Harris's pioneering study of the life and work of Thomas Dorsey, *The Rise of Gospel Blues: The Music of Thomas Andrew Dorsey in the Urban Church* (New York: Oxford

University Press, 1992) documents the development of the gospel blues, a term Harris uses to define "the blend of sacred texts and blues tunes." Harris sees the career of Thomas Dorsey as exemplifying the challenge gospel blues posed to and its triumph over old-line urban black Protestant denominations.

39. Allan Spear, *Black Chicago: The Making of a Negro Ghetto 1890–1920* (Chicago: University of Chicago Press, 1967), pp. 174–75.

40. Drake and Cayton, *Black Metropolis*, p. 157.

41. Pentecostalism itself was an urban religious movement founded by black holiness minister William J. Seymour. Seymour led the Azusa Street revivals in Los Angeles from 1906 to 1909. See C. Eric Lincoln and Lawrence Mamiya, *The Black Church in the African American Experience* (Durham, N.C.: Duke University Press, 1990), pp. 76–79.

42. See Drake and Cayton, *Black Metroplis*, pp. 416–23; Spear, *Black Chicago*, pp. 175–78; and James R. Grossman, *Land of Hope: Chicago, Black Southerners, and the Great Migration* (Chicago: University of Chicago Press, 1989), pp. 156–59.

43. Harris, *Gospel Blues*, pp. 120–21.

44. Grossman, *Land of Hope*, p. 128.

45. Ibid., p. 159.

46. Hazel Carby provides an insightful discussion of this conflict in "The Quicksands of Representation," the last chapter of *Reconstructing Womanhood: The Emergence of the Black Woman Novelist* (New York: Oxford University Press, 1987). Also see Carby, "Policing the Black Woman's Body." While Carby is correct in noting the class conflict between migrants and the Northern black middle class, she limits working-class black culture to blues culture. Gospel culture was another working-class–generated response to urban migration. Evelyn Higginbotham notes that there emerged within the working class a conflict over which voice best represented the migrant experience: that of the bluesmen and women or that of the church members. Evelyn Brooks Higginbotham, "'Out of the Age of the Voice': The Black Church and Discourses of Modernity," Paper delivered at the Conference on the Black Public Sphere in the Era of Reagan and Bush, October 14, 1993, University of Chicago.

47. Paul Oliver, *Songsters and Saints: Vocal Traditions on Race Records* (New York: Cambridge University Press, 1984).

48. Ibid., pp. 272–80.

49. *Preachin' the Gospel: Holy Blues*, Columbia Sony Entertainment, 1991.

50. Blind Willie Johnson was apparently "discovered" by Frank Walker of Columbia Records on a field recording trip to Dallas in 1927. According to Paul Oliver, Johnson had already gained a local reputation as a street singer and evangelist by the time he was recorded by Columbia. For an extensive study of early black religious recordings see Oliver's *Songsters and Saints*.

51. Mark A. Humphrey, "Holy Blues: The Gospel Tradition," in *Nothing But the Blues: The Music and the Musicians*, ed. Lawrence Cohn (New York: Abbeville Press, 1993), p. 125

52. Jean Toomer, *Cane*, (1923; reprint, New York: Liveright, 1975), p. 11; page numbers cited in the text refer to this edition.

53. Nellie McKay, *Jean Toomer, Artist: A Study of His Literary Life and Work, 1894–1936* (Chapel Hill: University of North Carolina Press, 1984), p. 129.

54. In seeing Avey as a repository of the Southern section, my reading departs from that of Houston Baker. Baker argues that Avey is "one of the more languorous and promiscuous members of the new urban black bourgeoisie" and that she is "hopelessly insensible to the artist's rendering of 'a larger life,' and one would scarcely expect her to respond to a beautiful heritage." "Journey Toward Black Art: Jean Toomer's *Cane*," in

Afro-American Poetics: Revisions of Harlem and the Black Aesthetic (Madison: University of Wisconsin Press, 1988), p. 34. Instead, I argue that her very "languorous" and "promiscuous" nature ties her to that "beautiful heritage" of the Southern section of the text. I think the narrator-artist is the one who appears to be most removed from that heritage. In this sense, my reading is probably closer to that of Nellie McKay, who argues, "Avey represents the creative elements of the black folk culture that were brought to the North. The narrator and his friends are the urban black people who recognize the culture's values but who exploit them for self-serving purposes that do not enhance or enrich themselves or others." Ibid., p. 132.

55. Baker, "Journey Toward Black Art," p. 37.

56. Wright, *American Hunger*, p. 1.

57. None of these images are race-specific; in utilizing them, Richard Wright brings naturalism to the task of creating an African-American migration narrative. They are forms and images used by other American naturalists like Theodore Dreiser.

58. Carla Cappetti and Michel Fabre have both documented the impact of the Chicago school on Wright's work. See Cappetti, *Writing Chicago: Modernism, Ethnography, and the Novel* (New York: Columbia University Press, 1993), and Michel Fabre, *The Unfinished Quest of Richard Wright* (New York: William Morrow, 1973). Capetti reads Wright's autobiographies as the "conjunction between literary autobiography and sociological life history" (p. 183). While Cappetti is right in stressing the influence of the Chicago school on Wright, in so stressing that influence she presents us with a Wright who is once again a "sociological" writer, missing the philosophical and political influences that are equally important in his art.

59. Robert E. Park, "Human Migration and the Marginal Man," in *Race and Culture: Essays in the Sociology of Contemporary Man* (London: Free Press of Glencoe, 1950), p. 355.

60. Ibid., pp. 354–56.

61. Drake and Cayton, *Black Metropolis*, pp. xviii–xix.

62. Nicholas Natanson explores in great detail those aspects of black life that Wright's narrative and Rosskam's accompanying phototext left out of *12 Million Black Voices*. For Natanson, the absence of a black middle class is especially significant. Given Wright's perspective about the possibilities inherent in black folk culture in his other writings, I think *12 Million Black Voices* emerges as the text where he is most willing to concede that the culture is a very rich one. However, even here he denies that it might offer any possibility for black agency in the North. Nicholas Natanson, *The Black Image in the New Deal: The Politics of FSA Photography* (Knoxville: University of Tennessee Press, 1992).

63. Ibid., p. 143.

64. The image of the clock takes on great significance in Wright's fiction, especially the opening alarm clock of *Native Son*. See Werner Sollors, "Modernization as Adultery: Richard Wright, Zora Neale Hurston, and American Culture of the 1930's and 1940's," *Hebrew University Studies in Literature and the Arts* 18 (1990): 1–37.

65. According to Natanson, Rosskam carefully selected and at times doctored the photographs so that they would better fit the grimness of Wright's narrative (*The Black Image*, p. 249). However, as this example illustrates, throughout the text, there is evidence that the photographs and the written narrative depart from one another.

66. Antonio Gramsci, *Selections from the Prison Notebooks*, ed. Quintin Hoare and Geoffrey Nowell Smith (New York: International Publishers, 1987).

67. Carla Cappetti's reading of Wright's autobiography is useful in discussing his position here in *12 Million Black Voices*. For Cappetti, Wright is an informant, a participant-observer, and "a kind of sociologist [who] gives meaning to his own life and to the lives of other black migrants" (*Writing Chicago*, p. 183).

68. Grossman, *Land of Hope*, p. 128.

69. Houston A. Baker, *Workings of the Spirit: The Poetics of Afro-American Women's Writing* (Chicago: University of Chicago Press, 1991), p. 117. Baker argues that black women fall victim to Wright's conception of history. According to Baker, Wright "did not simply miss the continent of black women during an innocent and objective voyage of discovery. No, in fact, he sighted the continent, then refigured it in accordance with his preferred historiographical strategies of scientific socialism" (p. 119).

70. Malcolm X with Alex Haley, *The Autobiography of Malcolm X* (New York: Ballantine Books, 1964), p. 63.

71. "Call of the Jitterbug," Filmstrip. Green Room Productions, 1988.

72. Wright, *12 Million Black Voices*, p. 126.

73. Ibid., p. 128.

74. Ibid., p. 147.

75. Significantly, Ann Petry's *The Street*, a text in which the visions of Wright and West often merge, did quite well commercially.

76. Lawrence R. Rodgers, "Dorothy West's *The Living Is Easy* and the Ideal of Southern Folk Community," *African American Review* 26 (Spring, 1992): 167.

77. Dorothy West, *The Living Is Easy* (1948; reprint, New York: The Feminist Press, 1982), p. 5; page numbers cited in the text refer to this edition.

78. Drake and Cayton, *Black Metropolis*, p. 662.

79. Ibid., p. 659.

80. Rodgers, "Dorothy West's *The Living Is Easy*," p. 169.

81. Charles Scruggs, *Sweet Home: Invisible Cities in the Afro-American Novel* (Baltimore: Johns Hopkins University Press, 1993), p. 139.

82. Although Baldwin's first novel seems to differ greatly from Wright's fictional portrayal of black life, it nonetheless is still greatly influenced by Wright's nonfiction and theoretical writing. In "Blueprint for Negro Writing," Wright encourages black writers to use the critical frameworks provided by Marxism, the literary techniques of modernism, and black folk culture in order to paint a complex picture of black life. In light of this, although we can see Baldwin's effort to distance himself from Wright in both his fiction and his nonfiction, Wright's influence on him remains. Once again, this suggests Wright's dominance.

83. For more on Baldwin's use of James, see Horace Porter, *Stealing the Fire: The Art and Protest of James Baldwin* (Middletown, Conn.: Wesleyan University Press, 1989), esp. Chapter 5, "James Baldwin and the Mighty Henry James."

84. James Baldwin, *Go Tell It on the Mountain* (1952; reprint, New York: Dell, 1985), p. 18; page numbers cited in the text refer to this edition.

85. Cornel West asserts: "When [Baldwin] looked closely into his own life, he saw almost precisely what Wright saw—terror, fear, and self-hatred. These qualities evolved from a rigid, fundamentalist Christian home in the heart of urban America—Harlem." *Prophesy Deliverance! An Afro-American Revolutionary Christianity* (Philadelphia: Westminister Press, 1982), p. 83.

86. Scruggs notes that in this section of the novel John also uses imagery from Charles Dickens's *A Tale of Two Cities* to make sense of the world about him (p. 153).

87. James Baldwin, "Down at the Cross: Letter from a Region in My Mind," in *The Fire Next Time* (New York: Dell Books, 1962), pp. 59–60.

88. Toni Morrison's *Song of Solomon* is the best example of this tendency. Morrison's *Bluest Eye* and Gloria Naylor's *The Women of Brewster Place* also provide evidence of the importance of Southern retentions for the Northern black.

89. Michael Awkward cites the connection between these two openings in *Inspiriting Influences: Tradition, Revision, and Afro-American Women's Novels* (New York: Columbia University Press, 1989), p. 100.

90. Gloria Naylor, *The Women of Brewster Place* (New York: Viking Press, 1982), p. 1; page numbers cited in the text refer to this edition.

91. Stevie Wonder, "Living for the City," *Innervisions* (Tamala Records, 9052MD, 1973).

92. Ellen Willis, "The Importance of Stevie Wonder," *New Yorker*, 30 December 1974, pp. 59–62.

93. Maureen Orth, "Stevie the Wonder Man," *Newsweek*, 28 October 1974, p. 62.

94. Other songs that were popular in the black community at the same time as "Living for the City" include Aretha Franklin's "Until You Come Back to Me" and James Brown's "Stoned to the Bone." Brown's "Funky President," which some suggest rivaled Wonder's portrayal of migration, did not come out until November 1974—a full year later. It spent fifteen weeks on *Billboard*'s rhythm and blues chart, and it peaked at number four. It never broke through the top forty on the pop chart. None of these songs has had the resonance of Wonder's "Living for the City."

Chapter 3

1. Werner Sollors, "Modernization as Adultery: Richard Wright, Zora Neale Hurston, and American Culture of the 1930's and 1940's," *Hebrew University Studies in Literature and the Arts* 18 (1990): 3.

2. Houston A. Baker, *Workings of the Spirit: The Poetics of Afro-American Women's Writing* (Chicago: University of Chicago Press, 1991), p. 104.

3. Spencer Crew, *Field to Factory: Afro-American Migration 1915–1940* (Washington, D.C.: Smithsonian Institution Press, 1987), p. 44.

4. Chicago Urban League Campaign of Education of Southern Migrants, quoted in Crew, ibid.

5. David Forgacs, ed., *An Antonio Gramsci Reader* (New York: Schocken Books, 1988), p. 275.

6. Richard Wright, *Lawd Today* (1963; reprint, Boston: Northeastern University Press, 1969), pp. 119–21.

7. Arna Bontemps, *Anyplace but Here* (1945; reprint, New York: Hill and Wang, 1966), p. 142.

8. Paula Giddings, *When and Where I Enter: The Impact of Black Women on Race and Sex in America* (New York: William Morrow, 1984), p. 204.

9. Ibid.

10. Hazel Carby, "Policing the Black Woman's Body in an Urban Context," *Critical Inquiry* 18 (Summer 1992): 746.

11. Michel Foucault, "The Subject and Power," *Critical Inquiry* 8 (Summer 1982).

12. bell hooks, "Homeplace: A Site of Resistance," in *Yearning: Race, Gender, and Cultural Politics* (Boston: South End Press, 1990).

13. Gwendolyn Brooks, *Blacks* (Chicago: The David Company, 1987), p. 20.

14. Gwendolyn Brooks, Ibid., p. 115.

15. "Kitchenette Building" was published in 1945 in Brooks's first collection of poetry, *A Street in Bronzeville*. At that time, she had been married for six years and had a five-year-old son.

16. Gwendolyn Brooks, *Blacks*, p. 331.

17. Hortense Spillers, "Gwendolyn the Terrible: Propositions on Eleven Poems," in *A Life Distilled: Gwendolyn Brooks, Her Poetry and Fiction*, ed. Maria K. Mootry and Gary Smith (Urbana: University of Illinois Press, 1987), p. 225.

18. Marita Bonner, "The Whipping," in *Frye Street and Environs* (Boston: Beacon Press, 1987), pp. 185–95.

19. In another story, "Light in Dark Places," Bonner does utilize a Southern-born grandmother figure whose presence and wisdom protects her Northern-born granddaughter. See Joyce Flynn and Joyce Occomy Stricklin, Introduction to Marita Bonner, *Frye Street and Environs* (Boston: Beacon Press, 1987).

20. Critics Bernard Bell and Majorie Pryse have addressed Petry's connection to and difference from Wright in their essays, "Ann Petry's Demythologizing of American Culture and Afro-American Character" and "Pattern against the sky: Deism and Motherhood in Ann Petry's *The Street*" respectively. Both essays are found in *Conjuring: Black Women, Fiction and Literary Tradition*, ed. Marjorie Pryse and Hortense Spillers (Bloomington: Indiana University Press, 1985).

21. Some might suggest that Mrs. Hedges represents a maternal elder who provides Lutie safe space which she also ignores. I argue that because Mrs. Hedges offers Lutie no alternative that allows her to maintain her dignity and integrity, she is, in fact, a threat to Lutie's well-being.

22. Karla Holloway, *Moorings and Metaphors: Figures of Culture and Gender in Black Women's Literature* (New Brunswick, N.J.: Rutgers University Press, 1992), p. 123.

23. Fisher, "Guardian of the Law" and "Miss Cynthie," in *City of Refuge: The Collected Short Stories of Rudolph Fisher*, ed. John McCluskey (Columbia: University of Missouri Press, 1987); Marita Bonner, "Light in Dark Places," in *Frye Street and Environs* (Boston: Beacon Press, 1987).

24. In "'Pattern against the Sky': Deism and Motherhood in Ann Petry's *The Street*, " Marjorie Pryse makes the connection between the name "Junto" and the historical figure Benjamin Franklin. According to Pryse, "Junto" was the name Franklin gave to "his secret group of friends." The group "served its members [powerful white males] as a central sphere of social and political influence" (p. 118).

25. Michel Foucault, "The Subject and Power," *Critical Inquiry* 8 (Summer 1982), and "Power and Strategies," in *Power/Knowledge: Selected Interviews and Other Writings 1972–77*, ed. Colin Gordon, (New York: Pantheon Books, 1980), p. 142.

26. Ann Petry, *The Street* (1946; reprint, Boston: Beacon Press, 1985), pp. 15–16; page numbers cited in the text refer to this edition.

27. Marjorie Pryse, "'Pattern against the Sky,'" p. 117.

28. This brick metaphor recalls the instance in Richard Wright's *Native Son* when Bigger uses a brick to murder Lutie's literary sister, Bessie. Interestingly, at the end of *The Street*, Lutie is headed for Chicago, home of Bigger. Her fate there might be worse than in New York, where white hands build a brick wall around her, for in Chicago, she might encounter the brick-wielding Bigger. This fate is one that is portrayed graphically in Naylor's text.

29. Gloria Naylor, *The Women of Brewster Place* (New York: Viking Press, 1982), pp. 103–4; page numbers cited in the text refer to this editin.

30. Michael Awkward notes: "Mattie's rocking 'above time' offers Ciel . . . a recognition of her connection with women throughout history, a sense in other words of membership in a timeless community of women united by a common suffering." *Inspiriting Influences: Tradition, Revision and Afro-American Women's Novels* (New York: Columbia University Press, 1989), p. 117.

31. Maya Angelou, *Gather Together in My Name*; Toni Morrison, *Song of Solomon*;

Toni Cade Bambara, *The Salt Eaters*; Ntozake Shange, *For Colored Girls Who Have Considered Suicide when the Rainbow Is Enuf*; Paule Marshall, *Praisesong for the Widow*.

32. Ann Rosalind Jones, "Towards an Understanding of l'Ecriture Féminin" in *The New Feminist Criticism: Essays on Women, Literature, and Theory*, ed. Elaine Showalter (New York: Pantheon Books, 1985), p. 345.

33. Ibid.

34. Awkward, *Inspiriting Influences*, p. 119.

35. Jill L. Matus, "Dream, Deferral, and Closure in *The Women of Brewster Place*." *Black American Literature Forum* 24 (Spring 1990): 50.

36. Melvin Dixon, *Ride Out the Wilderness: Geography and Identity in Afro-American Literature* (Urbana: University of Illinois Press, 1987), p. 57.

37. In *Go Tell It on the Mountain*, James Baldwin gives us another version of the urban black male in search of a critical consciousness, but nonetheless defeated by the city. His Richard, named for Richard Wright, is brilliant, bitter, and disdainful of black religion. Of Jesus, he says, "You can tell that puking bastard to kiss my big black ass." Instead of the Southern-inspired black church, Richard turns to other institutions, institutions of the city like the museum and the night school. Richard is falsely accused of robbery and, like Bigger and Malcolm, he ends up in the prison where he is the victim of police brutality. Instead of fulfilling his desire to live a resistant life, Richard is defeated by the injustices enacted upon him, and he commits suicide.

38. Wright attempts to portray more well-rounded interracial relationships in his later fiction; however, this is usually done at the expense of his portrayal of black women.

39. See Robert Stepto, *From Behind the Veil: A Study of Afro-American Narrative* (Urbana: University of Illinois Press, 1979), pp. 128–63.

40. Richard Wright, "How Bigger Was Born," in *Native Son* (New York: Harper and Row, 1987), p. xv; page numbers cited in the text refer to this edition.

41. In one of the best essays I have read on *Native Son*, "Bigger Thomas's Quest for Voice and Audience in Richard Wright's *Native Son*," James A. Miller argues that "it is within [the] world of 'authoritative discourse" symbolized by the billboard of the State's Attorney in the opening pages of the novel, the distortions of African reality at the Regal Theater, the liberal pieties of the Dalton family, the inflammatory rhetoric of the press, and the blatantly racist arguments of the State's Attorney—that Bigger must struggle to discover his voice, and, presumably, an audience which will give assent to his testimony." *Callaloo* 9 (Summer 1986): 503.

42. Valerie Smith, *Self-Discovery and Authority in Afro-American Narrative* (Cambridge, Mass.: Harvard University Press, 1987), p. 70.

43. Miller, "Bigger Thomas's Quest," p. 504.

44. Many critics have explored the manner in which the judicial system responds to the Biggers of these various public discourses and not to the flesh-and-blood human being behind the media distortion. Valerie Smith notes: "Bigger's misrepresentation in court and in the press epitomizes his lifelong struggle against other people's fictions. Buckley, the State Attorney, considers him violent and subhuman and prosecutes him according to collectively held stereotypes of black male behavior " (*Self-Discovery and Authority*, pp. 81–82). James Miller underscores Smith's assertion: "The public exchanges between Max and the State's Attorney Buckley represent two attempts to define, in opposing ideological terms, the meaning of Bigger Thomas's actions—and, by extension, his existence—in the public sphere of 'authoritative discourse'" (ibid., p. 505).

45. Rudolph Fisher is actually the first male author to assert the importance of such safe spaces and ancestors in the lives of urban black male characters. See *City of Refuge* and the especially useful introductory essay by John McCluskey.

46. Ralph Ellison, *Invisible Man* (1947; reprint, New York: Random House, 1990), p. 173; page numbers cited in the text refer to this edition.

47. Herbert Hill, ed., *Soon One Morning* (New York: Alfred A. Knopf, 1963), p. 243.

48. Stepto, *From Behind the Veil*, p. 194.

49. Malcolm X's autobiography spawned a spate of lesser urban male bildungsromans: Claude Brown's *Manchild in the Promised Land*, Piri Thomas's *Down These Mean Streets*, and Eldridge Cleaver's *Soul on Ice*.

50. Baldwin also seems to find these spaces provincial and stifling, suggesting that cosmopolitan education and the life of the street are two opposing alternatives. In his texts, there are often two young male characters who choose either of these. While the one choosing cosmopolitan education usually survives, it is the other, more violent choice which seems the most resisting one. Ellison and John Edgar Wideman suggest that homespaces do offer a viable alternative to objectification by the dominant society. However, it would take a woman to explore fully this possibility for the urban male: Morrison's Milkman. Writing on the heels of the Black Power Movement, Morrison creates an alternative definition of black manhood (as does Alice Walker in *The Third Life of Grange Copeland*).

51. Malcolm X with Alex Haley, *The Autobiography of Malcolm X* (New York: Ballantine Books, 1964), p. 39; page numbers cited in the text refer to this edition.

52. A *Boston Globe* article focusing on Malcom X's Boston years asserts Ella's role as the provider of safe space for Malcolm X throughout his life. According to the article, Ella was nurturing as well as disciplining. X himself acknowledged her significance. However, just as the editors of *Invisible Man* lessened Mary's role by deleting the rescue from the hospital, the Spike Lee film based on Malcolm X's life deletes her significance. *Boston Globe Sunday Magazine*, February 16, 1992.

53. Note that Malcolm X's description of this type of disciplinary activity comes years before the influence of Foucault on current understanding of this process.

54. My reading here owes a great deal to Foucault's "Technologies of the Self," in *Technologies of the Self: A Seminar with Michel Foucault*, ed. Luther H. Martin, Huck Gutman, and Patrick H. Hutton (Amherst: University of Massachusetts Press, 1988), p. 27. According to Foucault, activities like studying, reading, and writing were parts of the Care of the Self which classical thinkers valued. Such techniques of the self can lead individuals to constitute their own identities (p. 146).

55. Manthia Diawara elaborated on the role of the "good life" in *The Autobiography* and in African-American life in general in his provocative talk, "Malcolm X and the Black Public Sphere: Conversionists vs. Culturalists," Keynote address, "Seeking Ground: Figuring a Black Cultural Imaginary," graduate student conference in Afro-American studies, November 12–13, 1993, University of Pennsylvania.

56. *Stop the Violence: Overcoming Self-Destruction*, Nelson George, ed., for the National Urban League (New York: Pantheon Books, 1990).

57. According to Tricia Rose, "Samplers are computers that can digitally duplicate any existing sounds and play them back in any key or pitch, in any order, sequence and loop them endlessly." *Black Noise: Rap Music and Black Culture in Contemporary America*. (Middletown, Conn.: Wesleyan University Press, 1994), p. 73.

58. It is also significant that *The Autobiography* has never been out of print and that following the release of Spike Lee's film on X, the book once again emerged on best-seller lists.

59. Grand Master Flash and The Furious Five, "The Message," Sugar Hill Records, 1982.

Chapter 4

1. Gladys Knight and the Pips, "Midnight Train to Georgia," by James Weatherly (Motown Records, 5303MC, 1983).

2. This series claims to break old racial taboos by allowing four white women to share living and workspace with a black male. Anthony is a former convict, turned first handyman and then business partner and law student. At various times he seeks the women's advice, provides a shoulder on which they may lean, serves as escort, and even shaves one woman's legs. He is able to function in this way because of his desexualization. Like another Southern black man of contemporary American popular culture, Morgan Freeman's chauffeur in *Driving Miss Daisy*, Anthony may have a crush on his employers, but he never oversteps his racial or class position by asserting himself in an overtly sexual manner. Furthermore, Anthony is an ex-convict who is grateful to his employers for choosing to employ him and grace him with their company.

3. Ethel Waters, "Georgia on My Mind," *Ethel Waters 1938–1939: Foremothers Vol. 6* (Rosetta Cassettes, RC1314, 1986); Billie Holiday, "Georgia on My Mind," *Billie Holiday* (Joker, SM3966, 1982); Ray Charles, "Georgia on My Mind," *Genius Hits the Road* (ABC 334, 1960).

4. Nor are they above moments of blatant racism. Stereotypes about South American servants abound. In early episodes, there were racist jokes directed at African-Americans as well.

5. "The South Versus the Negro," *Negro Digest: A Magazine of Negro Comment* 3 (May 1945): 7.

6. Ibid., p. 53.

7. *New York Times*, September 23, 1991, p. A1; *Philadelphia Inquirer*, July 7, 1991, p. A1.

8. Alice Walker, *The Third Life of Grange Copeland* (1970), Albert Murray, *South to a Very Old Place* (1971), Toni Morrison, *Song of Solomon* (1977).

9. Critics have debated this point. Melvin Dixon argues that Kabnis fails to "become the voice of the South" but that the story creates a space for "others to sing." *Ride Out the Wilderness: Geography and Identity in Afro-American Literature* (Urbana: University of Illinois Press, 1987), p. 41. On the other hand, Houston Baker sees Kabnis as "the fully emergent artist—a singer of a displaced 'soilsoaked' beauty and an agent of liberation for his people." *Afro-American Poetics: Revisions of Harlem and the Black Aesthetic* (Madison: University of Wisconsin Press, 1988), p. 44.

10. Robert B. Stepto, *From Behind the Veil: A Study of Afro-American Narrative* (Urbana: University of Illinois Press, 1979), p. 167.

11. Ibid.

12. Quoted in Darwin Turner, "Introduction" to the 1975 edition of *Cane* (New York: Liveright, 1975); page nubers cited in the text refer to this edition.

13. Ibid.

14. Nellie McKay, *Jean Toomer, Artist: A Study of His Literary Life and Work, 1894–1936* (Chapel Hill: University of North Carolina Press, 1984), p. 168.

15. Dixon, *Riding Out the Wilderness*, p. 38.

16. John F. Callahan, *In the African-American Grain: Call-and-Response in Twentieth-Century Black Fiction* (Middletown, Conn.: Wesleyan University Press, 1988), p. 107.

17. Michael G. Cooke, *Afro-American Literature in the Twentieth Century: The Achievement of Intimacy* (New Haven: Yale University Press, 1984), p. 195.

18. Callahan, *In the African-American Grain*, p. 108.

19. Nella Larsen, *Quicksand* (1928; reprint, New Brunswick, N.J.: Rutgers University Press, 1985), page numbers cited in the text refer to this edition.

20. In contrast to Phyllis Rose, *Jazz Cleopatra: Josephine Baker in Her Time* (New York: Doubleday, 1989), I think that Josephine Baker was also incited into accepting her status as objective other.

21. Theater is used to illustrate moments of self-recognition in *Cane* as well: "Box Seat," "Theater," and "Kabnis."

22. James Weldon Johnson's Ex-Colored Man has a very similar experience. *The Autobiography of an Ex-Colored Man* (1912; reprint, New York: Hill and Wang, 1960).

23. For a thorough discussion of sexuality in *Quicksand*, see Deborah McDowell's pioneering introduction to the American Women Writers Series edition (New Brunswick: Rutgers University Press, 1986).

24. Richard Wright, *Black Boy: A Record of Childhood and Youth* (1945; reprint, New York: Harper and Row, 1966), p. 43.

25. Stepto, *From Behind the Veil*, p. 158.

26. Ibid.

27. Richard Wright, *12 Million Black Voices* (New York: Thunder's Mouth Press, 1988), p. 142; page numbers cited in the text refer to this edition.

28. Leroi Jones, *Blues People: The Negro Experience in White America and the Music That Developed From It* (New York: William Morrow, 1968), pp. 96–97.

29. William Stott, *Documentary Expression and Thirties America* (New York: Oxford University Press, 1973), pp. 234–35.

30. Kimberly W. Benston, *Baraka: The Renegade and the Mask* (New Haven: Yale University Press, 1976).

31. Amiri Baraka (Leroi Jones), *The System of Dante's Hell* (New York: Grove Press, 1965), p. 59; page numbers cited in the text refer to this edition.

32. Benston says: "Who are the 'Demons' who set Leroi against himself? . . . On a simplistic level they are the cavalcade of white Western poets and thinkers to whom the young poet was irresistibly drawn. . . . What afflicts him particularly, or actively, is the 'curse' of this demon tradition's own dichotomy: the intellect dreaming its dream of absolute freedom, and the soul knowing its terrible bondage" (*Baraka*, pp. 12–13).

33. Baraka's short story "The Screamers" creates a dance floor that is the site of rebellion and protest. It is the place where migrants and city-born blacks meet, meld, and form a consciousness of themselves as a people.

34. My positive reading of Leroi's sexual involvement with Peaches contrasts greatly with that of Melvin Dixon. Dixon sees Peaches as "Roi's principal antagonist" (*Riding Out the Wilderness*, p. 79).

35. Toni Morrison, *Song of Solomon* (New York: New American Library, 1978), p. 83; page numbers cited in the text refer to this edition.

36. Ibid., p. 296.

37. Both Michael Awkward and Valerie Smith have cited this passage as central to Milkman's personal growth.

38. Toni Morrison, "Rootedness: The Ancestor in Afro-American Fiction," in *Black Women Writers at Work: A Critical Evaluation*, ed. Mari Evans (Garden City, N.Y.: Anchor Press, 1984), p. 340.

39. Michael Awkward, "Unruly and Let Loose: Myth, Ideology, and Gender in *Song of Solomon*," Callaloo 13 (1990): 483.

40. Arrested Development, "Tennessee," EMI Records Group, FA-21929, 1992.

41. Charles Burnett's important film *To Sleep with Anger* challenges a romanticized

view of the South as site of the ancestor by portraying a devilish visitor from "home," who, with his superstition, wreaks havoc in the lives of Western migrants and their children.

42. Hazel Carby provides an insightful discussion of Hurston's choice in her *Reconstructing Womanhood: The Emergence of the Black Woman Novelist* (New York: Oxford University Press, 1987), pp. 164–65.

43. John Cromarte and Carol Stack, "Reinterpreting Black Migration to the South," *Geographic Review* 79 (1989): 3. Stack also argues for a redefinition of the notion of return migration, asserting that black children and adults born outside the South are in fact return migrants because they tend to migrate to areas where they have maintained strong family and communal ties, areas from which earlier generations of their family migrated. In this case, the Northern-born Milkman would be a return migrant to Shalimar.

44. Ronald Smothers, "South's New Blacks Find Comfort Laced with Strain," *New York Times*, September 23, 1991, p. A1.

45. Ibid. p. B10.

46. Ibid., p. B1.

Chapter 5

1. Susan Willis uses this term to describe the major characters of *Tar Baby*. See her *Specifying: Black Women Writing the American Experience* (Madison: University of Wisconsin Press, 1987).

2. The use of Old Testament names like Palestine and Rome signal a connection between black migration and the Jewish exodus. Both peoples migrate to escape persecution. Deborah McDowell makes this point in her dazzling review of the novel: "In naming these fictive cities of the pre-Migration past, Morrison forges her connection to that link the slaves made between themselves and the Israelites under Egyptian bondage, suggesting that even in Jazz Age Harlem the footprints of slavery have not been lost to time." "Harlem Nocturne," *Women's Review of Books* 9 (June 1992): 3.

3. Toni Morrison, *Jazz* (1992; reprint, New York: Plume, 1993), p. 98; page numbers cited in the text refer to this edition.

4. Jean Toomer's poem "Reapers," which appears in the Southern section of *Cane*, is especially fitting in this description of the cane cutters' fear of killing Wild:

> Black reapers with the sound of steel on stones
> Are sharpening scythes. I see them place the hones
> In their hip pockets as a thing that's done,
> And start their silent swinging, one by one.
> Black horses drive a mower through the weeds,
> And there, a field rat, startled, squealing bleeds,
> His belly close to ground. I see the blade,
> Blood-stained, continue cutting weeds and shade.

Cane (New York: Liveright, 1975), p. 5. The reapers' tools are masculine, penetrating the earth and the creatures that inhabit it, including a field mouse, and, in *Jazz*, Wild.

5. Again, references to *Cane* are apparent: In her inability to mother her child, Wild is like Karintha. Other references to *Cane* abound throughout Morrison's novel. Wild is a naturewoman, who turns Toomer's nature-defined women into surreal and absurd figures.

6. In numerous interviews and essays, Morrison has stressed the significance of the neighborhood and the specificity of place in her fiction. See especially Robert Stepto,

"'Intimate Things in Place': A Conversation with Toni Morrison," *Massachusetts Review* 18 (Autumn 1977); Thomas Leclair, "'The Language Must Not Sweat': A Conversation with Toni Morrison," *New Republic* 184 (Autumn 1977); Toni Morrison, "City Limits, Village Values: Concepts of the Neighborhood in Black Fiction," in *Literature and the Urban Experience*, ed. Jaye Michael and Ann Chalmers Watts (New Brunswick, N.J.: Rutgers University Press, 1981).

7. In her strength, sensuality, and determination, here Violet resembles Jean Toomer's "Carma, in overalls, and strong as any man, stand[ing] behind the old brown mule, driving the wagon home" (*Cane*, p. 12).

8. In *The Jazz Revolution: Twenties America and the Meaning of Jazz* (New York: Oxford Unversity Press, 1989), Kathy Ogren documents the media–pulpit debate about jazz music.

9. F. Scott Fitzgerald, "Echoes of the Jazz Age," in the *Crack-Up*, ed. Edmund Wilson (1941; reprint, New York: New Directions Press, 1945), p. 15.

10. Ogren, *Jazz Revolution*, pp. 149–50.

11. Toni Morrison, *Playing in the Dark: Whiteness and the Literary Imagination* (Cambridge, Mass.: Harvard University Press, 1992), p. vii.

12. Ibid., pp. 6–7.

13. Henry Louis Gates, Jr., Review of *Jazz*, in *Toni Morrison: Critical Perspectives Past and Present*, ed. Henry Louis Gates, Jr., and K. A. Appiah (New York: Amistad, 1993).

14. McDowell, "Harlem Nocturne," p. 4.

Bibliography

Literature

Attaway, William. *Blood on the Forge*. New York: Doubleday, 1941.

Baldwin, James. "Down at the Cross: Letter from a Region in My Mind." In *The Fire Next Time*. New York: Dell Books, 1962.

———. *Go Tell It on the Mountain*. 1953; reprint, New York: Dell Publishing, 1985.

———. "Nobody Knows My Name: A Letter from the South." *Nobody Knows My Name: More Notes of a Native Son*. New York: Dial Press, 1961.

Baraka, Amiri (Leroi Jones). *The System of Dante's Hell*. New York: Grove Press, 1965.

Bonner, Marita. *Frye Street and Environs*, edited by Joyce Flynn. Boston: Beacon Press, 1987.

Dunbar, Paul Lawrence. *Sport of the Gods*. 1902. Reprint. Miami: Mnemosyne Publishing, 1991.

Ellison, Ralph. *Invisible Man*. 1947; reprint, New York: Random House, 1990.

———. "Out of the Hospital, Under the Bar." In *Soon One Morning*, edited by Herbert Hill. New York: Alfred A. Knopf, 1963.

Fisher, Rudolph. *City of Refuge: The Collected Short Stories of Rudolph Fisher*, edited by John McCluskey. Columbia: University of Missouri Press, 1987.

Golden, Marita. *Long Distance Life*. New York: Ballantine Books, 1989.

Hughes, Langston. *Montage of a Dream Deferred*. New York: Henry Holt, 1951.

———. *One Way Ticket*. New York: Alfred A. Knopf, 1949.

Johnson, Charles. *Faith and the Good Thing*. New York: Viking Press, 1974.

Johnson, James Weldon. *The Autobiography of an Ex-Colored Man*. 1912. Reprint. New York: Hill and Wang, 1960.

Larsen, Nella. *Quicksand*. 1928; reprint, New Brunswick, N.J.: Rutgers University Press, 1986.

Marshall, Paule. *Brown Girl, Brownstones*. 1959; reprint, Old Westbury, N.Y.: Feminist Press, 1981.

Morrison. Toni. *The Bluest Eye*. New York: Holt, Rinehart and Winston, 1970.

———. *Jazz*. New York: Plume, 1992; reprint, 1993.

———. *Song of Solomon*. New York: New American Library, 1978.

Murray, Albert. *South to a Very Old Place*. New York: McGraw-Hill, 1971.

———. *Train Whistle Guitar*. New York: McGraw-Hill, 1974.

Naylor, Gloria. *The Women of Brewster Place*. New York: Viking Press, 1982.

Petry, Ann. *The Street*. 1946; reprint, Boston: Beacon Press, 1985.

Porter, Connie. *All Bright Court*. Boston: Houghton Mifflin, 1991.

Toomer, Jean. *Cane*. 1923; reprint, New York: Liveright, 1975.

West, Dorothy. *The Living Is Easy*. 1948; reprint, New York: Feminist Press, 1982.

Wright, Richard. *American Hunger.* New York: Harper and Row, 1977.

———. *Black Boy: A Record of Childhood and Youth.* New York: Harper and Row, 1945.

———. *Lawd Today.* Boston: Northeastern University Press, 1969.

———. *Native Son.* New York: Harper and Row, 1940.

———. *12 Million Black Voices.* New York: Viking Press, 1941.

——— . *Uncle Tom's Children.* New York: Harper and Row, 1940.

Literary and Cultural Criticism

Awkward, Michael. *Inspiriting Influences: Tradition, Revision, and Afro-American Women's Novels.* New York: Columbia University Press, 1989.

——— . "Unruly and Let Loose: Myth, Ideology, and Gender in *Song of Solomon*". *Callaloo* 13 (Spring 1990): 482–98.

Baker, Houston A. *Blues Ideology and Afro-American Literature.* Chicago: University of Chicago Press, 1984.

——— . *The Journey Back: Issues in Black Literature and Criticism.* Chicago: University of Chicago Press, 1980.

———. "Journey Toward Black Art: Jean Tommer's *Cane.*" In *Afro-American Poetics: Revisions of Harlem and the Black Aesthetic.* Madison: University of Wisconsin Press, 1988.

———. *Workings of the Spirit: The Poetics of Afro-American Women's Writing.* Chicago: University of Chicago Press, 1991.

Bawer, Bruce. "All That Jazz." *The New Criterion,* May 1992, pp. 10–17.

Benston, Kimberly W. *Baraka: The Renegade and the Mask.* New Haven: Yale University Press, 1976.

Blanchard, Marc Eli. *In Search of the City: Engels, Baudelaire, Rimbaud.* Saratoga, N.Y.: Anma Libri, 1985.

Bolton, Richard, ed. *The Contest of Meaning: Critical Histories of Photography.* Cambridge: MIT Press, 1989.

Bone, Robert. *Down Home: A History of Afro-American Short Fiction from Its Beginnings to the End of the Harlem Renaissance.* New York: Putnam, 1975.

Bottomley, Gillian. *From Another Place: Migration and the Politics of Culture.* Cambridge: Cambridge University Press, 1992.

Bremer, Sidney. *Urban Intersections: Meetings of Life and Literature in United States Cities.* Urbana: University of Illinois Press, 1992.

Buell, Lawrence. "American Pastoral Ideology Reappraised." *American Literary History,* Spring, 1989, pp. 1–29.

Callahan, John F. *In the African-American Grain: Call-and-Response in Twentieth-Century Black Fiction.* Middletown, Conn.: Wesleyan University Press, 1988.

Cappetti, Carla. *Writing Chicago: Modernism, Ethnography, and the Novel.* New York: Columbia University Press, 1993.

Carby, Hazel. "'It Jus Be's Dat Way Sometimes': The Sexual Politics of Women's Blues." In *Unequal Sisters: A Multicultural Reader in U.S. Women's History,* edited by Ellen Carol DuBois and Vicki L. Ruiz. New York: Routledge, 1990. First published in *Radical America* 20 (1986): 9–24.

———. "On the Threshold of the Woman's Era: Lynching, Empire and Sexuality in Black Feminist Theory." *Critical Inquiry* 12 (Autumn 1985): 266–77.

———. "Policing the Black Woman's Body in an Urban Context." *Critical Inquiry* 18 (Summer 1992): 738–55.

————. *Reconstructing Womanhood: The Emergence of the Black Woman Novelist.* New York: Oxford University Press, 1987.

Clarke, Graham, ed. *The American City: Literary and Cultural Perspectives.* New York: St. Martin's Press, 1988.

Cooke, Michael G. *Afro-American Literature in the Twentieth Century: The Achievement of Intimacy.* New Haven: Yale University Press, 1984.

Diawara, Manthia. "Malcolm X and the Black Public Sphere: Conversionists vs. Culturalists." Keynote address delivered at "Seeking Ground: Figuring a Black Cultural Imaginary," graduate student conference in Afro-American studies, November 12–13, 1993, University of Pennsylvania.

Dixon, Melvin. *Ride Out the Wilderness: Geography and Identity in Afro-American Literature.* Urbana: University of Illinois Press, 1987.

Fabre, Michel. *The Unfinished Quest of Richard Wright.* New York: William Morrow, 1973.

Fleischauer, Carl, and Beverly Brannan. *Documenting America 1935–1943.* Berkeley: University of California Press, 1988.

Gates, Henry Louis, Jr., and K. A. Appiah, eds. *Toni Morrison: Critical Perspectives Past and Present.* New York: Pantheon Books, 1990.

Harris, Trudier. *Black Women in the Fiction of James Baldwin.* Knoxville: University of Tennessee Press, 1985.

————. *Exorcising Blackness. Historical and Literary Lynching and Burning Rituals.* Bloomington: Indiana University Press, 1984.

Higginbotham, Evelyn Brooks. "'Out of the Age of the Voice': The Black Church and Discourses of Modernity." Paper delivered at the conference on the Black Public Sphere in the Era of Reagan and Bush, October 14, 1993, University of Chicago.

Holloway, Karla F. *Moorings and Metaphors: Figures of Culture and Gender in Black Women's Literature.* New Brunswick, N.J.: Rutgers University Press, 1992.

JanMohamed, Abdul R. "Negating the Negation as a Form of Affirmation in Minority Discourse: The Construction of Richard Wright as Subject." *Cultural Critique* 7 (Fall 1987): 245–66.

Jaye, Michael, and Ann Chalmers Watts, eds. *Literature and the Urban Experience.* New Brunswick, N.J.: Rutgers University Press, 1981.

Kern, Stephen. *The Culture of Time and Space, 1880–1918.* Cambridge, Mass.: Harvard University Press, 1983.

Klotman, Phyliss R. "Tearing a Hole in History: Lynching as Theme and Motif." *Black American Literature Forum* 19 (1985): 55–63.

Lenz, Gunter. "Symbolic Space, Communal Rituals and the Sureality of the Urban Ghetto. Harlem in Black Literature from 1920's to 1960's." *Callaloo* 2 (Spring 1988): 309–45.

MacKethan, Lucinda H. "Jean Toomer's Cane: A Pastoral Problem." In *Cane*, edited by Darwin Turner (New York: W. W. Norton, 1988).

Marx, Leo. *The Machine in the Garden: Technology and the Pastoral Ideal in America.* London: Oxford University Press, 1964.

Mason, Theodore O. "The Novelist as Conservator: Stories and Comprehension in Toni Morrison's *Song of Solomon*." *Contemporary Literature* 29 (1988): 564–81.

Matus, Jill L. "Dream, Deferral, and Closure in *The Women of Brewster Place*." *Black American Literature Forum* 24 (Spring 1990): 49–64.

McKay, Nellie. *Jean Toomer, Artist: A Study of His Literary Life and Work, 1894–1936.* Chapel Hill: University of North Carolina Press, 1984.

Meltzer, David. *Reading Jazz.* San Francisco: Mercury House, 1993.

Miller, James A. "Bigger Thomas's Quest for Voice and Audience in Richard Wright's *Native Son*." *Callaloo* 9 (Summer 1986): 501–6.

Morrison, Toni. "City Limits, Village Values: Concepts of the Neighborhood in Black Fiction." In *Literature and the Urban Experience*, edited by Michael Jaye and Ann Chalmers Watts. New Brunswick, N.J.: Rutgers University Press, 1981.

———. "Gone Home with Bitterness and Joy." Review of *South to a Very Old Place*, by Albert Murray. *New York Times Book Review*, January 2, 1972, p. 5.

———. *Playing in the Dark: Whiteness and the Literary Imagination*. Cambridge, Mass.: Harvard University Press, 1992.

——— . "Rootedness: The Ancestor in Afro-American Fiction." In *Black Women Writers at Work: A Critical Evaluation*, edited by Mari Evans. Garden City, N.Y.: Anchor Press, 1984.

Natanson, Nicholas. *The Black Image in the New Deal: The Politics of FSA Photography*. Knoxville: University of Tennessee Press, 1992.

Porter, Horce A. *Stealing the Fire: The Art and Protest of James Baldwin*. Middletown, Conn.: Wesleyan University Press, 1989.

Pryse, Marjorie, and Hortense Spillers, eds. *Conjuring: Black Women, Fiction and Literary Tradition*. Bloomington: Indiana University Press, 1985.

Reilly, John M. "Richard Wright Preaches the Nation: *12 Million Black Voices*." *Black American Literature Forum* 16 (Fall 1982): 116–19.

Rodgers, Lawrence R. "Dorothy West's *The Living Is Easy* and the Ideal of Southern Folk Community." *African American Review* 26 (Spring 1992): 161–72.

———. "Paul Laurence Dunbar's *The Sport of the Gods*: The Doubly Conscious World of Plantation Fiction, Migration, and Ascent. *American Literary Realism* 24 (Spring 1992): 42–57.

Scruggs, Charles. *Sweet Home: Invisible Cities in the Afro-American Novel*. Baltimore: Johns Hopkins University Press, 1993.

Sedgwick, Eve. *Between Men: English Literature and Male Homosexual Desire*. New York: Columbia University Press, 1985.

Sharpe, William Chapman. *Unreal Cities: Urban Figuration in Wordsworth, Baudelaire, Whitman, Eliot and Williams*. Baltimore: Johns Hopkins University Press, 1990.

Showalter, Elaine, ed. *The New Feminist Criticism: Essays on Women, Literature and Theory*. New York: Pantheon Books, 1985.

Smith, Valerie. *Self-Discovery and Authority in Afro-American Narrative*. Cambridge: Harvard University Press, 1987.

Sollard, Alain. "Myth and Narrative Fiction in *Cane*: 'Blood-Burning Moon.'" *Callaoo* 8 (Fall 1985): 551–62.

Sollors, Werner. "Modernization as Adultery: Richard Wright, Zora Neale Hurston, and American Culture of the 1930's and 1940's." *Hebrew University Studies in Literature and the Arts* 18 (1990).

Spillers, Hortense. "Gwendolyn the Terrible: Propositions on Eleven Poems." In *A Life Distilled: Gwendolyn Brooks, Her Poetry and Fiction*, edited by Maria K. Mootry and Gary Smith. Urbana: University of Illinois Press, 1987.

———. "An Order of Constancy: Notes on Brooks and the Feminine." *Centennial Review*, Spring 1985, pp. 223–48.

Squiers, Carol, ed. *The Critical Image. Essays on Contemporary Photography*. Seattle: Bay Press, 1990.

Stepto, Robert. *From Behind the Veil: A Study of Afro-American Narrative*. Urbana: University of Illinois Press, 1979.

Stott, William. *Documentary Expression and Thirties America*. New York: Oxford University Press, 1973.

Tagg, John. *The Burden of Representation: Essays on Photographies and Histories*. Amherst: University of Massachusetts Press, 1988.

Williams, Raymond. *The Country and the City*. New York: Oxford University Press, 1973.

Willis, Susan. *Specifying: Black Women Writing the American Experience*. Madison: University of Wisconsin Press, 1987.

Anthropology, History, Journalism, Sociology

Adero, Malaika, ed. *Up South: Stories, Studies and Letters of This Century's African-American Migrations*. New York: New Press, 1993.

Bontemps, Arna. *Anyplace but Here*. New York: Hill and Wang, 1966.

———. *They Seek a City*. New York: Doubleday, Doran, 1945.

Campbell, Daniel M., and Rex Johnson. *Black Migration in America: A Social Demographic History*. Durham, N.C.: Duke University Press, 1981.

Crew, Spencer. *Field to Factory: Afro-American Migration 1915–1940*. Washington, D.C.: Smithsonian Institution Press, 1987.

Cromartie, John, and Carol B. Stack. "Reinterpretation of Black Return and Nonreturn Migration to the South 1975–1980." *Geographical Review* 3 (1989): 297–370.

Drake, St. Clair, and Horace Cayton. *Black Metropolis*. New York: Harcourt, Brace, 1945.

Giddings, Paula. *When and Where I Enter: The Impact of Black Women on Race and Sex in America*. New York: William Morrow, 1984.

Grossman, James R. *Land of Hope: Chicago, Black Southerners, and the Great Migration*. Chicago: University of Chicago Press, 1989.

Hall, Jacquelyn Dowd. "'The Mind That Burns in Each Body': Women, Rape, and Racial Violence." In *Powers of Desire: The Politics of Sexuality*, edited by Ann Snitow, Christine Stansell, and Sharon Thompson. New York: Monthly Review Press, 1983, pp. 328–50.

———. *Revolt against Chivalry: Jessie Daniel Ames and the Women's Campaign against Lynching*. New York: Columbia University Press, 1979.

Haynes, George. "Negro Migration in 1916–1917." *The Survey* 4 (May 4, 1918), U.S. Department of Labor Division of Negro Education. Washington, D.C.: Government Printing Office, 1919.

Henri, Florette. *Black Migration: Movement North 1900–1920: The Road from Myth to Man*. New York: Anchor Press, 1976.

Hine, Darlene Clark. "Black Migration to the Urban Midwest: The Gender Dimension, 1915–1945." In *The Great Migration in Historical Perspective: New Dimensions of Race, Class and Gender*, edited by Joe William Trotter, Jr. Bloomington: Indiana University Press, 1991.

Huggins, Nathan. *The Harlem Renaissance*. New York: Oxford University Press, 1971.

Johnson, James Weldon. *Black Manhattan*. New York: Alfred A. Knopf, 1940.

Jones, Jacqueline. *Labor of Love, Labor of Sorrow: Black Women, Work and the Family from Slavery to the Present*. New York: Basic Books, 1985.

Katznelson, Ira. *Black Men, White Cities*. Chicago: University of Chicago Press, 1973.

Kennedy, Louise Venable. *The Negro Peasant Turns Cityward: The Effects of Recent Migrations to Northern Centers*. New York: Columbia University Press, 1930.

Lemann, Nicholas. *The Promised Land: The Great Black Migration and How It Changed America*. New York: Alfred A. Knopf, 1991.

Levine, Lawrence. *Black Culture, Black Consciousness: Afro-American Folk Thought*. New York: Oxford University Press, 1977.

Lincoln, C. Eric, and Lawrence H. Mamiya. *The Black Church in the African American Experience*. Durham, N.C.: Duke University Press, 1990.

Marks, Carol. *Farewell, We're Good and Gone*. Bloomington: Indiana University Press, 1989.

McKay, Claude. *Harlem: Negro Metropolis*. New York: E. P. Dutton, 1940.

Painter, Nell. *The Exodusters*. New York: Alfred A. Knopf, 1977.

Park, Robert E. *Race and Culture: Essays in the Sociology of Contemporary Man*. London: Free Press of Glencoe, 1950.

Parris, Guchard, and Lester Brooks. *Blacks in the City: A History of the National Urban League*. Boston: Little, Brown, 1971.

Pleck, Elizabeth. *Black Migration and Poverty*. New York: Academic Press, 1979.

Scott, Emmit, ed. "Letters of Negro Migrants of 1916–1918." *Journal of Negro History* 4 (July–October 1919): 290–340.

Sennett, Richard, ed. *Classic Essays on the Culture of Cities*. New York: Appleton-Century-Crofts, 1969.

————. *The Uses of Disorder: Personal Identity and City Life*. New York: Alfred A. Knopf, 1970.

Shapiro, Herbert. *White Violence and Black Response: From Reconstruction to Montgomery*. Amherst: University of Massachusetts Press, 1988.

Simmel, Georg. "The Metropolis and the Mental Life." In *Classic Essays on the Culture of Cities*, edited by Richard Sennett. New York: Alfred A. Knopf, 1970.

————. "The Stranger." In *On Individuality and Social Forms*, edited by Donald Levine. Chicago: University of Chicago Press, 1971.

Smith, Michael P. *The City and Social Theory*. New York: St. Martin's Press, 1979.

"The South Versus the Negro." *Negro Digest: A Magazine of Negro Comment* 3 (May 1945): 47–52.

Spear, Alan. *Black Chicago: The Making of a Negro Ghetto 1890–1920*. Chicago: University of Chicago Press, 1967.

Tolnay, Stewart E., and E. M. Beck. "Rethinking the Role of Racial Violence in the Great Migration." In *Black Exodus: The Great Migration from the American South*, edited by Alferdteen Harrison. Jackson: University Press of Mississippi, 1991.

Weiss, Nancy J. *The National Urban League*. New York: Oxford University Press, 1974.

Wells, Ida B. *Crusade for Justice*. Chicago: University of Chicago Press, 1970.

Williams, Brett. "The South in the City." *Journal of Popular Culture* 16 (1982): 30–41.

Woodson, Carter G. *A Century of Negro Migration*. 1916. Reprint. New York: Russell and Russell, 1969.

Woodward, C. Van. *The Strange Career of Jim Crow*. New York: Oxford University Press, 1974.

Music

Albertson, Chris. *Bessie*. New York: Stein and Day, 1972.

Barlow, William. *"Looking Up at Down": The Emergence of Blues Culture*. Philadelphia: Temple University Press, 1989.

Broonzy, Big Bill. *Big Bills Blues*. London: Cassell, 1955.

Chilton, John. *Billie's Blues*. London: Quartet Books, 1975.

Cohn, Lawrence, ed. *Nothing but the Blues: The Music and the Musicians*. New York: Abbeville Press, 1993.

Dahl, Linda. *Stormy Weather: The Music and Lives of a Century of Jazz Women*. New York: Pantheon Books, 1984.

George, Nelson. *The Death of Rhythm and Blues*. New York: E.P. Dutton, 1988.

———. ed. *Stop the Violence: Overcoming Self-Destruction*. New York: Pantheon Books for the National Urban League, 1990.

Harris, Michael. *The Rise of Gospel Blues: The Music of Thomas Andrew Dorsey in the Urban Church.* New York: Oxford University Press, 1992.

Holiday, Billie, and William Duffy. *Lady Sings the Blues*. Garden City, N.Y.: Doubleday, 1965.

Jones, Leroi. *Blues People: The Negro Experience in White America and the Music That Developed from It*. New York: William Morrow, 1968.

Keil, Charles. *Urban Blues*. Chicago: University of Chicago Press, 1966.

Lieb, Sandra. *Mother of the Blues: A Study of Ma Rainey*. Amherst: University of Massachusetts Press, 1981.

Murray, Albert. *Stomping the Blues*. New York: McGraw-Hill, 1976.

Ogren, Kathy J. *The Jazz Revolution: Twenties America and the Meaning of Jazz*. New York: Oxford University Press, 1989.

Oliver, Paul. *Blues Fell This Morning*. London: Cassell, 1960.

———. *Screening the Blues: Aspects of the Blues Tradition*. London: Cassell, 1968.

———. *Songsters and Saints: Vocal Traditions on Race Records*. New York: Cambridge University Press, 1984.

O'Meally, Robert. *Lady Day: The Many Faces of Billie Holiday*. New York: Little, Brown, 1991.

Ostronsky, Leroy. *Jazz City: The Impact of Our Cities on the Development of Jazz*. Englewood Cliffs, N.J.: Prentice-Hall, 1978.

Rose, Tricia. *Black Noise: Rap Music and Black Culture in Contemporary America*. Middletown, Conn.: Wesleyan University Press, 1994.

Sackheim, Eric. *The Blues Line: A Collection of Blues Lyrics from Leadbelly to Muddy Waters*. New York: Schermer Books, 1969.

Southern, Eileen. *The Music of Black Americans*. New York: W.W. Norton, 1971.

Taft, Michael. *Blues Lyric Poetry: An Anthology*. New York: Garland, 1983.

———. *Blues Lyric Poetry: A Concordance*, 3 vols. New York: Garland, 1984.

Recordings

Arrested Development. "Tennessee." *3 Years, 5 Months and 2 Days in the Life of . . . , EMI Records Group 1187–2–5, 1992.*

Charles, Ray. "Georgia on My Mind." *Genius Hits the Road*. ABC 334, 1960.

Gaye, Marvin. *What's Going On*. Motown Records TS310, 1971.

Grandmaster Flash and the Furious Five. *The Message* Sugar Hill Records, 1982.

Holiday, Billie. "Strange Fruit." *Jazz at the Philharmonic*. Verve VE 2–2504, 1976.

———. "Georgia on My Mind." *Billie Holiday*. Joker SM3966, 1982.

Knight, Gladys and the Pips. "Midnight Train to Georgia." Motown Records 5303MC, 1983.

Smith, Bessie. "Homeless Blues." *Bessie Smith the Empress*. Columbia Records CG30818, 1972.

———. "Poor Man's Blues."

Sorry but I Can't Take You: Women's Railroad Blues. Rosetta Records 1301, 1985.

Wonder, Stevie. "Living for the City" *Innervisions*. Tamala Records 9052MD, 1973.

Visual Arts

Lacy, Jean. *Welcome to My Ghetto Land*. Dallas Museum of Art, Dallas, Texas.

Lawrence, Jacob. *The Migration of the Negro* (60 paintings). The Phillips Collection, Washington, D.C.: Museum of Modern Art, New York.

"The Migration Series." *Fortune Magazine* 24 (November 1941): 102–11.

Perry, Regenia. *Free Within Ourselves: African-American Artists in the Collection of the National Museum of American Art*. Washington, D.C.: National Museum of American Art, Smithsonian Institution, 1992.

Prown, Jules David. "Mind in Matter: An Introduction to Material Culture Theory and Method." *Winterhur Portfolio* 17 (Spring 1982): 1.

Rozzelle, Robert, Alvia Wardlaw, and Maureen A. McKenna, eds. *Black Art—Ancestral Legacy: The African Impulse in African-American Art*. Dallas: Dallas Museum of Art, 1989.

Turner, Elizabeth Hutton, ed. *Jacob Lawrence: The Migration Series*. Washington, D.C.: Rappahannock Press in association with the Philips Collection, 1993.

Wheat, Ellen Harkins. *Jacob Lawrence: American Painter*. Seattle: University of Washington Press, 1986.

Critical Theory

Anderson, Perry. "The Atinomies of Antonio Gramsci." *New Left Review*, no. 100 (1976–77): 5–79.

Collins, Patricia Hill. *Black Feminist Thought: Knowledge, Consciousness and the Politics of Empowerment*. Cambridge: Unwin Hyman, 1990.

Forgacs, David, ed. *An Antonio Gramsci Reader*. New York: Schocken Books, 1988.

Foucault, Michel. *Discipline and Punish. The Birth of the Prison*. New York: Pantheon Books, 1977.

———. *Power/Knowledge: Selected Interviews and Other Writings 1972–77*. Edited by Colin Gordon. New York: Pantheon Books, 1980.

———. "The Subject and Power." *Critical Inquiry* 8 (Summer 1982): 777–95.

———. *Technologies of the Self: A Seminar with Michel Foucault*. Edited by Luther H. Martin, Huck Gutman, Patrick H. Hutton. Amherst: University of Massachusetts Press, 1988.

Gramsci, Antonio. *Selections from the Cultural Writings*. Edited by David Forgacs and Geoffrey Nowell-Smith. Cambridge, Mass.: Harvard University Press, 1985.

———. *Selections from the Prison Notebooks*. Edited by Quintin Hoare and Geoffrey Nowell Smith. (New York: International Publishers, 1987).

hooks, bell. "Homeplace: A Site of Resistance." In *Yearning: Race, Gender, and Cultural Politics*. Boston: South End Press, 1990.

Hoy, David Couzens. *Foucault: A Critical Reader*. Oxford: Basil Blackwell, 1986.

Kristeva, Julia. *Strangers to Ourselves*. New York: Columbia University Press, 1991.

———. "Women's Time." *Signs* 7 (Autumn 1981): 13–55.

West, Cornel. *Prophesy Deliverance! An Afro-American Revolutionary Christianity*. Philadelphia: Westminster Press, 1982.

Index

Adorno, Theodor, 151
Alabama, 158
Albertson, Chris, 21, 56
Allen, Lewis, 15
American Hunger, 51, 69, 75, 162
Ames, Jessie Daniel, 25
Ancestor, 4–6, 42, 130, 133, 148, 150, 152,
    153, 162, 177–79, 184, 186
  in the city, 8, 42, 114–18
  in floating blues verse, 56
  Malcolm X as, 139–40
  migrants as, 195–96
  text as, 8, 46
Angelou, Maya, 121,146
Arrested Development, 139, 148, 178–79
  Faris, Dionne, 179
  speech, 148, 179
  Taree, Aerle, 179
Autobiography of an Ex-Colored Man, 25
Autobiography of Malcolm X, 123, 130–39,
    214n58
"Avey," 66–67, 209n54
Awkward, Michael, 77, 111, 121, 202n59,
    212n30

"Backwater Blues," 21
Baker, Josephine, 156
Baker, Houston, 68, 81, 102–3, 208n54,
    210n69
Baldwin, James, 8, 37–40, 46, 87–91, 146,
    167, 186, 204n51, 205n53, 213n37,
    214n50
  on the black church, 87–91
  "Down at the Cross," 88
Baraka, Amiri (Leroi Jones), 18, 24, 52–54,
    57, 60, 146, 148, 163, 166–71, 177,
    207n26, 216n33
Barker, Donny, 55
Barlow, William, 19, 56, 58
Bambara, Toni Cade, 121
Benston, Kimberly, 166, 167, 168, 216n32
"Big Boy Leaves Home," 29–31
Black Arts Movement, 43, 170

Black Boy, 69, 161
Black family, patriarchal nature of, 37
Black leadership, 132, 134, 138
Black masculinity, 43, 169, 171–78, 214n50
Black Metropolis, 68, 72, 73, 85
Black middle class
  Jacob Lawrence on, 197
  Malcolm X on, 136
  managing migrants, 103
  organizations, 103, 106
  reaction to migrants, 49, 53, 84–87
  service tradition of, 107
Black Power Movement, 11, 40, 43, 46, 119,
    123, 169
Black press, 103. *See also* Chicago Defender
Black women's clubs assisting migrants, 106
Black women writers, 111
  black feminist literary movement, 119,
    142
Blood, 16, 37, 65
"Blood-Burning Moon," 25–28, 39, 153,
    203n33
Blue note, 56
"Blueprint for Negro Writing," 7, 28, 210n82
Blues
  lyrics, 19, 22, 106, 202n12
  as migrant, 52, 56
Bluest Eye, 102
Billboard, 92, 142
body, 13, 15, 16, 20, 52
  attempts to control in the urban setting,
    102, 105, 155, 158
  focus on in Southern setting, 24–45
Boogie Woogie Blues, 58–59
Bone, Robert, 27
Bonner, Marita, 111–14, 178
Bontemps, Arna, 72
Boston, 83–87, 135–36
"Bourgeoisie Blues," 53, 66
Big Bill Broonzy, 56, 57, 58
Brewster Place
  compared to "Seventh Street," 92
  maternal nature of, 92

Brooks, Gwendolyn, 7, 94–110, 111–13, 117, 137, 189
Burnett, Charles, 216n41

Cafe society, 15
Callahan, John, 151, 153
Cane, 24, 64–68, 147–54, 194, 196, 208n54, 217nn4,5, 218n7
Carby, Hazel, 4, 19, 106–7, 199n2, 207n32, 208n46, 214n42
Carmichael, Hoagy, 144
Carraway, Nick, 51, 65
Cayton, Horace, 62, 68, 72, 73, 85
Charles, Ray, 144
Chaney, James, 146
Chicago, 48, 49, 51, 62, 69, 112–14, 124
  packing houses, 106
  Race Riots of, 50
Chicago Defender, 22, 106, 202n23
Chicago School of Sociology, 72
Church
  free of white control, 62
  migrant founded, 61
  migrant impact upon, 61
  Mount Olive Baptist, 62
  as safe space, 62, 95, 190
  in *12 Million Black Voices*, 79
City
  impact on migrants in American Hunger, 73
  sounds, 65, 70
  as unknown terror, 70
"City of Refuge"
  song, 63
  story, 51
Civil Rights Movement, 11, 40, 142–43, 144, 145, 166
Cixous, Hélène, 121
Clock, 68, 102, 195, 209n64
Collins, Patricia Hill, 8, 9
Communist Party, 165
Cooke, Michael, 152
Critical consciousness
  acquisition of in *12 Million Black Voices*, 72, 78
  as resistance in black male narrative, 123–39, 162, 165

Dash, Julie, 5, 6, 179–80, 182
"Dead Cat on the Line," 63
Dead, Macon, 40, 42, 172
Dead, Pilate, 5, 40, 173, 177
Death of a Salesman, 148–49
  Willie Loman, 148
Demby, William, 10
Denmark, 155–58

Designing Women, 144, 215n2
Detroit, 103
Diawara, Manthia, 214n55
Dixon, Melvin, 42, 43, 123, 150, 215n9, 216n34
Dorsey, Thomas, 62
Douglass, Frederick, 150
"Down at the Cross," 88
Drake, St. Clair, 62, 68, 72, 73, 85
Dr. Dre, 139
Driving Miss Daisy, 144, 215n2
DuBois, W. E. B., 146, 148, 194
Dunbar, Paul Lawrence, 3, 25, 146

Ebony, 114
Elder, 5, 173
Eliot, T. S., 108
Ellison, Ralph, 8, 37, 54, 87, 123, 130–34, 149
"Ethics of Living Jim Crow," 29
Europeans, 155–58

Farm Securities Administration, 31, 76
Fauset, Jessie, 83, 112
Finn, Huckleberry, 20
Fisher, Rudolph, 51, 114, 213n45
Fitzgerald, F. Scott, 51, 193–94
Flynn, Joyce, 111, 113
Ford Motor Company, 105, 106
  blues lyrics about, 106
  Fordism, 105
Foucault, Michel, 16, 76, 199n5, 214n54
Franklin, Benjamin, 114–15
Fried Green Tomatoes, 144

Gaines, Ernest, 146
Gates, Henry Louis, 40
Gaye, Marvin, 97
Georgia, 142, 148, 152
  Atlanta, 143
  Sea Islands, 180
  site of black renaissance, 182–83
"Georgia on My Mind," 144
Ghetto Boyz, 139
Go Tell It On the Mountain, 10, 37–40, 87–91, 186, 204n51, 205n53
Goodman, Andrew, 146
Gone With the Wind, 144
Gramsci, Antonio, 77, 104–5
Grandmaster Flash, 141, 178
Great Depression, 59
Great Gatsby, 51, 193–94
Great Migration, 49, 51, 61
Great Migration novel, 4
Grimes, Florence, 37–38

Grimes, John, 87–91
Gospel music, 61–63
Gordy, Berry, 99

Haley, Alex, 44, 134
Hall, Jacquelyn Dowd, 25, 47
Harlem, 108, 114–18, 130–34, 185–97
Harlem Renaissance, 10, 14, 196
Harper, Frances, 71
Harris, Michael, 62, 207n38
Harris, Trudier, 29, 45, 199n4, 204n51
Higginbotham, Evelyn, 208n46
Himes, Chester, 10, 12, 114
Hine, Darlene Clark, 37, 45
Holiday, Billie, 11–17, 54, 57, 144, 179
Hollow Men, 108
Holloway, Karla, 5, 114, 212n22
Home, 53, 55, 94, 179, 182, 189, 190
Homeless Blues, 19
Homespace, 107–8
Hooker, John Lee, 56
hooks, bell, 108
Hopper, Edward, 72
Hottentot Venus, 156
"How Bigger Was Born," 7, 124
Hughes, Langston, 18, 45, 51, 108
Humphrey, Mark, 63
Hunter, Alberta, 56
Hurston, Zora Neale, 8, 111, 148, 160

Identity, 53
Interracial sex, 26
Invisible Man, 10, 54, 87, 123, 130–34, 159
Irigaray, Luce, 121

Jazz, 3, 10, 184–97
jazz, 184, 191
   as metaphor for migrants, 192
Jazz Age, 191, 193, 194, 196
Jet Magazine, 166
Jim Crow, 20, 22
Johnson, Blind Willie, 63, 208n50
Johnson, Etta Mae, 44, 93–94
Johnson, James P., 55
Johnson, James Weldon, 25, 72, 148
Johnson, Lutie, 114–18
Jones, Gayle, 114
Judson, Cleo, 83–87
Jungle Fever, 98

"Kabnis," 147–54
Kabnis, Ralph, 27, 68, 147–54, 160, 167, 177,
   215n9
Keil, Charles, 54
Kern, Stephen, 51, 68

Kitchenette. *See also* Brooks, Gwendolyn
   as one of Foucault's institutions, 76
   in Jean Lacy's "Welcome to My Ghetto
      Land," 100–102
   in *12 Million Black Voices,* 75
Kitchenette Building, 76, 108, 122
Knight, Gladys, 142–43
Kristeva, Julia, 7, 121
KRS-1, 139

Lacy, Jean, 100–101, 189
Lady Sings the Blues, 54
Language
   black innovation in, 32
   medium of alienation, 74
Larsen, Nella, 84, 112, 146, 149, 154–60
Lawd Today, 29, 69, 102, 161
Lawrence, Jacob, 13, 14, 46, 48, 69, 76, 107,
   179, 186, 205n1
Layin' on of hands, 93, 119–23
Ledbetter, Huddy (Leadbelly), 53, 66
Lee, Russell, *Negro Family,* 76–77
Levine, Lawrence, 18, 22, 206n22
Lindy hop (jitterbug), 59, 78, 81
Living for the City, 52, 94–99, 179, 211n94
Locke, Alain, 194
Love Song of J. Alfred Prufrock, 148–49
Lynching, 5, 13–47, 153

Madness, 185, 190
Map, 50, 51, 64, 73, 187
   for survival, 115
Marginal man, 7, 72
Marshall, Paule, 12, 121, 148
Marxism, 28
Matus, Jill, 122
MC Lyte, 139
McCall, Nathan, 108
McDowell, Deborah, 196, 217n2
McKay, Claude, 36, 72
McKay, Nellie, 65, 203n34, 209n54
McPherson, James, 146
Michael, Mattie, 44, 93–94, 119–22
Midnight Train to Georgia, 142–43
Migrants
   agency of, 18, 32, 102, 157
   as ancestor, 196
   impact on cities, 49, 84
   influence of the city on, 49
   letters of, 19, 22, 23
   male defined in Cane, 65
   psyche of, 52, 71, 74, 75
   reader as, 65
   resistance of, 107
   return of, 181–83

Migrants (*continued*)
  spaces of, 107, 135–37
Migration narrative, 3, 16, 24, 48
  characteristics of, 3, 24, 122, 140, 177, 184
  film and rap, 183
  interdisciplinary nature of, 4
  repository of the ancestor, 6
  re-written by black women, 171
  rhythm and blues, 94
  urban spaces in, 102
Migration of the Negro Series, 13–15
  #1, 49
  #7, 48
  #15, 14, 186
  #53, 107, 206n15
Milkman, 42, 171–78
Miller, James A., 35, 128–29, 213n41, 213n44
Mississippi River flood, 20
Moon, 26, 154
Morrison, Toni, 3, 5, 6, 11, 40–43, 46, 112,
  122, 146, 171–78, 184–97, 199n6,
  210n88
Motown, 99
Muhammed, Elijah, 138
Murray, Albert, 11, 146
Museum of Modern Art, 14, 201n1
Mydans, Carl, *Backyard of Alley Dwelling,* 164

Natanson, Nicholas, 36, 209n62
Nation of Islam, 135
National Association of Colored Women,
  106–7
Native Son, 7, 15, 69, 73, 74, 76, 112, 118,
  102, 123–30, 160, 213n41
Naylor, Gloria, 40, 43–45, 46, 53, 83, 111,
  118–23, 189, 210n88
NdegeOcello, Me'Shell, 139
Negro Digest, 145
New Challenge, 83
New Jack City, 98
New York Times, 145, 181, 184

Ogren, Kathy, 193
Oliver, Paul, 53, 63, 208n50
O'Meally, Robert, 15, 201n4
Outsider, 161

Park, Robert, 7, 72
Peazant, Nana, 5, 6, 180
Petry, Ann, 7, 10, 71, 83, 93, 111, 114–18,
  146
Philadelphia Inquirer, 145
Phillips Collection, 14
Playing in the Dark, 194
Police brutality, 5

Poor Man's Blues, 58, 60
"Portrait in Georgia," 24
Post office, 105
Pryse, Marjorie, 117, 212n20, 212n24

Queen Latifah, 139
Quicksand, 11, 154–60. *See also* Larsen, Nella

Railroad, 19, 30
Rainey, Ma, 57
Rape, 5
Redemption, South as site of, 26
Return migration, 181–82, 217n43
Resistance, 21, 100–41
Rodgers, Lawrence, 4, 86, 100n2
Rose, Tricia, 214n57
Rosskam, Edwin, 31, 209n65. *See also* Farm
  Securities Administration
Rothstein, Arthur
  Interior, 76, 77
  Steelworker, 34–35

Safe space, 8, 9, 103, 173, 188
  blues performance as, 56
  church, 62
  dance hall, 79
  defined, 111–23
  food and cooking as, 131, 135
  friendship as, 90–91
  Malcolm X as, 134
  memory and dreams, 114–23
  nicknames as, 93, 135
  return to mother as, 93
  ritual as, 119–20
  stifling nature of, 130
  tenements as, 101
  in *12 Million Black Voices,* 78–79
Salt and Pepa, 139
Scarlett, 144
Schuyler, George, 145
Schwerner, Michael, 146
Scottsboro Boys, 28
Scruggs, Charles, 4, 87, 199n2, 210n86
Sermons
  recorded, 63
  Stevie Wonder, 95
"Seventh Street," 64–66, 110, 188
Shange, Ntozake, 44
Simmel, Georg, 6, 72, 78
Slave narrative, 3, 20, 24
Slavery, 20, 148, 160
Smith, Bessie, 19–22, 56
  performance, 55
Smith, Valerie, 127, 213n44
Snoop Doggy Dog, 139

Sollors, Werner, 209n64
Sometimes I Feel Like a Motherless Child, 21
Song of Solomon, 6, 42–45, 171–78, 205n59
  response to *Song of the Son*, 176
Song of the Son, 147–48
South, 24
  beauty and horror of, 16
  feminine nature of, 67
  landscape, 33
  return to, 183
  site of ancestors, 5
  as symbolic space, 148
South in the city
  defined, 52, 206n10
  embodied in migrant, 52
  in *Go Tell It On the Mountain*, 87–91
  in *Jazz*, 189
  in *Living is Easy*, 83–87
  as site of resistance, 87
  in *12 Million Black Voices*, 82
Spear, Allen, 61
Spillers, Hortense, 110
Spirituals, 20, 159, 162, 206n14
Spivey, Victoria, 56
Sport of the Gods, 3
Stack, Carol B., 181, 217n43
Stepto, Robert, 4, 134, 162, 147–48
Stewart, Sallie, 106
Stott, William, 31, 165
Strange Fruit, 15, 30, 33, 127, 201n4
  performance of, 15
  poem, 15
  recording, 15
  See also Holiday, Billie
Stranger, 4, 6, 7, 113, 200n11, 207n26
The Street, 7, 93, 102, 114–18, 212n20
  compared to *Native Son*, 114
  compared to "The Whipping," 114
Strickland, Joyce Ocomy, 11
Survey Graphic, 104
System of Dante's Hell, 146, 166–71

Tagg, John, 31
Taylor, Frederic, 105
Taylorism, 104–5
Technology, 51, 60, 66
Tennessee, 178–79
Third Life of Grange Copeland, 44
Thomas, Bigger, 7, 29, 110, 123–30
Till, Emmett, 42, 146, 165, 171
Time and space, 52, 60, 65, 120, 173
Toomer, Jean, 24–28, 52, 64–68, 91, 95, 110,
  138, 142, 146, 147–54, 160, 165, 167,
  172, 179, 188

Trees
  ancestors as, 26
  black bodies and, 26
  as site of lynching, 26
Turner, Nat, 150
12 Million Black Voices, 29, 31–36, 69, 71–82,
  129, 161, 162–66, 209n62
  relationship between photographic and
    written narrative, 34–36, 73, 76
Troop, singing *"Living for the City,"* 98

Uncle Tom's Children, 15, 27–28, 29, 69, 75
  reviews of, 28
Urban League
  Chicago, 17, 103, 106, 107, 135
  Education of the Migrants Project, 103
  National Industrial Department, 104
  Stop the Violence Campaign, 139
Urban space
  site of the ancestry, 107
  workplace, 103, 105
"Unemployment Stomp," 58–60

Van der Zee, James, 196
Virginia, 185–86

Walker, Alice, 11, 43–44, 46, 146, 171
Washington, Booker T., 146, 149
Washington, D.C., 65, 114, 153
Waters, Ethel, 144
Waters, Muddie, 56
Watts, Jerry, 200n11
Weatherly, James, 142
We Real Cool, 108
Welcome to My Ghetto Land, 100–101
  compared to *Women of Brewster Place*, 100
  compared to Richard Wright, 101
  tenement as sacred space, 100–101
Wells, Ida B., 25, 42
West, Cornel, 210n85
West, Dorothy, 52, 91, 136
  Living is Easy, 83–87
  and Richard Wright, 83
"The Whipping," 112–14
White Rose Mission, 106–7
White women
  Designing Women, 144
  interracial relationships with black men,
    124–37
  and lynching, 24–30, 102
  maintaining racist stereotypes of black
    women, 116
Williams, Brett, 206n10
Winfrey, Oprah, 44
Wirth, Louis, 72

Women of Brewster Place, 43–45, 91–94
Wonder, Stevie, 52, 94–99, 142, 179
Wright, Richard, 7, 10, 27–37, 46, 51, 69, 78,
    95, 105, 108, 112, 113, 123–30, 146,
    160–66, 171, 177, 205n3, 209n57,
    213n41
  on black dance, 81
  and *Black Metropolis,* 73
  on black music, 60
  on black women, 81–82
  as bluesman, 70
  on church, 79–80
  and Dorothy West, 83
  as migrant, 70

Willis, Susan, 4, 199n2, 205n59

Vesey, Denmark, 150

X, Malcolm, 130–41, 214nn49–52
  on black dance, 81
  as resisting ancestor for hip-hop generation,
    139–40
  as safe space, 134

Young Negroes' Progressive Association, 103,
    107